RESEARCHING
SENSITIVE
<u>TOPICS</u>

OTHER RECENT VOLUMES IN THE
SAGE FOCUS EDITIONS

RESEARCHING
SENSITIVE
TOPICS

Claire M. Renzetti
Raymond M. Lee
editors

SAGE Publications
International Educational and Professional Publisher
Newbury Park   London   New Delhi

For information address:

SAGE Publications, Inc.
2455 Teller Road
Newbury Park, California 91320

SAGE Publications Ltd.
6 Bonhill Street
London EC2A 4PU
United Kingdom

SAGE Publications India Pvt. Ltd.
M-32 Market
Greater Kailash I
New Delhi 110 048 India

Printed in the United States of America

Library of Congress Cataloging-in-Publication Data

Renzetti, Claire M.
   Researching sensitive topics/ Claire M. Renzetti, Raymond M. Lee, editors
        p.   cm.   —(Sage focus editions : 152)
   Includes bibliographical references and index.
   ISBN 0-8039-4844-1.   —ISBN 0-8039-4845-X (pbk.)
   1. Social sciences—Research. 2. Political correctness—Research.
I. Lee, Raymond M. II. Title.
H62.R43   1993
300'.72—dc20   92-33022

93 94 95 96 10 9 8 7 6 5 4 3 2 1

Sage Production Editor: Diane S. Foster

Contents

This book is dedicated to the memory of
John L. Martin
(1954-1992)

Preface

Social scientists are increasingly being called upon to carry out research on topics that are "sensitive" in the sense that they deal with behavior that is intimate, discreditable, or incriminating. Such topics not only pose difficult technical problems, they also pose wider issues having to do with the ethics and politics of research that are common to most kinds of study but that are most clearly seen in research on sensitive topics. Methodological work on sensitive topics, however, is often fragmented because researchers are usually unaware of the ways that their colleagues in different substantive areas, different disciplines, or different parts of the world are addressing specific methodological difficulties.

The purpose of the current volume is to bring together articles devoted to issues and problems surrounding research on sensitive topics so that researchers in various fields and various specialties may benefit from the experiences of their colleagues. It began as a special issue of the *American Behavioral Scientist* (May/June, 1990). Many of the articles that originally appeared in the *ABS* issue are reprinted here; most have been revised and updated to reflect the authors' more recent experiences in researching a sensitive topic. In addition, however, this volume explores three areas of concern not explicitly examined in the *ABS* issue. More specifically, two chapters have been added that examine problems of sensitivity in cross-cultural research (Curran and Cook in Part II and

Brink in Part V). The contributions of feminist methodologies to researching sensitive topics are addressed in the three chapters that constitute Part IV of this volume (Edwards, Kennedy Bergen, and Bendelow). And issues regarding disclosure and dissemination of research findings are the focus of Part V of the book (the chapters by Brink, Adler and Adler, and Channels).

The chapters that appear in this volume were written by researchers from a variety of academic disciplines—sociology, psychology, criminology, economics, anthropology, public policy, public health, and nursing—who are working in the United States, Great Britain, Canada, and Australia. We wish to take this opportunity to thank these authors for their contributions and for their efforts to comply with our imposed deadlines. Thanks as well to Joann Devlin, who assisted in preparing the manuscript for submission to the publisher.

We also wish to thank Charles (Terry) Hendrix, Vice President and Editorial Director at Sage Publications, for his support of the project, and Deborah Laughton, Research Methods Editor at Sage, for her editorial expertise in bringing the project to completion.

—*Claire M. Renzetti*
Raymond M. Lee

PART I

What Is Sensitive Research?

1

The Problems of Researching Sensitive Topics

An Overview and Introduction

RAYMOND M. LEE
CLAIRE M. RENZETTI

Defining "Sensitive" Topics

One difficulty with the notion of a *sensitive topic* is that the term is often used in the literature as if it were self-explanatory. In other words, the term usually is treated in a commonsensical way, with no attempt at definition. Consider the substantive topics addressed by the chapters in this volume. Child abuse, AIDS, and policing in Northern Ireland, for instance, are topics that most social scientists would generally regard without much reservation as sensitive. Why? What is it about these topics that makes them "sensitive" relative to other research topics?

A starting point for answering these questions is provided by Sieber and Stanley (1988). They define "socially sensitive research" as

AUTHORS' NOTE: An earlier version of this chapter appeared as "The Problems of Researching Sensitive Topics: An Introduction and Overview," in the *American Behavioral Scientist, 33,* 510-528.

studies in which there are potential consequences or implications, either directly for the participants in the research or for the class of individuals represented by the research. For example, a study that examines the relative merits of day care for infants against full-time care by the mother can have broad social implications and thus can be considered socially sensitive. Similarly, studies aimed at examining the relation between gender and mathematical ability also have significant social implications. (p. 49)

A major advantage of defining sensitive research in this way is that it is broad in scope, thereby allowing for the inclusion of topics that ordinarily might not be thought of as "sensitive." In addition, it alerts researchers to their responsibilities to the wider society. This is entirely appropriate, given the ethical and professional issues that form the primary focus of Sieber and Stanley's article. The difficulty is that Sieber and Stanley do not specify the scope or nature of the kinds of consequences or implications that they have in mind. As a result, their definition logically encompasses research that is consequential in any way. This would include presumably almost any kind of applied research, even where it had limited scope or was wholly beneficial. Therefore the term *sensitive,* as used by Sieber and Stanley, almost seems to become synonymous with *controversial.* Moreover, while the importance of ethical issues should not be diminished, one needs to remember that research on sensitive topics raises a whole range of problems, including those of a more specifically technical or methodological kind. The definition proposed by Sieber and Stanley tends to draw attention away from these problems.

An alternative approach to defining sensitive topics would be to start with the observation that those topics that social scientists generally regard as sensitive are ones that seem to be threatening in some way to those being studied. Another way to put this is to say that sensitive topics present problems because research into them involves potential costs to those participating in the research. It is true, of course, that all research involves some costs to those who participate, if only in terms of time and possible inconvenience. While there are cases in which research makes demands on participants that are quite substantial, the potential costs in the case of sensitive topics go beyond the incidental or merely onerous. Thus, for a topic to be sensitive, the threat it poses should at least be moderate, although probably more often it is severe.

At the same time, sensitive topics seem to involve particular kinds of costs. On one hand, these may take the form of psychic costs, such as guilt, shame, or embarrassment. Alternatively, sensitive topics are threatening because participation in research can have unwelcome consequences. For instance, wrongdoing uncovered by research might bring with it the possibility of discovery and sanction. As a result, the relationship between the researcher and the researched may become hedged with mistrust, concealment, and dissimulation. This, in turn, has obvious detrimental effects on levels of reliability and validity and raises a concomitant need for ethical awareness on the part of the researcher.

Finally, it is important to remember that research can be threatening to the *researcher* as well as the researched. Researchers may be placed in situations in which their personal security is jeopardized, or they may find themselves stigmatized by colleagues and others for having studied particular topics (e.g., sexual deviance).

We are now in a position to offer at least a preliminary definition of a sensitive topic. The threatening character of the research, and its potential consequences for both researcher and researched, suggest that *a sensitive topic is one that potentially poses for those involved a substantial threat, the emergence of which renders problematic for the researcher and/or the researched the collection, holding, and/or dissemination of research data.* Although one could attempt to develop a comprehensive list of sensitive topics based on this definition, it seems more fruitful to look at the conditions under which "sensitivity" arises within the research process.

Sensitive Topics and the Research Process

The sensitive nature of a particular topic is emergent. In other words, the sensitive character of a piece of research seemingly inheres less in the topic itself and more in the relationship between that topic and the social context within which the research is conducted. It is not uncommon, for example, for a researcher to approach a topic with caution on the assumption that it is a sensitive one, only to find that those initial fears had been misplaced. Neither is it unusual for the sensitive nature of an apparently innocuous topic to become manifest once research is under way. Just as Goyder (1987) hypothesized that different social groups attribute different meanings to requests for participation in research, it may well be that a study seen as threatening by one group will be thought innocuous by another.

It is probably possible for *any* topic, depending on context, to be a sensitive one. Experience suggests, however, that there are a number of areas in which research is more likely to be threatening than in others. These include (a) where research intrudes into the private sphere or delves into some deeply personal experience, (b) where the study is concerned with deviance and social control, (c) where it impinges on the vested interests of powerful persons or the exercise of coercion or domination, and (d) where it deals with things sacred to those being studied that they do not wish profaned.

Intrusions into the private sphere need not always be threatening. Day (1985), for instance, concluded that there is no fixed private sphere. Topics and activities regarded as private vary cross-culturally and situationally. Commonly, however, areas of social life concerned with sexual or financial matters remain shielded from the eyes of nonintimates. Other areas of personal experience, such as bereavement, are not so much private as emotionally charged. Research into such areas may threaten those studied through the levels of emotional stress they produce.

Research involving the investigation of deviant activities has frequently been regarded as having a sensitive character. Those studied are likely to fear being identified, stigmatized, or incriminated in some way. Areas of social life that are contentious or highly conflictual often produce topics for research that are sensitive. Normally, this is because in such situations research can be seen by those involved as threatening the alignments, interests, or security of those in a conflict, especially those who are in positions of relative power. Finally, the values and beliefs of some groups are threatened in an intrinsic way by research. Some religious groups—fundamentalists, for example—quite literally regard research into their beliefs and activities as anathema (Homan, 1978; Homan & Bulmer, 1982).

Sensitivity, as we have used the term here, affects almost every stage of the research process from formulation through design to implementation, dissemination, and application (Brewer, this volume; Seigel & Bauman, 1986; Sieber, this volume; Sieber & Stanley, 1988). Perhaps only the actual process of data analysis is likely to remain relatively untouched (although considerations relating to the confidentiality of data can add complexities even here). The problems that arise at each stage can take a variety of forms. Sensitive research raises methodological, technical, ethical, political, and legal problems as well as having potential effects on the personal life of the researcher (Plummer, 1983), not least in some contexts at the level of personal security (Brewer, this volume; Curran & Cook, this volume; Kennedy Bergen, this volume).

Research on sensitive topics has tended to have two rather contradictory outcomes. First, the difficulties associated with sensitive research have tended to inhibit adequate conceptualization and measurement (Herzberger, this volume). The problems raised by sensitive topics have also led to technical innovation, however, in the form of imaginative methodological advances (e.g., see Caplan, 1982). As a result, research on sensitive topics has contributed to methodological development in both the widest and the narrowest senses. Good examples here are the development of strategies for asking sensitive questions on surveys (Bradburn & Sudman, 1979) and technical means for preserving the confidentiality of research data (Boruch & Cecil, 1979).

As Sieber makes clear in Chapter 2, sensitive topics also raise wider issues related to the ethics, politics, and legal aspects of research. As an example of the extent to which political pressures may impinge on the research process, Sieber discusses the controversy over large-scale surveys of sexual behavior. Surveys of this kind, prompted by the need to understand more fully the factors involved in the transmission of HIV infection, have clear social benefits. It is also clear that reliable and valid data can be produced from such studies without anxiety or hostility to the research on the part of those studied. Yet, in Britain as well as in the United States, such surveys have incurred opposition that has persuaded politicians to withdraw funding. Sieber notes that such situations are not uncommon. Research on difficult issues is frequently open to misinterpretation by those who see political opportunities in denigrating social science. Moreover, such misinterpretations are often recycled and amplified by sensationalist reporting in the media. Echoing a point made by Channels (this volume), Sieber stresses the importance of social scientists making active efforts to educate politicians, journalists, and opinion formers about research on issues of social sensitivity. At the same time, she cautions social scientists against hasty overreaction to attacks. As she puts it, "It is best to speak wisely and with good counsel, or to say nothing."

In recent years, the ethical and legal aspects of social research have become increasingly salient. In many countries, there has been a growing concern for individual rights, including those of research participants, and for the rights of social groups who may be affected by the research. Such trends are likely to intensify as researchers move toward more complex research designs (Kimmel, 1988) and a greater involvement in applied research. Again, as Sieber makes clear, such issues impinge on all research, whatever its character, but they may impinge most forcefully in the case of sensitive topics.

Ethical debates in the social sciences have tended to be conducted between, on one hand, those who espouse teleological conceptions of ethics, frequently based around a utilitarian calculus of costs and benefits (see, for instance, Bertilson, 1990), and, on the other hand, those whose underlying ethical conceptions are deontological in character (Kimmel, 1988). By its very nature, research on sensitive topics, because it sharpens ethical dilemmas, tends to reveal the limits of existing ethical theories.

Where sensitive topics are involved, utilitarianism can lead to a lessened rather than a heightened ethical awareness, while deontological theories may be too restrictive, replacing the sin of callousness with the sin of scrupulosity. Thus MacIntyre (1982) argued that one difficulty with a utilitarian approach to ethical decision making is that there is no consensus among social scientists about what counts as a benefit. Moreover, apparently disinterested assertions about risks and rewards may actually be self-serving because researchers have greater power than research participants to define costs and benefits. One can also note that, to assume that there are substantial benefits to society from a particular piece of research is also to assume that the relationship between the production of knowledge and its applicatiton is linear and non-problematic with no scope for misuse. At the same time, however, if one follows the kind of line taken by MacIntyre, there is the danger of excluding as legitimate research a number of areas that may be judged sensitive. According to MacIntyre (1982, p. 188):

> The study of taboos by anthropologists and of privacy by sociologists show how important it is for a culture that certain areas of personal and social life should be specially protected. Intimacy cannot exist where everything is disclosed, sanctuary cannot be sought where no place is inviolate, integrity cannot be seen to be maintained—and therefore cannot in certain cases be maintained—without protection from illegitimate pressures.

For MacIntyre, to violate those sanctuaries is to do a wrong to those one studies. This is despite the fact that, as MacIntyre acknowledges, research into the areas of human life he wants to protect—he uses bereavement as an example—would lead to substantial good in terms of increasing knowledge. Whatever the benefits accruing from these gains, however, MacIntyre insists that it cannot be right to do a wrong to anyone. One difficulty with MacIntyre's position is that his assertion of the inviolability of the intimate sphere is justified by reference to empirical research by anthropologists and sociologists on the functions of privacy. If MacIntyre's point of view is accepted, however, research of this kind would be unethical. It also would not be possible to assess MacIntyre's own claims empirically. At the same time, permitting research on the private sphere might reveal that in many instances, particularly in sensitive areas, research participants desire catharsis rather than sanctuary (Bendelow, this volume; Kennedy Bergen, this volume; Lee, 1981). That is, research on sensitive topics may produce not only gains in knowledge but also effects that are directly beneficial to research participants.

A complicating factor in all of this is that empirical studies of researchers' ethical decision making are surprisingly lacking (Stanley, Sieber, & Melton, 1987). One suspects, though, that relatively few researchers actually desist from research either because the costs involved exceed the benefits or on grounds of moral principle. Paradoxically, this may be especially true where research has a sensitive character. In sociology, for example, the sensitive nature of a study has frequently been used as a justification for the use of covert methods, a practice that many regard as ethically dubious.[1] The argument is made that, because the topic under investigation is sensitive, research into it can be conducted only in a covert way (see, for example, Humphreys, 1970).

While research participants should, in general, expect their rights to privacy, anonymity, and confidentiality to be protected, maintaining confidentiality of research data is especially important where informants or respondents are being asked to reveal intimate or incriminating information. Recently, AIDS researchers have begun to be concerned about public health reporting laws and the power of courts to subpoena research data (Melton & Gray, 1988). This last is an issue that at various times has attracted considerable interest and concern among researchers involved in the study of deviant and criminal behavior. As Ayella indicates in her chapter in this volume, the law also has impinged on scholars researching the plethora of "new" or "alternative" religious movements that emerged as a novel social phenomenon in the West in the 1960s and 1970s.

The legal system both regulates research and intervenes in the research process. The state, for instance, regulates the relationships that researchers have to those they study either, as is common in Europe, through data protection legislation (Akeroyd, 1988) or, to take the U.S. case, by compelling prior ethical review. There have been a number of suggestions that legal regulations lead to research of a sensitive nature being inhibited or sanitized. Thus the Data Inspection Board in Sweden has required researchers to remove questions judged to be sensitive from questionnaires (Flaherty, 1979; Hammar, 1976; Janson, 1979), while researchers in the United States have charged that government regulations and censorship have increased the difficulty of undertaking research on deviance or controversial topics (Ceci, Peters, & Plotkin, 1985; Hessler & Galliher, 1983; Reiss, 1979; Sieber, this volume).

Although malpractice suits against researchers apparently remain only a theoretical possibility (Reiss, 1979; Useem & Marx, 1983), the law has intervened in the research process on a number of occasions. In the United States, legal intervention has been seen most commonly in attempts by prosecutors and courts to subpoena research data (Brajuha & Hallowell, 1986; Knerr, 1982). In contrast, legal threats in Britain usually have taken the form of actual or threatened libel actions (Braithwaite, 1985; Punch, 1986; Wallis, 1977). In both instances, the risks of legal intervention are felt most keenly by those researching sensitive topics. Thus attempts have been made to subpoena data relating to criminal activities, while powerful groups on occasion have been able to use the threat of libel litigation to suppress or substantially modify the accounts that social scientists give of their activities (Adler & Adler, this volume; Ayella, this volume; Braithwaite, 1985). In neither Britain nor the United States are research data legally privileged, although some limited protection does exist in the United States (Melton & Gray, 1988; Nelson & Hedrick, 1983). Again, few researchers will have the resources to fight cases or to pay the necessary penalties if they lose. This is particularly so in Britain, where libel laws are stringent and where libel damages can be substantial.[2]

At this point, it may appear to readers that researching sensitive topics is a daunting enterprise. Brewer (this volume) notes that the many problems that arise in studying a sensitive topic may indeed defeat the researcher unless she or he brings a tough, single-minded, tenacious but pragmatic attitude to the task. Moreover, the fact that sensitive topics pose complex issues and dilemmas for researchers does not imply that such topics should not be studied. As Sieber and Stanley (1988, p. 55) convincingly argues,

Sensitive research addresses some of society's most pressing social issues and policy questions. Although ignoring the ethical issues in sensitive research is not a responsible approach to science, shying away from controversial topics, simply because they are controversial, is also an avoidance of responsibility.

Likewise, we argue that ignoring the methodological difficulties inherent in researching sensitive topics is also socially and scientifically irresponsible because this ignorance may potentially generate flawed conclusions on which both theory and public policy subsequently may be built. If social scientists are not to opt out of research on sensitive topics, they must confront seriously and thoroughly the problems and issues that these topics pose. This volume constitutes a step in that direction.

Notes

1. A range of articles debating this issue may be found in Bulmer (1982).
2. Of course, problems of confidentiality do not arise only in relation to raw data. What Boruch and Cecil (1979) referred to as "deductive closure" is also possible. Here, particular or distinctive combinations of attributes permit the identification of individuals by secondary analysts and readers of published reports. For a range of strategies for preserving the confidentiality of research data, see Boruch (1979), Boruch and Cecil (1979), and Campbell, Boruch, Schwartz, and Steinberg (1977). There are some situations in which these strategies may not be useful, such as when the identity of research participants is itself sensitive information. It is also the case that it is more difficult to maintain the confidentiality of qualitative data by technical means than it is for quantitative data. Yet qualitative researchers are facing mounting pressure to protect confidentiality of their data, both from the growth of field research in applied settings, where there may be greater likelihood of legal intervention (Broadhead, 1984), and from the increasing use of computers to analyze qualitative data (Tesch, 1988). This last advance, in particular, has come about at a time when national data protection laws are becoming increasingly common (Akeroyd, 1988).

References

Akeroyd, A. V. (1988). Ethnography, personal data, and computers: The implications of data protection legislation for qualitative social research. In R. G. Burgess (Ed.), *Studies in qualitative methodology: Vol. 1. Conducting qualitative research.* Greenwich, CT: JAI.

Bertilson, H. S. (1990). Can aggression be justified to study aggression? *American Behavioral Scientist, 33,* 594-607.

Boruch, R. F. (1979). Methods of assuring personal integrity in social research: An introduction. In M. Bulmer (Ed.), *Censuses, surveys, and privacy.* London: Macmillan.

Boruch, R. F., & Cecil, J. S. (1979). *Assuring the confidentiality of social research data.* Philadelphia: University of Pennsylvania Press.

Bradburn, N. M., & Sudman, S. (1979). *Improving interview method and questionnaire design.* San Francisco: Jossey-Bass.

Braithwaite, J. (1985). Corporate crime research: Why two interviewers are needed. *Sociology, 19,* 136-138.

Brajuha, M., & Hallowell, L. (1986). Legal intrusion and the politics of fieldwork: The impact of the Brajuha case. *Urban Life, 14,* 454-478.

Broadhead, R. S. (1984). Human rights and human subjects: Ethics and strategies in social science research. *Sociological Inquiry, 54,* 107-123.

Bulmer, M. (1982). *Social research ethics.* London: Macmillan.

Campbell, D. T., Boruch, R. F., Schwartz, R. D., & Steinberg, J. (1977). Confidentiality-preserving modes of access to files and interfile exchange for useful statistical analysis. *Evaluation Quarterly, 1,* 269-300.

Caplan, A. L. (1982). On privacy and confidentiality in social science research. In T. L. Beauchamp, R. R. Faden, R. J. Wallace, Jr., & L. Waters (Eds.), *Ethical issues in social science research.* Baltimore, MD: Johns Hopkins University Press.

Ceci, S. J., Peters, D., & Plotkin, J. (1985). Human subjects review, personal values and the regulation of social science research. *American Psychologist, 40,* 994-1002.

Day, K. J. (1985). *Perspectives on privacy: A sociological analysis.* Unpublished doctoral dissertation, University of Edinburgh.

Flaherty, D. (1979). *Privacy and governmental data banks: An international comparison.* London: Mansell.

Goyder, J. (1987). *The silent minority: Non-respondents on sample surveys.* Cambridge: Polity.

Hammar, T. (1976). The political resocialization of immigrants project. In T. Dalenius & A. Klevamarken (Eds.), *Personal integrity and the need for data in the social sciences.* Stockholm: Swedish Council for Social Research.

Hessler, R. M., & Galliher, J. F. (1983). Institutional review boards and clandestine research: An experimental test. *Human Organization, 42,* 82-87.

Homan, R. (1978). Interpersonal communication in Pentecostal meetings. *Sociological Review, 26,* 499-518.

Homan, R., & Bulmer, M. (1982). On the merits of covert methods: A dialog. In M. Bulmer (Ed.), *Social research ethics.* London: Macmillan.

Humphreys, L. (1970). *Tearoom trade: Impersonal sex in public places.* Chicago: Aldine.

Janson, C. (1979). Privacy legislation and social research in Sweden. In E. Mochman & P. J. Mullaer (Eds.), *Data protection and social science research: Perspectives from ten countries.* Frankfurt: Campus Verlag.

Kimmel, A. J. (1988). *Ethics and values in applied social research.* Newbury Park, CA: Sage.

Knerr, C. R. (1982). What to do before and after a subpoena of data arrives. In J. Sieber (Ed.), *The ethics of social research: Surveys and experiments.* New York: Springer-Verlag.

Lee, R. M. (1981). *Interreligious courtship and marriage in Northern Ireland.* Unpublished doctoral dissertation, University of Edinburgh.

MacIntyre, A. (1982). Risk, harm, and benefit assessment as instruments of moral evaluation. In T. L. Beauchamp, R. R. Faden, R. J. Wallace, Jr., & L. Waters (Eds.), *Ethical issues in social science research*. Baltimore: Johns Hopkins University Press.

Melton, G. B., & Gray, J. N. (1988). Ethical dilemmas in AIDS research: Individual privacy and public health. *American Psychologist, 42,* 735-741.

Nelson, R. L., & Hedrick, T. E. (1983). The statutory protection of confidential research data: Synthesis and evaluation. In R. F. Boruch & J. S. Cecil (Eds.), *Solutions to ethical and legal problems in social research*. New York: Academic Press.

Plummer, K. (1983). *Documents of life: An introduction to the problems and literature of a humanistic method*. London: Allen & Unwin.

Punch, M. (1986). *The politics and ethics of fieldwork*. Beverly Hills, CA: Sage.

Reiss, A. J. (1979). Government regulation in scientific inquiry: Some paradoxical consequences. In C. B. Klockars & F. W. O'Connor (Eds.), *Deviance and decency: The ethics of research with human subjects*. Beverly Hills, CA: Sage.

Seigel, K., & Bauman, L. J. (1986). Methodological issues in AIDS-related research. In D. A. Feldman & T. M. Johnson (Eds.), *The social dimensions of AIDS*. New York: Praeger.

Sieber, J. E., & Stanley, B. (1988). Ethical and professional dimensions of socially sensitive research. *American Psychologist, 43,* 49-55.

Stanley, B., Sieber, J. E., & Melton, G. B. (1987). Empirical studies of ethical issues in research: A research agenda. *American Psychologist, 42,* 735-741.

Tesch, R. (1988). Computer software and qualitative analysis: A reassessment. In G. Blank, J. L. McCartney, & E. Brent (Eds.), *New technology in sociology*. New Brunswick, NJ: Transaction.

Useem, M., & Marx, G. T. (1983). Ethical dilemmas and political considerations. In R. B. Smith (Ed.), *Handbook of social science methods: Vol. 1. An introduction to social research*. Cambridge, MA: Ballinger.

Wallis, R. (1977). The moral career of a research project. In C. Bell & H. Newbury (Eds.), *Doing sociological research*. London: Allen & Unwin.

2

The Ethics and Politics
of Sensitive Research

JOAN E. SIEBER

Ethics has to do with application of a system of moral principles to prevent harming or wronging others, to promote the good, to be respectful, and to be fair. Politics has to do with the methods and strategies used to gain a position of power and control. Ethics and politics are intertwined in sensitive research, especially that performed in community settings.

Both ethics and politics are about the manifold of interests and feelings—one's own and those of others—that must be recognized, understood, and taken into consideration to achieve optimally good results. Nowhere is this more true than in sensitive social research, where individuals or communities may be helped or harmed by the conduct, publicity, and results of the research. Moreover, the task of recognizing and resolving ethical and political problems is made difficult, and at times impossible, because other parties have motives and perceptions quite different than those of the researcher and sometimes at odds with the facts. One reason that the social sciences are so vital and interesting is that they so often deal with the immediate and difficult problems of real

AUTHOR'S NOTE: This work was carried out with the support of NSF grant DIR 9012185 and with funds provided by the State of California and allocated on the recommendation of the Universitywide Task Force on AIDS (Grant C89CSH01). This chapter benefited greatly throughout its development from the suggestions and critical comments that Bruce E. Trumbo graciously offered.

people. As a consequence, politicians and the press require no special technical expertise to know what is being studied, even if they misinterpret the nuances.

For example, consider some of the differences between social research on a sensitive topic such as teen pregnancy versus research on molecular bonds. Research on molecular bonds requires special expertise to understand, or even to care about, the topic. Interests of politicians and the press, if any, are largely limited to the amount spent, the administration of the spending, and perhaps whether the results are considered a breakthrough of some kind. The molecular bonds, themselves, are presumably oblivious to and unaffected by the research process. The laws that molecular bonds obey are descriptive. In contrast, laws that legislatures pass for human behavior (possibly based on the perceived results of social research) proscribe and punish or legitimize, encourage, and sanction.

Being ethical and being "political" go hand in hand when seeking to conduct sensitive research. Research that harms or offends, or that appears to be conducted incompetently, invalidly, or without due regard for consequences, is likely to result in someone (e.g., a politician, journalist, or community leader) questioning the prerogative of the scientist to conduct such research. Thus the National Opinion Research Center (NORC) was being both ethical and political as it sought to design, and obtain government clearance for, its research on Americans' sex lives. As described by Booth (1989), this was to have been the first representative survey of the sex life of Americans. This survey was to ask people, in plain English, how many partners they've had and just exactly what they did. It would ask about homosexuality, contraception, fertility, religion, and sexual abuse. People would be asked to describe their own sex lives and to discuss why they have sex and what they think about it.

During the pilot study, NORC interviewers would field test methods and procedures to discover, for example, whether it is necessary that people be interviewed by someone of the same sex, age, and race; where the interviews should take place; and what words should be used to describe various sexual practices. The NORC interviewers would develop a long list of every possible term for every imaginable sex act, because what is intelligible to an 18-year-old black male in the inner city might be meaningless to a 62-year-old white female in rural Nebraska. The NORC researchers would try handing subjects a card listing by number all kinds of sexual practices. For example, the number 1 might represent kissing, 2 hugging, 3 touching, 4 licking, and so on. The subject could thus describe a sexual encounter without using the actual words. He or she could simply respond to a question about a recent event by saying: "We did 2, 5, 7, 13, 21, and then 5 again."

Booth noted that, with Office of Management and Budget (OMB) clearance of the project, the pilot study would likely reach the field by March 1989, about two years after the survey was strongly recommended by the National Academy of Sciences and the Institute of Medicine, and pilot data would be expected by summer 1989. After that, the whole project would go back to the bureaucracy for another round of clearance for the final study, and results would begin to appear during the 1990s, a decade after the AIDS epidemic began (Booth, 1989).

As the NORC "sex study" illustrates, those who intend to do sensitive research must design the research for maximum validity and minimum offensiveness and must then negotiate with many gatekeepers, perhaps including institutional review boards (IRBs) or human subjects ethics review committees as they are variously called, the OMB, funding review panels, funding agencies, city governments, community leaders, and the subjects themselves. The success of the research may depend on the cultural sensitivity, research design skills, and political sophistication with which the researchers shape their research plans and present their research proposal. Sensitive research evokes a wide range of responses from those who learn about it. Research such as the "sex study" might be discussed on talk shows, in editorial columns, from the pulpit, and in letters to members of Congress. And even the most sophisticated of investigators may be "outpoliticked" by those who would oppose the research. Indeed, that is what happened to the NORC study of adult sexuality, as well as to a study of adolescent sexuality, as described on the front page of the *APA Monitor*:

> Congress and the administration have derailed funding for studies on sexual behavior, a move psychologists say threatens effective AIDS prevention programs and raises disturbing questions about political interference with peer-reviewed research. Surveys on adult and adolescent sexual behavior . . . are "deader than a doornail," said Brian Wilcox, director of the American Psychological Association's Office of Public Policy. . . .
>
> What some find worrisome is the politicizing of science. . . . "It's a threat to the peer-review process." . . . "A small political group [conservatives] managed to prevent a whole area of research from happening." . . . "What seemed

before to be something you could look at as a topic of public-health research now becomes subject to political intervention." (Youngstrom, 1991, pp. 1, 29)

Obviously, the values and interests of scientists versus politicians are widely disparate in this case. While everyone involved would agree that the proposed research is sensitive, there is disagreement as to whether the research is warranted and whether enough care was taken to respect the sensitivities of the respondents. One suspects that it is not the respondents' sensitivities that are at issue. This is reminiscent of the upset that was created when the so-called Kinsey reports were published.

The Kinsey reports of sexual behavior in the human male (Kinsey, Pomeroy, & Martin, 1948) and female (Kinsey, Pomeroy, Martin, & Gebhard, 1953) were based on interviews in which subjects responded readily and without offense to questions about their sexual behavior. Many who later heard about the Kinsey reports objected, however. It is unclear whether they were objecting primarily because survey researchers asked a nationwide sample about their sexual behavior or because the respondents acknowledged sexual practices that "nice people" were supposed to deny. Most who objected had not read the actual report but had heard about it secondhand. The press stirred much interest by reporting people's shock at the Kinsey report. Some politicians and clergy expressed a sense of outrage, but it remains unclear how many people were really offended.

Indeed, "sensitivities" are sometimes created to promote the interests of opinion leaders (e.g., politicians, ministers, or journalists) who may use the media to establish their views to their constituencies and thus to benefit their careers. Ultimately, the best strategy for protecting the sensitivities of research participants and community members and for avoiding the wrath of zealous opinion leaders is to design ethical and culturally sensitive research and to interpret findings tactfully and judiciously, with concern for the interests of the research participants, the gatekeepers, and society. Sensitivities that are created by opinion leaders for their own political purposes, however, are sometimes unavoidable.

Sensitivity and the Perception of Risk

The fate of the "sex surveys" illustrates that different groups are likely to perceive research differently. A key challenge facing the investigator of sensitive topics is that of gaining insight into the way others are likely to perceive the research and designing the research so that sensitivities are minimized.

Sensitivity and the perception of risk are highly subjective. What the research participant or gatekeeper perceives as a risk or as a sensitive matter may not be perceived as such by the investigator. Some perceived risks or sensitivities may be connected only with *imagined* outcomes and not with outcomes that will actually arise. And, as illustrated by the "sex study" example above, some sensitivities have to do with differences in values and political agendas.

Stated otherwise, the sensitivities and research risks that the investigator must recognize are not necessarily sensitivities and risks that the investigator considers to be real. The challenge, then, is to learn the perspective of those who will be the participants and gatekeepers of the intended research and to design the research with those perspectives in mind. Similarly, the researcher should learn what kinds of outcomes community members would consider a benefit and plan to give back to the participants and to their community as many of those benefits as possible.

The potential risks, sensitivities, and benefits in sensitive research are the same as those in any social research but greater in magnitude. Key risks of harm include invasion of privacy, breach of confidentiality, and embarrassment. Issues of competency and validity are acute given that the dissemination of invalid conclusions might lead to harmful policy decisions. Informed consent means far more than a consent statement—it means communicating respectfully and openly with participants and community members throughout the project, respecting autonomy and life-style, and providing useful debriefing about the nature, findings, and value of the research and its likely dissemination. Deception and concealment, while perhaps acceptable in some laboratory research, are generally unacceptable and infeasible in sensitive research. Procedures should benefit different populations equally; and, in return for participation, respondents should receive something (information, referrals, services) of actual value to them. The researcher must be respectful and responsive to the perspectives and needs of the gatekeepers and the community.

The chapters that follow in this volume present compelling cases that help the reader to anticipate potential risks and sensitivities. A detailed discussion of types of risks in socially sensitive research is beyond the scope of this chapter; such a discussion may be found in Chapter 8,

"Recognizing Elements of Risk," in *Planning Ethically Responsible Research* (Sieber, 1992).

The Ethics of Sensitive Research

A prerequisite of ethical problem solving is accurate assessment of the potential for such risks and sensitivities. This entails recognizing how issues may arise in all phases of the research process from theory to application, recognizing the vulnerability of each of the persons or institutions that may be affected by the research, and understanding the kinds of ethical issues that may arise. These issues include privacy and confidentiality, safety of individuals, validity of the research, respectful communication including consent and debriefing, avoidance of deception, equitable treatment of the parties involved, responsible stewardship of the data and of the knowledge that is gained, and responsible relationships with relevant gatekeepers and opinion leaders.

Being ethical in the conduct of sensitive research also means being *culturally sensitive* in the way one designs the research and interacts with research participants, community members, gatekeepers, and relevant others. This means learning to perceive risk factors from the perspective of the persons who will be affected, remembering that not everyone perceives things as the researcher would.

Cultural sensitivity is used here to refer to the understanding and approaches that enable one to gain access to individuals in a given culture or subculture, to learn about their actual life-styles (beliefs, habits, needs, fears, risks), and to communicate in ways that the individuals understand, believe, regard as relevant to themselves, and are likely to act upon.

For example, within the generic cultures of each ethnic group, there are distinct subcultures, some of which are at high risk for HIV infection. These high-risk subcultures include intravenous drug users, prostitutes, the homeless, gay men, women in relationships with men who are at risk, and runaway children. The specific issues to which one needs to be sensitive depend partly on the nature of the research. For example, if one is experimenting with AIDS interventions in community settings, it is vital to understand the basic assumptions that the population holds about such things as health, illness, AIDS and other STDs, sexuality, personal adequacy and self-worth, sin and salvation, science, whose advice to take about medical or sexual matters, masculinity, femininity, and so on. These assumptions may vary with education, age, ethnicity, religion, neighborhood, and occupation.

Apart from such overarching basic assumptions, community-based researchers must stay in touch with current opinions that are circulating in the community. These views may be about the researcher's motives, the risks or benefits of participating in the research, and so on. These views may be true or false and may make or break the research. Good communication is vital to keeping abreast of the views that are being disseminated, to addressing them appropriately, and to learning appropriate ways to benefit one's research participants and others in the community.

The *needs and fears* of the target population will affect their (a) basic assumptions and (b) current views. Understanding and responding constructively to these needs and fears is an important part of cultural sensitivity and is vital to the success of the research. It does not necessarily seem "rational" from the perspective of the well-educated professional that some fears would arise; the professional is likely to bring different background information, including a different understanding of causality and probability, to bear on some issues. Issues of control, autonomy, and fear of exploitation are involved in any attempt of one group to study or influence the characteristics of another group. These need to be understood. Trust, multilateral and shared decision making, and an equal-status, respectful relationship between intervener and target population need to be established.

There are effective processes for gaining rapport and trust, for establishing equal status relationships, and for learning about people and reducing barriers to effective communication. Processes for establishing trust and rapport include serving meals and eating with people when discussing the project as well as asking people what they want the program to do for them and how they want the program to operate (e.g., Case, 1990). A variety of ethnographic methods may be used to learn about people. Approaches to creating effective communication include holding focus group sessions in which participants are asked to help design the research, enlisting participants as assistants, and giving the results of the research to the community in regular and highly understandable terms (Bowser & Sieber, Chapter 10, this volume). Effective approaches to informing and obtaining the consent of individuals and communities are discussed in Melton, Levine, Koocher, Rosenthal, and Thompson (1988) and Sieber (1992).

Ethical problem solving requires that one avail oneself of the relevant techniques of research design and data management. These include, for example, procedures for protecting confidentiality (e.g., Boruch & Cecil, 1979) and procedures for valid research design in field settings (e.g., Cook & Campbell, 1979).

Finally, ethical problem solving requires mindfulness of the way in which the interests and perspectives of powerful others can create political problems for the applied researcher who does sensitive research, the topic to which we now turn.

The Politics of Sensitive Research

Most investigators of sensitive problems have had occasion to worry that their honest efforts to investigate human characteristics would result in misunderstanding, social backlash, or bad public policy. Such outcomes may, in fact, occur, and many parties may be harmed in the process, including the investigator.

The Researcher's Relationship with Politicians

Although physical science researchers have often received respect and support from politicians, social researchers often encounter hostility and conscious distortion of their work by "cheap shot" politicians. A dreaded outcome of media coverage is that a misconstrued version of one's research will be read by a politician who will then demand to know why public funds are being spent on such arrant nonsense—or on such offensive activities (see also Adler & Adler, this volume; Channels, this volume). Social scientists are in a no-win situation. If they discover that people behave just as one might suppose, they are accused of studying the obvious. But, if they discover the nonobvious, they are accused of even worse. For example, Laud Humphreys (1970) discovered that many of the men who engage in fellatio in public rest rooms are upstanding citizens who are heterosexual. He was regarded as a voyeur and troublemaker. The broader implications of the knowledge are often ignored, and a tawdry view of the particular treatments and operational definitions are emphasized.

Social scientists need to make a conscious effort to communicate effectively with politicians, whether via the mass media, through public testimony, or through other carefully planned efforts to educate politicians about the social sciences. The main misperceptions to be overcome are the notions that social science deals with the obvious, that social scientists are advocates rather than scientists, and that they do not contribute to a lasting knowledge base for social understanding (Wells, 1982). Apart from not appearing foolish in public, perhaps the two best ways to help overcome these views of social scientists are as follows:

> to participate in educational forums organized by one's professional society to educate politicians and
>
> to provide one's funder with evidence that the research has improved society.

Both professional societies and funders need evidence with which to persuade government to fund social research.

Press-Mediated Sensitivity

Press-mediated sensitivity on the part of members of the public who know little about the actual research is not uncommon. Research on sensitive topics makes exciting news and is often seized upon by reporters. The researcher's interpretation of the findings is not necessarily what gets reported in the press, however. A recent example is illustrative. Shedler and Block (1990) report a study of adolescent drug use and psychological health. The abstract of their study states:

> The relation between psychological characteristics and drug use was investigated in subjects studied longitudinally from preschool through age 18. Adolescents who had engaged in some drug experimentation (primarily with marijuana) were the best-adjusted in the sample. Adolescents who used drugs frequently were maladjusted, showing a distinct personality syndrome marked by interpersonal alienation, poor impulse control, and manifest emotional distress. Adolescents who, by age 18, had never experimented with any drug were relatively anxious, emotionally constricted, and lacking in social skills.
>
> Psychological differences between frequent drug users, experimenters, and abstainers could be traced to the earliest years of childhood and related to the quality of parenting received. The findings indicate that (a) problem drug use is a symptom, not a cause, of personal and social maladjustment, and (b) the meaning of drug use can be understood only in the context of an individual's personality structure and developmental history. It is suggested that current efforts at drug prevention are misguided to the extent that they focus on symptoms, rather than on the psychological syndrome underlying drug use. (p. 612)

Shedler and Block wisely close their article with the following admonition:

> In presenting research on a topic as emotionally charged as drug use, there is always the danger that findings may be misinterpreted or misrepresented. Specifically, we are concerned that some segments of the popular media may misrepresent our findings as indicating that drug use might somehow improve an adolescent's psychological health. Although the incorrectness of such an interpretation should be obvious to anyone who has actually read this article, our concern about media misrepresentation requires us to state categorically that our findings do not support such a view, nor should anything we have said remotely encourage such an interpretation. (p. 628)

Even so, headlines in the *San Francisco Chronicle* on May 14, 1990 (Furor over report, 1990, p. A10) read, "Furor over Report on Teenage Drug Use: Researchers said those who experimented were healthier than abstainers or abusers." The press went on to report that drug counselors were outraged and made to feel foolish. "What does this do to the kids who made a commitment to be abstinent? Now they're being told they're a bunch of dorks and geeks," said Dr. Gary Levine, director of Marin General Hospital's adolescent recovery center. "You can imagine how much more peer pressure is going to be put on them." Drug counselors were quoted as saying that Shedler and Block had harmed society by broadcasting their destructive ideas (see also Channels, this volume).

The principle of scientific freedom and responsibility holds that a scientist may research any question so long as it is done rigorously and responsibly. Shedler and Block more than fulfilled their social and scientific responsibilities, and ultimately their excellent research can be expected to aid society in its struggles with drug addiction. It should be noted, however, that Shedler and Block spent considerable time answering false criticisms based not on what they had said but on misrepresentation of them in the press. The lesson for researchers is clear: Think twice about whether socially sensitive research is being conducted in the most responsible manner possible and whether one is ready for the criticism and misrepresentation that may ensue in any case.

The Researcher's Relationship With the Press

Scientists sometimes make the mistake of expecting journalists to help them with their public image or to help disseminate their findings (Goodfield, 1981). Journalists, however, want information that is newsworthy, that is, likely to interest their audience, and that runs counter to everyday expectations, or that contains elements of dispute and contention among parties (Channels, this volume; Tunstall, 1971). Given this basic difference between the publicity goals of scientists and the reporting goals of journalists, it is hardly surprising that scientists are often shocked at what they find in print and then wish they had refused to be interviewed.

Research on the accuracy of science reporting in the print media indicates that errors of *fact* are less frequent than errors of *emphasis*. Typically, the headline is flashy and misleading; what is unique about the research is overemphasized, and essential contextual information is omitted (Tichenor, Olien, Harrison, & Donohue, 1970). Fortunately, scientists can affect the accuracy of reporting by insisting on face-to-face interviews, having the reporter's notes read back to them, and insisting on seeing the article before it is printed (Tichenor et al., 1970). Owing to the exigencies of deadlines and reporters' dislike of anything resembling censorship, however, they may not be eager to submit their article to the scientist before it goes to press.

Stocking and Dunwoody (1982) offer several other useful suggestions about dealing with the press: As journalists often lack training in the social sciences, it would be useful to ask about the reporter's background to learn how much relevant training he or she brings to the interview, and then to do as much educating of the reporter as seems necessary during the interview. Even if the reporter has a background in social science, a researcher must never assume the reporter is knowledgeable in a particular area of specialization. It is a good idea to educate oneself about what the journalist is looking for by asking the reporter questions such as the following: What interests you in this research? Why did you decide to talk to me? What will be the angle of your story? The reporter who has clear ideas about the purpose of the interview probably deserves an interview. When describing the research, the researcher should use simple, direct, jargon-free language. When providing the reporter with information that should not appear in print, the researcher must announce, *before* giving the information, that it is "off the record"; reporters are not obligated to honor that request after the information has been given. When the reporter asks a poor question, the scientist might politely respond, "A better question would be . . ." Finally, the scientist should consider issuing a press release; the American Psychological Association has produced a booklet that tells psychologists how to prepare press releases (Olean, 1977; see also Channels, this volume).

The Researcher and Special Interest Groups

Politicians and journalists are the most visible opinion leaders, but they are often only the purveyors of opinions expressed by special interest groups. For example, the press probably would have said little about the Kinsey report had not certain clergy galvanized their congregations into writing letters to newspapers and politicians.

The importance of educating the press and politicians about social research is underlined by the fact that there are a large number of talk show hosts, religious opinion makers, and leaders of special interest groups who are also "educating" people about social research and urging people to write to their politicians and newspapers to protest our "sins" and "injustices." Any talk show host can invite listeners to phone in their opinions on, say, "those Berkeley psychologists who say kids who use drugs are better adjusted." Scientists must be prepared to respond.

No one thinks clearly when under public attack, especially when the attack is personal and absurd. What a scientist feels like saying under such circumstances may well be counterproductive. Social scientists who plan to publish research that invites such distortion would benefit from wise counsel before they publish. One's scientific or professional society, university legal counsel, and colleagues who have ventured into sensitive areas may have sound advice to offer and may help one to retain a calm and balanced perspective if an attack is launched. The dignity of science and its ability to exert an enlightened influence on public policy are affected by the way scientists respond to attack. It is best to speak wisely and with good counsel, or to say nothing.

References

Booth, W. (1989, January 20). Asking America about its sex life. *Science, 243,* 304.

Boruch, R. F., & Cecil, J. S. (1979). *Assuring the confidentiality of social research data.* Philadelphia: University of Pennsylvania Press.

Case, P. (1990). The prevention point needle exchange program. In J. E. Sieber, Y. Song-Kim, & P. Kelzer (Eds.), *Vulnerable populations and AIDS: Ethical and procedural requirements for social and behavioral research and intervention.* [Available from the Pioneer Bookstore: (510) 881-3507.]

Cook, T. D., & Campbell, D. T. (1979). *Quasi-experimentation: Design and analysis issues for field settings.* Chicago: Rand McNally.

Furor over report on teenage drug use. (May 14, 1990). *San Francisco Chronicle,* p. A10.

Goodfield, J. (1981). *Reflections on science and the media.* Washington, DC: American Association for the Advancement of Science.

Humphreys, L. (1970). *Tearoom trade: Impersonal sex in public places.* Chicago: Aldine.

Kinsey, A. C., Pomeroy, W. B., & Martin, C. E. (1948). *Sexual behavior in the human male.* Philadelphia: W. B. Saunders.

Kinsey, A. C., Pomeroy, W. B., Martin, C. E., & Gebhard, P. H. (1953). *Sexual behavior in the human female.* Philadelphia: W. B. Saunders.

Melton, G. B., Levine, R. J., Koocher, G. P., Rosenthal, R., & Thompson, W. C. (1988). Community consultation in socially sensitive research: Lessons from clinical trials on treatments for AIDS. *American Psychologist, 43,* 573-581.

Olean, M. M. (1977). *Communicating with the public—via the media—about psychology.* Washington, DC: American Psychological Association.

Shedler, J., & Block, J. (1990). Adolescent drug use and psychological health: A longitudinal study. *American Psychologist, 45,* 612-630.

Sieber, J. E. (1992). *Planning ethically responsible research.* Newbury Park, CA: Sage.

Stocking, S. H., & Dunwoody, S. L. (1982). Social science in the mass media: Images and evidence. In J. Sieber (Ed.), *The ethics of social research: Fieldwork, regulation and publication.* New York: Springer-Verlag.

Tichenor, P., Olien, C., Harrison, A., & Donohue, G. A. (1970). Mass communication systems and communication accuracy in science news reporting. *Journalism Quarterly, 47,* 673-683.

Tunstall, J. (1971). *Journalists at work.* London: Constable.

Wells, W. G., Jr. (1982). Politicians and social scientists. *American Behavioral Scientist, 26,* 235-249.

Youngstrom, N. (1991). Sex behavior studies are derailed. *APA Monitor, 22*(11), 1, 29.

PART II

Designing Research on Sensitive Topics

Duelli Klein (1983, p. 38) points out that "the 'what' to investigate must come prior to the decision of 'how' to go about doing one's research." In a number of important respects, what is studied can be constrained in significant ways by the sensitive character of the topic. For example, powerful gatekeepers can impose restrictions on researchers in ways that constrain their capacity to produce or report on findings that threaten the interests of the powerful. Funding agencies, it has been argued, tend to prefer research having a particular character: research that is relevant to the policymaking process (Abrams, 1981; Sjoberg & Nett, 1968); based on individualistic rather than structural explanations (Hanmer & Leonard, 1984; Galliher & McCartney, 1973); and quantitative or positivistic in its methodology (Broadhead & Rist, 1976; Ditton & Williams, 1981). One lesson that some writers have drawn from this is that the organization of research funding tends to serve the interests of powerful groups in society by excluding support for research on topics that they might consider sensitive or detrimental to their interests. The institutional context within which researchers operate is also seen to abet this tendency because, it is argued, universities and research institutions dislike offending local elites or putting in jeopardy sources of possible funding (Broadhead & Rist, 1976; Moore, 1973; Record, 1967).

Sensitivity can also affect "what to investigate" in other ways. According to Sieber and Stanley (1988, p. 50), the very fact that a researcher poses a particular theory or research question can have major social implications even if the research is never performed. Thus framing a specific research question about a sensitive topic presents an initial set of problems. Consider, for instance, research on domestic violence. The question that has dominated this area of inquiry for more than two decades has been this: Why do battered women stay with partners who abuse them? Regardless of the answers generated, posing the question itself establishes the parameters of the problem of partner abuse in terms of the behavior of battered women. Attention is deflected from batterers onto victims. It is battered women who are defined as deviant for remaining in abusive relationships, not their partners who are deviant for battering them (Loseke & Cahill, 1984). In short, asking: "Why do battered women stay?"—rather than "What factors make battering possible or even permissible in our society and others?"—creates a scientific and popular milieu for blaming the victim. To paraphrase Sieber and Stanley (1988, p. 50), faulty ideas drawn from social science research may powerfully affect social conceptions of significant social problems and issues regardless of the adequacy of the research findings.

This is a point taken up in this part in Sharon Herzberger's chapter on studying child abuse. Herzberger examines the methodological difficulties that arise when studying this sensitive topic. She is especially concerned with empirical tests of the widely accepted "cyclical hypothesis," the notion that individuals who were physically abused by their parents tend to become child abusers themselves. Herzberger argues that research on child abuse has been plagued by four major problems: inconsistent operational definitions, lack of control or comparison groups, failure to use multivariate analysis, and the limits of retrospective studies. These are problems that occur in many research areas, and the deficiencies that Herzberger identifies can be generalized to research on other sensitive topics. For example, Renzetti (1992) notes in her research on homosexual partner abuse that vague and inconsistent definitions of the behavior in question make comparisons of findings across studies difficult at best and also give rise to difficulties and confusion over important "facts," such as the incidence of the behavior.

In the case of child abuse, Herzberger argues, the methodological flaws that she identifies seriously undermine many of the early studies of the cyclical hypothesis. Later, better designed research has provided only modest support for the proposition. As Sieber and Stanley (1988, p. 53), point out, "Sensitive research topics are more likely to have applications in the 'real' world that society will enthusiastically embrace, irrespective of the validity of the application." Perhaps for this reason many social scientists and lay people continue to treat the cyclical hypothesis as fact. Herzberger contends, however, that this has serious consequences: It provides a shaky foundation on which to build future research and inhibits accurate theory building by researchers; it misguides social service personnel and policymakers as they attempt to develop effective programs; and it arouses stress and fear in many formerly abused adults who are misled into believing that they will inevitably abuse their own children.

Economist J. J. Thomas, in his chapter in this part, focuses on the difficulties of studying the hidden or underground economy. There are many respects in which Thomas's chapter echoes the concerns about implementation and measurement raised by Herzberger. He notes that disagreements over definitions of the underground economy have led to considerable confusion. More important, however, is his point that two factors have constrained research on this sensitive topic and have inhibited the development of a comprehensive understanding of it: the training of economists to analyze rather than collect data and mainstream economists' lack of interest in criminal behavior.

After reviewing several indirect measures of the underground economy using both macro- and microeconomic data sources, and delineating the strengths and weaknesses of each, Thomas suggests that an interdisciplinary approach to the study of the underground economy may be more fruitful. While mindful of the problems involved, he urges economists to adopt various methods used by other social scientists, such as the use of surveys and participant observation techniques, and he encourages collaborative research between economists and other social scientists. We share his optimism that interdisciplinary research endeavors may generate higher quality data, not only in studies of the underground economy but in studies of other sensitive topics as well.

In some countries—the United Kingdom is an example—research on the underground economy is sensitive because of its political implications. The extent of participation in the underground economy has, for instance, entered into heated debates about the incidence of welfare fraud. Whatever heat or light has been generated by these controversies, however, research on the topic itself has still remained possible. There are some contexts, though, in which political circumstances massively constrain the ability to do research. In their chapter in this part, Curran and Cook consider how research on the juvenile justice system in the People's Republic of China was affected by the massacre in Tiananmen Square. They discuss how, in the aftermath of Tiananmen, the Chinese government increased control over the publication and circulation of research and over activities of domestic and foreign scholars. According to Curran and Cook, the conflict in Tiananmen Square also had effects in the West. Funding agencies and others began to look askance at continued research activity in China. Curran and Cook suggest that in some respects this reaction, while understandable, was misplaced. They argue that continued involvement in research on China is both appropriate and necessary, while recognizing that there are costs and difficulties in this involvement.

Other problems that are especially acute for researchers investigating sensitive topics are those deriving from the recruitment of study participants. In studies of relatively innocuous behavior or issues, complete sampling frames are often available that allow for random sampling and a sound estimate of sampling bias. This is rarely the case, however, in studies of sensitive topics. Indeed, the more sensitive or threatening the topic under examination, the more difficult sampling is likely to be, because potential participants have greater need to hide their involvement.

Systematic treatments of sampling issues related to deviant populations can be found in Becker (1970) and, for rare populations, in Kish (1965), Sudman and Kalton (1986), Sudman, Sirken, and Curran (1988). The major strategies that can be used, singly or in combination, for sampling "special" populations that are rare and/or deviant in some way are (a) the use of lists, (b) multipurpose surveys, (c) household screening procedures, (d) the location of locales within which sample members congregate as sites for the recruitment of respondents, (e) the use of networking or "snowballing" strategies, (f) advertising for respondents, and (g) obtaining study participants in return for providing a service of some kind. In the study of deviant populations, probably the most common method used has been the "snowball" sample. Ironically, though, as qualitative researchers have begun to develop a more critical assessment of the limitations of this method (Biernacki & Waldorf, 1981), survey researchers have become more open to using similar network sampling methods to locate rare or elusive populations (Rothbart, Fine, & Sudman, 1982; Sudman & Kalton, 1986; Sudman et al., 1988).

Martin and Dean had both ethical and technical reasons for rejecting screening procedures to generate a sample for their study of the impact of the AIDS epidemic on the emotional and behavioral functioning of gay men. As they point out in their chapter in this part, there was a likelihood that the stigma attached to homosexuality, along with growing antigay harassment and violence, would likely bias the sampling frame

toward gay men who were self-assured and open about their sexual preference. Neighborhood screening would also produce biases, because the
logical choice—in this case, Greenwich Village—is a predominantly
white, upper middle-class neighborhood of highly visible gay men. (In
any case, a number of researchers—e.g., Hope, Kennedy, & DeWinter,
1976; McRae, 1986—have recorded that the costs of having to screen
large populations to uncover individuals possessing relatively rare traits
are a major limitation on such methods.)

Martin and Dean's choice was to use network sampling including a
variety of sources to "seed" their initial sample. Sudman and Kalton
(1986) recently demonstrated that lists that provide only partial coverage of some populations may still be a useful starting point for the development of an adequate sample. Among the sources that Martin and
Dean used for the base, or "generation zero" as they call it, of their
sample was the membership lists of gay organizations in New York City.
Although they tried to control for many of the difficulties inherent in
network or snowball sampling, they were unable to determine precisely
to what extent they had been successful in generating a reliable sample.
Nevertheless, cross-group comparison and comparisons with two random samples of gay men indicate that they obtained a fairly representative sample of gay men who had not been diagnosed as having AIDS.
Their chapter is likely to be helpful to researchers interested in developing a workable sampling strategy for a survey of a hidden population.
Martin and Dean's work suggests that, even in the absence of external
validating criteria, it is possible to go a long way despite imperfect
circumstances. It is, however, with sadness that we must report that
John Martin died of AIDS while this book was in the final stages of
preparation.

References

Abrams, P. (1981). Visionaries and vituosi: Competence and purpose in the education of
    sociologists. *Sociology, 15,* 530-538.
Becker, H. S. (1970). Practitioners of vice and crime. In R. Haberstein (Ed.), *Pathways
    to data.* Chicago: Aldine.
Biernacki, P., & Waldorf, D. (1981). Snowball sampling: Problems and techniques of
    chain referral sampling. *Sociological Methods and Research, 10,* 141-163.
Broadhead, R. S., & Rist, R. C. (1976). Gatekeepers and the social control of research.
    Social Problems, 23, 325-336.

Ditton, J., & Williams, R. (1981). *The fundable versus the doable* (Occasional paper). Glasgow: University of Glasgow, Department of Sociology.

Duelli Klein, R. (1983). How to do what we want to do: Thoughts about feminist methodology. In G. Bowles & R. Duelli Klein (Eds.), *Theories of women's studies.* London: Routledge & Kegan Paul.

Galliher, J. F., & McCartney, J. L. (1973). The influence of funding agencies on juvenile delinquency research. *Social Problems, 21,* 77-90.

Hanmer, J., & Leonard, D. (1984). Negotiating the problem: The DHSS and research on violence in marriage. In C. Bell & H. Roberts (Eds.), *Social researching: Politics, problems and practice.* London: Routledge & Kegan Paul.

Hope, E., Kennedy, M., & DeWinter, A. (1976). Homeworkers in North London. In D. L. Barker & S. Allen (Eds.), *Dependence and exploitation in work and marriage.* London: Longman.

Kish, L. (1965). *Survey sampling.* New York: John Wiley.

Loseke, D. R., & Cahill, S. E. (1984). The social construction of deviance: Experts on battered women. *Social Problems, 31,* 296-310.

McRae, S. (1986). *Cross-class families.* Oxford: Clarendon.

Moore, J. (1973). Social constraints on sociological knowledge: Academics and research concerning minorities. *Social Problems, 21,* 65-77.

Record, J. C. (1967). The research institute and the pressure group. In G. Sjoberg (Ed.), *Ethics, politics and social research.* Cambridge, MA: Schenckman.

Renzetti, C. M. (1992). *Violent betrayal: Partner abuse in lesbian relationships.* Newbury Park, CA: Sage.

Rothbart, G. S., Fine, M., & Sudman, S. (1982). On finding and interviewing the needles in a haystack: The use of multiplicity sampling. *Public Opinion Quarterly, 45,* 408-421.

Sieber, J. E., & Stanley, B. (1988). Ethical and professional dimensions of socially sensitive research. *American Psychologist, 43,* 49-55.

Sjoberg, G., & Nett, R. (1968). *A methodology for social research.* New York: Harper & Row.

Sudman, S., & Kalton, G. (1986). New developments in the sampling of special populations. *Annual Review of Sociology, 12,* 401-429.

Sudman, S., Sirken, M. G., & Curran, C. D. (1988). Sampling rare and elusive populations. *Science, 240,* 991-996.

3

The Cyclical Pattern of Child Abuse

A Study of Research Methodology

SHARON D. HERZBERGER

The beginnings of modern concern about child abuse are attributed to Kempe and his colleagues, who in 1962 identified the "battered child syndrome." This paper was rapidly followed by others that addressed the causes of child battering (e.g., Bennie & Sclare, 1969; Steele & Pollock, 1968; see Gelles, 1979, and McLeer, 1988, for reviews). These papers tended to concentrate on the characteristics of the parents who perpetrated this egregious act. Soon it was discovered that many of these parents reported being maltreated themselves (Curtis, 1963; Spinetta & Rigler, 1972) and, lo and behold, we witnessed the birth of the "cyclical hypothesis": Children who have experienced abuse at the hands of their parents tend to grow up to abuse their own children. And the hypothesis was transformed into "fact" as article after article cited it as though the hypothesis had been tested and confirmed.

The influence of the cyclical hypothesis rapidly extended beyond the professional and academic communities as child abuse became a popular topic for media presentation. Busses in Chicago during the 1970s

AUTHOR'S NOTE: An earlier version of this chapter appeared in the *American Behavioral Scientist, 33,* 529-545.

carried posters saying, "Stop the cycle of violence," which urged violent individuals to call local self-help groups. It became common (and indeed today still is common) for researchers and practitioners to overhear conversations about the cross-generational transmission of abuse at social gatherings or even at the hairdresser, or to be questioned about the phenomenon when giving public lectures (e.g., Gelles & Straus, 1988).

Today we know that the cyclical hypothesis is overly simplistic and fails to tell much of the truth about the transmission of violence from one generation of a family to the next. Whereas, 20 years ago, researchers attempted to make generalizations from selected case studies and were not concerned about issues of definition and control, today's child abuse researchers are more sophisticated in their approach to testing hypotheses. As excellent recent surveys of the methodological problems extant in this field have shown (Geffner, Rosenbaum, & Hughes, 1988; Weis, 1989), however, much improvement in research methodology remains to be instituted and researchers need to be much more self-conscious and explicit about the limitations imposed by the methods they have chosen for their work.

This chapter first reviews some of the methodological and theoretical problems that afflict child abuse research in general. I concentrate on four main concerns: definitional problems, the lack of appropriate control or comparison groups, the failure to address child abuse from a multitheoretical and multivariate perspective, and the difficulties imposed by retrospective designs. Next, I apply these criticisms to research on the cyclical hypothesis. The chapter examines the history of research on the cyclical pattern, reviews the state of our current knowledge, and suggests future directions for investigation.

This review is motivated by the recognition that child abuse is a sensitive research topic. Its sensitivity is evident in two respects. First, the research requires extraordinary delicacy in eliciting information from respondents. Although respondent confidentiality is often promised, participants in most interview or survey studies are also told that disclosure of some types of information will nullify this promise and that the researcher will be required to report such information to the authorities. Even under conditions when the researcher can guarantee anonymity, respondents may not believe it or fully understand how it will be achieved. Thus it is difficult or perhaps even impossible to ensure that research participants will provide honest answers to questions. This difficulty renders the methodological problems noted in this chapter to some extent unremediable. Second, disseminating information that stems from research on child abuse is highly consequential. Such information may affect public policy and may influence how professionals and policymakers view abusive parents and their victims as well as how victims view themselves. Therefore it is imperative to conduct valid investigations and to disseminate accurate interpretations of the results in a manner that is sensitive to these potentialities.

Overview of Methodological Problems

Definition of Child Abuse

Virtually every review of research on the topic of child abuse bemoans the lack of precise operational definitions. Definitions are needed not only to distinguish among various forms of abuse (e.g., physical, sexual, emotional) but to distinguish abuse from nonabuse or at least to allow researchers to understand the characteristics that underlie the continuum from nonabuse to severely abusive behavior. The ambiguity involved in specifying what constitutes the behavior under study leads to difficulties in comparing results across studies and disagreements about the "facts" pertinent to the phenomenon. Weis (1989), for example, reports that estimates of the amount of child maltreatment run from 1% of the child population of the United States to 30%, depending upon one's definition. Fromuth and Burkhart (1987) report that from 4% to 24% of male college students have been sexually abused, again depending upon the restrictiveness of the category. The age of the victim and perpetrator, the differences in their ages, the acts involved, and the victim's perspective on the acts may or may not be taken into account by researchers when they label cases of sexual abuse, thus leading to variations in the incidence rates reported.

Variations in the definition emerge because some researchers concentrate on the perpetrator's act (e.g., Straus, 1979), while others examine the act, the consequences, and the circumstances surrounding the victimization (see Weis, 1989). Weis (1989) urges that acts should be distinguished from attempted actions and from threats to perform the action, and all should be monitored and their significance to the phenomenon under study analyzed.

In addition, the degree of victimization, including information about the frequency and severity of injuries, should be noted. Knowing that a father beat a child twice with a stick seems insufficient compared with knowing that the first time the child suffered welts on the arm that lasted for two days, while the second time she suffered multiple facial cuts.

Bradley and Lindsay (1987) suggest that the etiology of the abusive incident is an important component of the definition. Abuse due to parental psychopathology, poor anger control, neglect, hatred toward the child, and inadequate parenting skills may not lead to different parental acts but may lead to widely divergent consequences as the child develops and therefore should be part of the definition and labeling. In addition, the parent's and child's interpretation of the act may mediate the consequences that follow (Corbin, 1987; Herzberger, 1983; Herzberger, Potts, & Dillon, 1981). A child who believes that the parent hurt him or her for positive reasons (out of love or wanting to teach an important lesson) may respond differently in the long and short term than one who rejects the violence as the act of a malicious person. A vivid example of the former is the child of Vietnamese American parents who bruise him by rubbing his body with coins to cure minor illnesses (Gray & Cosgrove, 1985). The social context in which this "victimization" occurs is such that the child's perspective on it may differ greatly from the perspective of another child whose body was bruised in other circumstances.

Failure to define the phenomenon in question leads to ignorance about the facts, as noted previously, but it also prevents precise theory building and testing and leads to inaccurate generalizations about child abuse. For example, we find reports that abused children suffer from loss of self-esteem, become wary, and are likely to become aggressive (e.g., Martin & Rodeheffer, 1976). But, does one act of child abuse result in this personality change? Which types of acts produce such change and under what circumstances? Without explicit instruction about the process by which researchers label an act of abuse, we cannot answer such questions from the literature. As stated previously, the sensitive nature of this research topic renders it more difficult to gather the wealth of information that would lead to a full understanding of the circumstances that surround and define the abusive act. When this is done, however, better comparisons across investigations can be made and better tests of theory are permitted.

Inadequate Comparison Groups

When trying to understand the etiology or consequences of child abuse, it is essential to compare a group that has been abused with a group that has not been abused but that is identical in all other important respects. This basic methodological principle has been violated in much research on child abuse. Some of our early knowledge stemmed from uncontrolled case studies (e.g., Steele & Pollock, 1968) in which the characteristics of only perpetrators or victims were examined. Even researchers who have used control or comparison groups have not done so adequately (see Geffner et al., 1988). For example, researchers who are interested in studying the long-term emotional consequences of physical abuse must compare a group of abused subjects with a group that did not suffer physical abuse. The difficulty arises in the ability to ensure that no physical abuse occurred to subjects in the comparison group. Often, researchers check police and social service records and permit the absence of substantiated reports of abuse to serve as the determining criterion. Given that we know many more cases of abuse exist than are reported and substantiated, however, this method is inadequate. One solution is to supplement and confirm the official record by interviewing subjects in both samples about their experience with violence, especially through a widely used instrument, such as the Conflict Tactics Scale (Straus, 1979). This procedure will identify some of the unofficial cases of abuse, although it will not catch people who wish to keep their violence hidden from the interviewer and will thus underestimate the true incidence of abuse. Thus, because of the sensitive information requested, comparison groups no doubt will contain abused or abusive individuals who have not provided an accurate history.

Other forms of abuse that accompany the abuse under consideration should also be examined. Gelles and Straus (1988) suggest that verbal violence almost always accompanies physical abuse. Similarly, many cases of sexual abuse of children may be labeled psychological abuse as well (Finkelhor, 1984; Garbarino, Guttmann, & Seeley, 1986). Thus researchers should attempt to measure all forms of abuse experienced by individuals in their sample (another way of stating this is that researchers should measure *how* abuse is *experienced* by individuals). It may be impossible to sort the separate effects of one type of violence from another, and researchers in such cases need to be careful about claiming that specific consequences are due to one particular form of abuse.

Multivariate Approach to Research

As the literature on child abuse has expanded from clinical case studies to involve several disciplines, the theoretical perspectives on the problem have multiplied. Primarily psychodynamic approaches have been supplanted by integrated theoretical perspectives that take into account sociological (Gelles & Straus, 1979), biological (Burgess & Draper, 1989), and social ecological (Belsky, 1980) or social cognitive (Dodge, Bates, & Pettit, 1990; Herzberger, 1983) factors. The recognition that there are various causes of abuse, however, has not greatly affected research in this area. Most research still uses simple correlation or analysis of variance designs and examines the contributions of one or two variables at a time rather than using a multivariate approach. The use of only one or a small set of predictors may exaggerate a variable's relationship to abuse. In contrast, through multiple regression, the contributions of other variables also believed to predict the behavior are measured simultaneously, which permits a more accurate assessment of the relative contribution of a given variable (however, see Briere, 1988, for a discussion of potential hazards of multivariate techniques).

Failure to adopt an integrated, multivariate approach has led to a repetitive and fragmented literature on child abuse (Ohlin & Tonry, 1989). Studies that address the myriad causes and consequences of aggression toward children will contribute more to our knowledge than studies of single variables out of context and in isolation. When we consider the difficulties of securing permission to work with abused children, abusive parents, or data from social service archives, the collection of extensive data bases from each study should be the top priority of researchers.

Research Designs

Much of the research on child abuse involves the collection of data at one time point by noting current behavior and asking respondents for a self-report of their history. Although researchers attempt to draw causal conclusions by questioning respondents about the antecedents and consequences of the abusive episode, there are great dangers in doing so (Weis, 1989). Freud (1955) said it well:

> So long as we trace a development from its final outcome backwards, the chain of events appears continuous and we feel we have gained an insight which is completely satisfactory or even exhaustive. But if we proceed the reverse way, then we no longer get the impression of an inevitable sequence of events . . . there might have been another result, and that we might have been just as well able to understand and explain the latter. (p. 167)

Thus, in retrospective studies, it is too easy to believe that one is verifying some causal hypothesis. Furthermore, people have trouble recalling the time period in which events occurred, the frequency of events, and their reactions (Sudman & Bradburn, 1982). Some researchers avoid self-reported histories by using data archives (e.g., Widom, 1989b). The use of archives may be problematic, however, due to selective and biased entry of such sensitive information, and the validity of the information in the archives is often untestable (Webb, Campbell, Schwartz, & Sechrest, 1969; Weis, 1989). For these reasons, the accuracy of conclusions drawn from archival information is often questionable.

Prospective studies are, of course, an excellent alternative to retrospective research. Given that child abuse is a relatively infrequent occurrence, however, it is expensive to monitor the prevalence of abuse and the circumstances that predict it among a randomly selected sample or even a stratified sample selected for its higher probability of abuse (Egeland & Sroufe, 1981). A less expensive, but still useful, alternative is to follow a sample of recently abused children and a comparison group, monitoring along the way other experiences that may promote aggressive parenting styles. Such studies provide us with an opportunity to observe how the experience of abuse influences the child's development, compared with other experiences that children have. As Dodge et al. (1990) have pointed out, however, children whose treatment has been brought to the attention of social service officials may lead different lives and therefore generalizations of research findings with such groups to other abused children are unwise. Thus prospective studies on randomly selected samples of children are most useful.

In the preceding pages, I have provided an overview of some of the major methodological problems that impede theory building and testing in the area of child abuse. This discussion provides a context in which to understand the difficulties of doing research on the cyclical hypothesis. As we will see, methodological problems have pervaded this subarea for the last 20 years and these problems have seriously affected the thinking of researchers, policymakers, and lay people.

Cyclical Hypothesis

In 1972, Spinetta and Rigler remarked, "One basic factor in the etiology of child abuse draws unanimity: abusing parents were themselves abused or neglected physically or emotionally as children" (p. 298). Similarly,

Kempe, Silverman, Steele, Droegemueller, and Silver (1962) state: "It has long been recognized by psychologists and social anthropologists that patterns of child rearing, both good and bad, are passed from one generation to the next in relatively unchanged form. . . . It would appear that one of the most important factors to be found in families where parental assault occurs is 'to do unto others as you have been done by' " (p. 106).

What was the evidence that led to such strong assertions? One of the studies cited often was that of Silver, Dublin, and Lourie (1969), who studied 34 suspected or confirmed child abuse cases. They found evidence in four (12%) of the cases that the abuser had been an abused child. Gibbins and Walker (1956) studied 39 people imprisoned for cruelty to children, finding parental rejection and hostility in their histories but only 2 cases of physical abuse. Similarly, Easson and Steinhilber (1961) reported eight case studies of boys who had committed violent crimes. In three cases, the boys had been physically assaulted by their parents. Easson and Steinhilber concluded that parental approval of the boys' aggression led to the violent crimes and that child abuse was just one of the many factors that created the problems noted.

Review of these and other studies led several investigators (Jayaratne, 1977; Potts, Herzberger, & Holland, 1979; Widom, 1989a) to suggest that there might not be sufficient evidence for such confidence in the cyclical pattern. First, none of the early studies compared the histories of abusive or violent individuals with those of nonabusive people. Second, the use of a conveniently selected, rather than a randomized, sample of individuals overestimated the relationship between childhood abuse and parental or adult violence. Furthermore, as Potts et al. (1979) pointed out, some of the studies cited as evidence for the cyclical process presented no empirical evidence whatsoever (e.g., Harper, 1963; Lystad, 1975; Morris, Gould, & Matthews, 1964) and the results of other studies that did contain empirical findings have been exaggerated by subsequent writers (see also Widom, 1989a). Thus some of the lore about the strength of the evidence in favor of the cyclical hypothesis stems from inaccurate reading and reporting of the results of early studies.

The first controlled attempt to verify the cyclical hypothesis was a survey by Straus and his colleagues (Straus, 1979; Straus, Gelles, & Steinmetz, 1980) of a random sample of the population of the United States. They found that 17.6% of the adults surveyed who had been physically punished twice or more a year as teenagers "abused" their own children. In contrast, 12.5% of the adults who had been physically punished less frequently abused their own children. There are at least two ways to interpret these data. One is that having been abused oneself leads to a 40% increase in the likelihood that one will become an abuser, thus confirming the cyclical hypothesis. A second interpretation is that the cyclical hypothesis is wrong; more than 80% of adults who experienced physical punishment did not abuse their own children.

This study, the first to use a comparison group, was important for a number of reasons. First, the study demonstrated the importance of testing hypotheses in a controlled fashion and the folly of drawing conclusions from select case studies. Second, Straus explicitly stated his criteria for testing the cyclical hypothesis. Although some researchers have questioned the generality of the findings, given the age limitations and the criteria for abuse, the circumstances under which these percentages were found were made explicit. Thus subsequent researchers were able to adopt or alter this definition and could easily compare results across studies.

Combining the Straus results with those of other investigations (Egeland, Jacobvitz, & Papatola, 1987; Hunter & Kilstrom, 1979), Kaufman and Zigler (1989) estimated the proportion of abusive parents who had been abused themselves to be approximately 30%, compared with a rate of 5% in the population in general. Finding that estimates ranged from 18% to 70% of abusive parents having experienced abuse in childhood, Kaufman and Zigler graphically demonstrate how differences in methodology affect the degree of support for the cyclical hypothesis. Studies using samples of known abusers or other high-risk samples (e.g., Egeland et al., 1987) find greater proportions of abused parents than studies using random samples of the population because parents abused as children are likely to suffer other stresses that enhance the likelihood of abuse. Similarly, studies starting with a sample of abusive and nonabusive parents and retrospectively studying their histories find more support for the cyclical hypothesis than studies beginning with a randomly drawn, prospective sample. Finally, studies that broadly define abuse (e.g., Egeland et al., 1987, added "borderline" cases to their number of cases of abuse and thereby added 30% to the total percentage of abusers who had been abused) or that measure only "abuse potential" (Miller & Challas, 1981) also find more support.

The findings of Straus and others confirm that receiving harsh physical treatment leads some people to treat others harshly. As Kaufman and Zigler (1989) have advised, "The time has come for the intergenerational myth to be placed aside; and for researchers to cease to ask, 'Do abused children become abusive parents?' " Instead, they urge researchers to ask, "under what conditions is the transmission of abuse most likely to occur?" (p. 191). I would like to suggest that there are at least three major directions for research needed to address this question. One set of questions pertains to the *specificity of reactions to abuse:* What forms of maltreatment lead to maltreatment of others, and can one form of maltreatment lead to a different form? A related second set of questions pertains to the *exact conditions under which abuse is transmitted.* In other words, why are some people ill-affected by their treatment as youth while others escape the cyclical pattern? A third set of questions pertains to the *role of the family as a special contributor to the transmission process:* Is abuse inflicted by a family member more likely to feed into an intergenerational pattern? Furthermore, are family members specifically targeted for the abuse that was transmitted from the previous generation? Or is abuse just as likely to lead an individual to behave violently outside the family?

Let us first address the specificity of reactions to abuse and the conditions that promote or impede the transmission process. Those who espouse the cyclical hypothesis never claim that an abusive act has a narrow range of effects when transmitted from one generation to the next, but neither do they specify the behaviors that would or would not be expected to be transmitted. The failure to deal with these matters is due largely to a lack of reflection and to theoretical ambiguity and not to a deliberate effort to be all inclusive. Little effort has been made to specify the degree, type, and frequency of maltreatment that will operate to the child's disadvantage (see Brassard, Germain, & Hart, 1987, and Garbarino et al., 1986, for discussion of the difficulty of deriving operational definitions of emotional abuse). This leads to problems. For example, Steele and Pollock (1968) claimed that their group of abusing parents consisted of some adults who had been physically beaten and some who had never experienced physical violence from a parent. In contrast, all reported feeling emotionally mistreated. Thus they, as well as Spinetta and Rigler (1972), claimed that emotional abuse as a child led to physical abuse as an adult. But Garbarino et al. (1986) have noted that all of us have suffered from emotional mistreatment at some time. The trick is to determine under what conditions a particular type, severity, and frequency of treatment will affect our interactions with others and in what way.

Research has begun to identify these conditions. Simons, Whitbeck, Conger, and Chyi-In (1991), using partially retrospective methods, found that mothers' "harsh parenting" (not necessarily "abusive") was more predictive of their adult children's severe treatment of offspring than was fathers' harsh parenting. Egeland and his colleagues (Egeland & Sroufe, 1981; Egeland, Sroufe, & Erickson, 1984) have compared the characteristics of children who have suffered different forms of maltreatment. They found that, although children from physically abusive, verbally abusive, psychologically unavailable, and neglectful homes were all likely to suffer, some differences were found and that children of "psychologically unavailable" mothers were found to be the most disturbed. Although these studies did not follow the children until they became parents, their later research with abusive and nonabusive mothers found that any form of maltreatment in childhood—physical, emotional, sexual, neglectful—may lead to maltreatment of one's own children (Egeland et al., 1987). Other research, however, suggests that the family circumstances of parents who engage in various forms of abuse differ (Martin & Walters, 1982), indicating that different theories may be needed to account for the circumstances that promote the transmission of different forms of abuse.

The almost universal mention of emotional support or love as a factor missing in the childhood history of abusive parents (Brassard et al., 1987; Egeland, Jacobvitz, & Sroufe, 1988; Garbarino et al., 1986; Herrenkohl, Herrenkohl, & Toedter, 1983; Hunter & Kilstrom, 1979; Kaufman & Zigler, 1987; Spinetta & Rigler, 1972) suggests that this may be a central ingredient in the transmission process. Also important are the current presence of an emotionally supportive other and a relatively low level of stress. Furthermore, some attempt to gain perspective on one's abusive history helps, either through therapy (Egeland et al., 1988) or self-reflection. Hunter and Kilstrom (1979) report that abused parents who did not abuse their children provided better accounts of their own abuse and were more angry about it than parents who engaged in abuse themselves. Egeland et al. (1988) found that nonabusive mothers were more likely to recognize the consequences of their own abused history and how it might relate to their own parenting practices.

If it is true that emotional maltreatment is the key to the transmission process, then research methods that tap only the existence of physical violence in each generation are inadequate. It is possible that the effect of physical abuse, if important at all, is secondary to the traumas inflicted by the accompanying emotional maltreatment (Jayaratne, 1977).

Because we might expect emotional maltreatment to accompany physical maltreatment, but would not expect all cases of emotional maltreatment to have a coexisting physical component, it is thus critical to monitor the presence of all forms of maltreatment when studying the transmission process.

Perhaps the most provocative set of recent studies are those that examine the consequences of viewing violence within the family as opposed to being victimized oneself (see Fantuzzo & Lindquist, 1989). Certainly the implied message of the cyclical hypothesis is that children adopt the behaviors they observe parents perform. Therefore we should not be surprised that seeing one's parents engaged in spousal abuse affects the child as much as, if not more than, being victimized personally. Caesar (1988), for example, compared a group of wife abusers to nonabusers who also sought therapy. Batterers were more likely than nonbatterers to have experienced some form of child abuse (38% versus 11%, respectively), but they were also more likely to have viewed violence between their parents (50% versus 17%, respectively). Caesar did not report multivariate analyses wherein the separate and combined effects of own victimization and witnessing the victimization of others were assessed. It appears, however, that the witnessing of violence or the combination of witnessing and being victimized seemed best to distinguish batterers and nonbatterers.[1] Similarly, Kalmuss (1984) found that observing violence between one's parents related more strongly to violence in one's own marriage than did being hit as a teenager. When both forms of exposure to violence were present, Kalmuss found the highest amount of current marital violence (see also Miller, Handal, Gilner, & Cross, 1991). Not all studies support this evolving model of the transmission process (e.g., MacEwen & Barling, 1988), and Cappell and Heiner (1990) have suggested that observing spousal aggression may increase one's vulnerability to victimization more than one's likelihood of becoming a perpetrator. But this body of research argues strongly that future studies of the cyclical pattern must include an assessment of various forms of violence to which the children might be exposed.

Studies have also examined which children are more likely to be affected adversely by the parent's victimization. Wolfe, Jaffe, Wilson, and Zak (1984) found that boys were more likely to be affected by their mother's abuse than girls and that the mother's well-being significantly moderated the child's adjustment. Simons et al.'s (1991) recent study that explicitly assessed intergenerational parenting styles, however, found that mothers pass on ill parenting to both sons and daughters.

Caesar (1988) used the descriptions of the violence experienced or witnessed by batterers and nonbatterers to understand why similar childhood experiences lead to different adult behaviors. We must be cautious about overgeneralizing from these results because this study used retrospective methods. The results are somewhat predictable, however: Batterers tended to idolize aggressive parents, to feel protective of them, and to have become involved in their parents' fights on the side of one or the other parent. Nonbatterers, in contrast, recognized their parents' faults and remained distant from marital fights.

The reviewed research suggests that various forms of maltreatment within the family may lead to similar *and* to different forms of maltreatment of other family members. These studies also remind us of the importance of examining the individual's own violent treatment in comparison with the contributions of other variables. The social context in which abuse occurs and the characteristics of the abused child may be as important as the abuse itself. As we develop an understanding of the consequences produced by different forms of maltreatment and the circumstances that surround the maltreatment, we can begin to formulate more detailed theories about the specific conditions under which abuse is transmitted.

Research that examines only the patterns of violence within the family, however, may underestimate dramatically the consequences of victimization. Recent studies (Dodge et al., 1990; Hotaling & Straus, 1989; Kruttschnitt, Ward, & Sheble, 1987; Widom, 1989b; see also the review by Fagan & Wexler, 1987) suggest that violence within the family can lead to violence outside the family. Dodge et al. (1990) found that physical abuse by parents predicts children's aggressive behavior in school. Widom (1989b), using multiple regression to control for other characteristics related to the commission of crime, notes that neither physical abuse nor neglect is as important in predicting criminal arrest as age, gender, or race. Abused and neglected young adults, however, were significantly more likely to have been arrested for a violent crime than controls. Hotaling and Straus (1989) suggest that, although the cycle of violence may generalize outside the home for any group of children, it is most likely to happen among boys and children from blue-collar families. And Widom (1989a) notes that abused children are often self-destructive, suggesting that the cycle of violence may be directed inward as well as outward. Thus, to fully understand the cycle of violence, researchers must simultaneously assess familial and nonfamilial manifestations of the consequences of abuse.

Parental violence is not the only source of violent behavior. Because some people who are violent toward family members never experienced violence within their family of origin (Straus, 1979), we might expect that exposure to nonfamilial violence contributed to some extent to the current violence. Social learning theorists (Bandura, 1973) may believe that family members are in a position to serve as ideal models of aggressive behavior, but they also recognize that children and adults are exposed to a variety of influential people, both inside and outside the family.

The manner or extent to which there is something unique about *family* violence that distinguishes it from violence in general is not known (Gelles & Straus, 1979; Weis, 1989). Gelles and Straus (1979) suggest that characteristics such as role relationships, intensity of contact, involuntary membership, and stress mark the family as different than other social groups. Whether these characteristics affect the transmission process, however, remains to be determined.

Concluding Remarks

We know that violence breeds some form of violence among some people and that there are myriad ways in which violence can be transmitted. We do not yet know the limitations to this relationship. We cannot say with confidence what amount or frequency of abuse, administered by whom and under what conditions, will promote the transmission or inhibit it. We do know, however, that the relationship between childhood history of abuse and adult violence is not simple and that efforts to study it should be multifaceted.

It is abundantly clear, however, that not all people who have experienced violence will grow up to be violent. In fact, a minority of maltreated children grow up to maltreat their own children (Kaufman & Zigler, 1989; Straus, 1979). Less than a third of teenagers abused or neglected as children have a record of delinquency, and less than a third of the same children will grow up to have an adult criminal record (Widom, 1989a). We might expect substantial overlap between those who engage in violent behaviors within the family and outside. If this expectation is confirmed, many children who have been exposed to violence remain nonviolent.

To test fully the cyclical hypothesis, we must develop prospective, longitudinal studies that follow children through their own parenting years. Such studies must monitor the child's and adult's exposure to violence from family members and from other sources and must control for other factors known to be associated with violent acts.[2] Obviously, this type of study is expensive, and results will not come quickly. But such a study is needed to assess accurately the extent to which violence begets violence and the family's role in the cyclical pattern.

Current research methods are more sophisticated than in the original studies, but the current failure to understand the circumstances under which abuse is transmitted from generation to generation stymies policymakers and social service workers in their efforts to develop prevention or intervention programs narrowly targeted to those who would most benefit. Furthermore, policymakers do not know whether to target limited resources to families or to the society-at-large. Thus more and better research is needed and, until we can be more confident about our conclusions, we should be more humble about the implications of our findings.

Many of us who have talked to lay people about child abuse have been startled by the undue influence of the cyclical hypothesis (see Gelles & Straus, 1988). Let me recount one of my earliest and one of my most recent experiences in this regard. In 1979, Potts et al. delivered a paper in which we criticized the nonreflective acceptance of the cyclical hypothesis and cited Straus's (1979) evidence that abused children do not necessarily become abusers. Abstracts from the paper were published by news services and broadcast on radio stations. Shortly thereafter, we received mail from adults around the country thanking us for giving them hope. They had been alarmed ever since they began hearing that, because they had been abused, they were going to abuse their children. One parent reported that she always thought that "someday" she would harm her children, even though until then she had been a loving, nonviolent parent. These parents were happy to hear that someone believed that they could conquer the influence of their past.

Then, recently, as I was having my hair cut, a woman in the next chair was discussing with her hairdresser a television special about an abusive husband and father that both of them had watched the night before. I waited silently for the inevitable and was not disappointed. When one of them mentioned that the child involved would no doubt grow up to be abusive himself, the other concurred. I felt compelled to announce that this was not necessarily true and explained the rationale underlying my statement. But, when they asked how to tell which children would be so affected, I was disappointed that in the last quarter century we have not made better progress in answering this question.

These are examples of the consequences of the insensitive dissemination of study findings and the poor methodology used to study the cyclical hypothesis. The widespread propagation and acceptance of the cyclical hypothesis distorted professional and lay perspectives on the consequences of abuse victimization. And the extent of the damage done will never be known. Sound methodology is important for research on nonsensitive topics as well; therefore, in a sense, the concerns of this chapter are universal. Research findings related to sensitive topics such as child abuse, however, are influential far beyond the academic and social service communities. As researchers, we should minimize the chances of repeating the mistakes by learning from our checkered past.

Notes

1. Another difference between these two groups, however, was corporal punishment. Caesar (1988) reports that, among those who did not witness violence among parents, batterers were more likely than nonbatterers to have experienced such corporal punishment as being hit with a belt or switch (62% versus 8%, respectively). Thus, although this author did not label this form of punishment abuse (preferring instead to rely upon the respondent's own assessment of whether he had been abused), others (e.g., Straus, 1979) have. If we added batterers who had received corporal punishment to the group of abused batterers, the differences between own victimization and witnessing as predictors of battering would diminish.

2. Widom's (1989b) and Dodge et al.'s (1990) data are exciting because, if they follow their current samples to parenthood, they can address these issues. To test the relative importance of the parent's abuse on the child's development, however, the authors must continue to gather information about the participants' exposure to other forms of violence and to other experiences that are known to predict aggressive behavior.

References

Bandura, A. (1973). *Aggression: A social learning analysis.* Englewood Cliffs, NJ: Prentice-Hall.

Belsky, J. (1980). Child maltreatment: An ecological integration. *American Psychologist, 35,* 320-335.

Bennie, E. H., & Sclare, A. B. (1969). The battered child syndrome. *American Journal of Psychiatry, 125,* 975-979.

Bradley, E. J., & Lindsay, R. C. L. (1987). Methodological and ethical issues in child abuse research. *Journal of Family Violence, 3,* 239-255.

Brassard, M. R., Germain, R., & Hart, S. N. (1987). *Psychological maltreatment of children and youth.* New York: Pergamon.

Briere, J. (1988). Controlling for family variables in abuse effects research: A critique of the "partialling" approach. *Journal of Interpersonal Violence, 3,* 80-89.

Burgess, R. L., & Draper, P. (1989). The explanation of family violence: The role of biological, behavioral, and cultural selection. In L. Ohlin & M. Tonry (Eds.), *Family violence.* Chicago: University of Chicago Press.

Caesar, P. L. (1988). Exposure to violence in the families-of-origin among wife-abusers and maritally nonviolent men. *Violence and Victims, 3,* 49-63.

Cappell, C., & Heiner, R. B. (1990). The intergenerational transmission of family aggression. *Journal of Family Violence, 5,* 135-152.

Corbin, J. E. (1987). Child abuse and neglect: The cultural context. In R. E. Helfer & R. S. Kempe (Eds.), *The battered child* (4th ed.). Chicago: University of Chicago Press.

Curtis, G. C. (1963). Violence breed violence—perhaps? *American Journal of Psychiatry, 120,* 386-387.

Dodge, K. A., Bates, J. E., & Pettit, G. S. (1990). Mechanisms in the cycle of violence. *Science, 250,* 1678-1683.

Easson, W. M., & Steinhilber, R. M. (1961). Murderous aggression by children and adolescents. *Archives of General Psychiatry, 4,* 1-10.

Egeland, B., Jacobvitz, D., & Papatola, K. (1987). Intergenerational continuity of abuse. In R. Gelles & J. Lancaster (Eds.), *Child abuse and neglect: Biosocial dimensions.* New York: Aldine de Gruyter.

Egeland, B., Jacobvitz, D., & Sroufe, L. A. (1988). Breaking the cycle of abuse. *Child Development, 59,* 1080-1088.

Egeland, B., & Sroufe, L. A. (1981). Developmental sequelae of maltreatment in infancy. *New Directions for Child Development, 11,* 77-92.

Egeland, B., Sroufe, L. A., & Erickson, M. (1984). The developmental consequence of different patterns of maltreatment. *International Journal of Child Abuse and Neglect, 7,* 459-469.

Fagan, J., & Wexler, S. (1987). Crime at home and in the streets: The relationship between family and stranger violence. *Violence and Victims, 2,* 5-23.

Fantuzzo, J. W., & Lindquist, C. U. (1989). The effect of observing conjugal violence on children: A review and analysis of research methodology. *Journal of Family Violence, 4,* 77-94.

Finkelhor, D. (1984). *Child sexual abuse.* New York: Free Press.

Freud, S. (1955). The psychogenesis of a case of homosexuality in a woman. (Reprinted in J. Strachey, A. Freud, A. Strachey, & A. Tyson, Eds., *The standard edition of the complete psychological works of Sigmund Freud.* London: Hogarth.)

Fromuth, M. E., & Burkhart, B. R. (1987). Childhood sexual victimization among college men: Definitional and methodological issues. *Violence and Victims, 2,* 241-253.

Garbarino, J., Guttmann, E., & Seeley, J. W. (1986). *The psychologically battered child.* San Francisco: Jossey-Bass.

Geffner, R., Rosenbaum, A., & Hughes, H. (1988). Research issues concerning family violence. In V. B. Van Hasselt, R. L. Morrison, A. S. Bellack, & M. Hersen (Eds.), *Handbook of family violence.* New York: Plenum.

Gelles, R. J. (1979). *Family violence.* Beverly Hills, CA: Sage.

Gelles, R. J., & Straus, M. A. (1979). Determinants of violence in the family: Toward a theoretical integration. In W. R. Burr, R. Hill, F. I. Nye, & I. L. Reiss (Eds.), *Contemporary theories about the family.* New York: Free Press.

Gelles, R. J., & Straus, M. A. (1988). *Intimate violence.* New York: Simon & Schuster.

Gibbins, T. N., & Walker, A. (1956). Violent cruelty to children. *British Journal of Delinquency, 6,* 260-277.

Gray, E., & Cosgrove, J. (1985). Ethnocentric perception of childrearing practices in protective services. *Child Abuse and Neglect, 9,* 389-396.

Harper, F. V. (1963). The physician, the battered child and the law. *Pediatrics, 31,* 899-902.

Herrenkohl, E. C., Herrenkohl, R. C., & Toedter, L. J. (1983). Perspectives on the intergenerational transmission of violence. In D. Finkelhor, R. J. Gelles, G. T. Hotaling, & M. A. Straus (Eds.), *The dark side of families: Current family violence research.* Beverly Hills, CA: Sage.

Herzberger, S. D. (1983). Social cognition and the transmission of abuse. In D. Finkelhor, R. J. Gelles, G. T. Hotaling, & M. A. Straus (Eds.), *The dark side of families: Current family violence research.* Beverly Hills, CA: Sage.

Herzberger, S. D., Potts, D. A., & Dillon, M. (1981). Abusive and nonabusive parental treatment from the child's perspective. *Journal of Consulting and Clinical Psychology, 49,* 81-90.

Hotaling, G. T., & Straus, M. A. (1989). Intrafamily violence, and crime and violence outside the family. In L. Ohlin & M. Tonry (Eds.), *Family violence.* Chicago: University of Chicago.

Hunter, R., & Kilstrom, N. (1979). Breaking the cycle in abusive families. *American Journal of Psychiatry, 136,* 1320-1322.

Jayaratne, S. (1977). Child abusers and children: A review. *Social Work, 22,* 5-9.

Kalmuss, D. (1984). The intergenerational transmission of marital aggression. *Journal of Marriage and the Family, 46,* 11-19.

Kaufman, J., & Zigler, E. (1987). Do abused children become abusive parents? *American Journal of Orthopsychiatry, 57,* 186-192.

Kaufman, J., & Zigler, E. (1989). The intergenerational transmission of child abuse. In D. Cicchetti & V. Carson (Eds.), *Child maltreatment: Theory and causes and consequences of child abuse and neglect.* Cambridge: Cambridge University Press.

Kempe, C. H., Silverman, F. N., Steele, B. F., Droegemueller, W., & Silver, H. K. (1962). The battered-child syndrome. *Journal of the American Medical Association, 181,* 17-24.

Kruttschnitt, C., Ward, D., & Sheble, M. A. (1987). Abuse resistent youth: Some factors that may inhibit violent criminal behavior. *Social Forces, 66,* 501-519.

Lystad, M. H. (1975). Violence at home: A review of the literature. *American Journal of Orthopsychiatry, 45,* 328-344.

MacEwen, K. E., & Barling, J. (1988). Multiple stressors, violence in the family of origin, and marital aggression: A longitudinal investigation. *Journal of Family Violence, 3,* 73-87.

Martin, H. P., & Rodeheffer, M. A. (1976). Effects of parental abuse and neglect on children: The psychological impact of abuse on children. *Journal of Pediatric Psychology, 1,* 12-16.

Martin, M. J., & Walters, J. (1982). Familial correlates of selected types of child abuse and neglect. *Journal of Marriage and the Family, 44,* 267-276.

McLeer, S. V. (1988). Psychoanalytic perspectives on family violence. In V. B. Van Hasselt, R. L. Morrison, A. S. Bellack, & M. Hersen (Eds.), *Handbook of family violence*. New York: Plenum.

Miller, D., & Challas, G. (1981, July). *Abused children as adult parents: A twenty-five year longitudinal study*. Paper presented at the National Conference for Family Violence Researchers, Durham, NH.

Miller, T. R., Handal, P. J., Gilner, F. H., & Cross, J. F. (1991). The relationship of abuse and witnessing violence on the Child Abuse Potential Inventory with black adolescents. *Journal of Family Violence, 6*, 351-363.

Morris, M. G., Gould, R. W., & Matthews, P. J. (1964). Toward prevention of child abuse. *Children, 11*, 55-60.

Ohlin, L., & Tonry, M. (1989). Family violence in perspective. In L. Ohlin & M. Tonry (Eds.), *Family violence*. Chicago: University of Chicago Press.

Potts, D. A., Herzberger, S. D., & Holland, A. E. (1979, May). *Child abuse: A cross-generational pattern of child rearing?* Paper presented at the annual meetings of the Midwestern Psychological Association, Chicago.

Silver, L. B., Dublin, C. C., & Lourie, R. S. (1969). Does violence breed violence? Contributions from a study of the child abuse syndrome. *American Journal of Psychiatry, 126*, 404-407.

Simons, R. L., Whitbeck, L. B., Conger, R. D., & Chyi-In, W. (1991). Intergenerational transmission of harsh parenting. *Developmental Psychology, 27*, 159-171.

Spinetta, J. J., & Rigler, D. (1972). The child-abusing parent: A psychological review. *Psychological Bulletin, 77*, 296-304.

Steele, B., & Pollock, C. B. (1968). A psychiatric study of parents who abuse infants and small children. In R. E. Helfer & C. H. Kempe (Eds.), *The battered child* (2nd ed.). Chicago: University of Chicago Press.

Straus, M. A. (1979). Family patterns and child abuse in a nationally representative sample. *International Journal of Child Abuse and Neglect, 3*, 213-225.

Straus, M. A., Gelles, R. J., & Steinmetz, S. K. (1980). *Behind closed doors: Violence in the American family*. Garden City, NY: Doubleday.

Sudman, S., & Bradburn, N. M. (Eds.). (1982). *Asking questions*. Washington, DC: Jossey-Bass.

Webb, E. J., Campbell, D. T., Schwartz, R. D., & Sechrest, L. (Eds.). (1969). *Unobtrusive measures: Nonreactive research in the social sciences*. Chicago: Rand McNally.

Weis, J. G. (1989). Family violence research methodology and design. In L. Ohlin & M. Tonry (Eds.), *Family violence*. Chicago: University of Chicago Press.

Widom, C. S. (1989a). Does violence beget violence? A critical examination of the literature. *Psychological Bulletin, 106*, 3-28.

Widom, C. S. (1989b). The cycle of violence. *Science, 244*, 160-166.

Wolfe, D., Jaffe, P., Wilson, S., & Zak, L. (1984, August). *Predicting children's adjustment to family violence: Beyond univariate analyses*. Paper presented at the Second Family Violence Research Conference, Durham, NH.

4

Measuring the
Underground Economy

A Suitable Case for
Interdisciplinary Treatment?

J. J. THOMAS

The Economic Approach
to the Underground Economy

Although pioneering studies by Cagan (1958) and Machesich (1962) had appeared earlier, economists' interest in the underground economy did not blossom until after the publication of "The Subterranean Economy" by Peter Gutmann in 1977. Two features of this article caught the attention of both academics and politicians: (a) It proposed a procedure for measuring the size of the underground economy that was simple to apply to easily obtainable data and (b) the estimates of the size of the underground economy it produced were dramatic and well publicized. Activities in the underground economy involve breaking the law through tax evasion, working "off the books," and/or social security fraud, and most economists were skeptical about obtaining data on such sensitive activities through sample surveys and direct questioning. The appeal about

AUTHOR'S NOTE: This chapter was originally published in the *American Behavioral Scientist, 33,* 621-637.

Gutmann's approach was the neat way in which it proposed an indirect method of measurement that did not require interviews or direct data collection. The upsurge of publications on this subject that followed represents an interesting example of "measurement without theory" and raises a number of methodological questions concerning the nature of the phenomena that economists are able and willing to analyze both theoretically and empirically.

From the outset, there has been little agreement over precisely what is meant by the *underground economy.* Some economists (particularly those involved in government and concerned with tax evasion) have taken the view that it represents income not reported to the tax authorities, whether or not this income has been measured in the national income accounts. Others have viewed it as the difference between the actual total of economic activity in a country and the estimated size of the economy as measured by the national income accounts.

These differing viewpoints have led to disagreements over the definition of the underground economy, especially on the question of where to draw the line between the underground economy and the criminal sector. For those interested primarily in tax evasion, the distinction would be that, in the underground economy, while the goods and services being produced are legal, there is some element of illegality in the process of either production or distribution, such as the evasion of taxes. In contrast, in the criminal sector, the goods and services being produced, as well as the process of production and distribution, are illegal. If detected, those working in the underground economy would not be discouraged, as long as they paid their taxes and conformed to any relevant regulations. Those operating in the criminal sector, however, would be put out of business if possible, hence it is argued that their activities should not be included in the underground economy.

Among economists interested primarily in measuring total economic output, there is less agreement over what should be done about crime and the income it produces. On one hand, as Blades (1985) points out, most countries have adopted the U.N. System of National Accounts (SNA) and this system, at least in principle, covers illegal as well as legal activities. His list of activities that could be entered in the national income accounts covers the production and distribution of illegal goods and services, smuggling, theft by employees from their place of work, bribery, shoplifting, theft of other goods, theft of money, check and credit card fraud, and extortion.

On the other hand, there are those who question the inclusion of the wages of sin in the national accounts on the grounds that it seems wrong that gross domestic product (GDP), as a measure of economic welfare, should increase as a result of an increase in crime. For example, Carter (1984) suggested that it would seem inconsistent to include income from the production and distribution of illegal drugs, given that the economy expends considerable resources to suppress these activities. On the whole, this view predominates, and, as a result, the economic gains generated by most criminal activities are excluded from both the national income accounts and the problems of measurement generally considered by economists.

In summary, the current state of economic research on the underground economy is characterized by a lack of agreement over what the concept means and also what to call it. Among economists, it is referred to as *underground, subterranean, black, hidden, shadow, irregular, informal, unrecorded,* and so on. Given that economists are not alone in studying the activities that are included in the broad definition discussed earlier, further confusion is caused by the fact that some of these terms (e.g., the *hidden economy*) already have technical meanings in other subject areas, such as social anthropology.

The lack of interest by economists in criminal activities has had two important effects. First, while some Chicago-trained economists set out to show that the neoclassical paradigm of constrained optimization could explain any activities from the supply of murders (Ehrlich, 1975) to marriage and the family (Becker, 1981), mainstream economic theory ignored deviant behavior. In particular, macroeconomics took no account of how criminal activities might impinge on key relationships, such as the aggregate demand for money. Second, the emphasis of economics on the collection of data that were "legal" and could be obtained easily as a routine by-product of normal economic activity meant that the majority of economists were not trained in methods of statistical data collection. As Reuter (1982, p. 137) points out:

> Economists are unique among social scientists in that they are trained only to analyze, not to collect, data. While psychologists are taught experimental techniques, sociologists learn the vagaries of interviewing, and anthropologists devote much of their training to field work, economists are provided only with the tools for data analysis. One consequence is a lack of skepticism about the quality of data.

One can go further; not only is there a lack of healthy skepticism about the quality of much economic data, but there is an unhealthy skepticism on the part of many economists, often based on ignorance, concerning the possibilities of collecting quantitative data on criminal activities from samples of individuals through the use of survey techniques.

As interest in the underground economy grew, economists were concerned with a number of different questions. The macroeconomic question related to the size of the underground economy: Was it so large that it represented a serious problem? There were also policy issues that required microeconomic analysis. For example, if the underground economy was growing, why was it growing? Was tax evasion the major activity, and, if so, was this because the burden of taxation had become oppressive, or was it the result of growing disillusionment with the efficiency of government expenditure? With growing unemployment during the post-OPEC oil-shock period, questions were raised about whether those officially without jobs were really unemployed or whether they were working "off the books." Who were the tax evaders and the social security defrauders, and how did they get away with it? Were workers and/or employers being hoodwinked, or was it a grand conspiracy by both against the government?

These were important questions, and a number of microeconomic theorists responded by extending the analysis of tax evasion (see Cowell, 1987) and labor market behavior, but economists were handicapped by their lack of expertise in data collection, which led most to argue against taking a direct empirical approach. The view was that any attempt to collect data on the scale of activities in the underground economy through samples and questionnaires would fail because either those involved would be nonrespondents or, if they agreed to take part in a study, they would not tell the truth. The solution was seen to lie in an indirect, macroeconomic approach that would look for the statistical fingerprints of the underground economy at the aggregate level and make use of macroeconomic data, which, because they had not been collected specifically to analyze the underground economy, were felt to be free from some of the problems inherent in the direct approach.

It may be argued that the indirect methods of measurement represent the major empirical contribution of economists to the analysis of the underground economy. These indirect methods are evaluated in the next section. In contrast, some information concerning the underground economy has been obtained through sample surveys, and this is reviewed in the third section of this chapter. The fourth section discusses a number of experimental techniques developed in other social sciences that might be relevant to economists in their analysis of the underground and also suggests some topics in which an interdisciplinary approach might be taken.

Macroeconomic Measures of the Underground Economy

Critical surveys of the various methods developed by economists to measure the size of the underground economy already exist (e.g., Feige, 1989; Smith, 1986; Thomas, 1988), so here I will outline only the two indirect monetary approaches that have been most widely applied. The first is known as the cash-deposit ratio method and was used by Gutmann (1977), while the second, known as the monetary transactions approach, was proposed by Feige (1979). The first, which is the easier of the two to apply, assumed that cash alone is used in the underground economy. In contrast, Feige assumed that both cash and checks are used in the underground economy and based his estimate on the quantity theory of money.

The Cash-Deposit Ratio Approach

Here, the argument is that, to conceal income generated in the underground economy, people will prefer to be paid in cash and that, in the absence of an increase in the velocity of circulation of money or a fall in the level of deposits, the cash-deposit ratio will rise. Given an assumption concerning a base year in which the underground economy did not exist (or in which it is assumed to be some known percentage of national income, or GDP), increases in the cash-deposit ratio are used to measure the size of the underground economy. The method works as follows: Let C represent the amount of cash and D the level of deposits, with the quantity of money defined as $M = C + D$. Then:

1. A year must be specified in which the underground economy is assumed not to exist. Call this year 0, calculate the cash-deposit ratio $(C/D)0$ and denote this ratio as λ. This is taken as the ratio expected in the absence of the underground economy.
2. For the other years, calculate the amount of cash that would have been demanded in the absence of the underground economy as $C_t^0 = \lambda \cdot D_t$,

where the superscript o indicates the "overground" (i.e., nonunderground) economy, and t is any other year.

3. Then the amount of cash demanded each period for use in the underground economy, C_t^u, is given by $C_t^u = C_r - C_t^o$.

4. Denoting national income by Y, calculate the velocity of circulation of money in the overground economy as $V_t = [Y/(C^o + D)]t$.

5. Finally, if it is assumed that the velocity for the circulation of cash in the underground economy is the same as the velocity of money with respect to income in the overground economy, an estimate of the size of income in the underground economy is obtained as $Y_t^u = V_t \cdot C_t^u$.

The attraction of the method is clear; it only requires data on C, D, and Y, and, because all of these are easily available in most countries, it is not surprising that the method has been widely applied. There are, however, a number of difficulties in applying this method of estimation.

The first is that, while it may be plausible to assume that those involved in the underground economy prefer to use cash in their activities, the same assumption is even more plausible for those engaged in criminal activities. Because the cash-deposit ratio method cannot be sensitive to whether the cash it detects is underground or criminal, it is clear that what the method actually measures is broader than even the broad concept of the underground discussed earlier.

The second is that the choice of the cash-deposit ratio as the variable of interest does not follow from any economic theory but is arbitrary. Trundle (1982) made a convincing case for using the ratio of consumers' expenditures to cash as a more appropriate variable for detecting underground economic activity and showed that this ratio has risen in the United Kingdom during the period 1963 to 1981.

The third is the assumption that the only reason for changes in the cash-deposit ratio is the growth of the underground economy. New developments in payment methods, such as the introduction of credit cards, took place that would be expected to affect the cash-deposit ratio, but their effect cannot be allowed for in this approach.[1]

The fourth is the sensitivity of the results to the choice of the base year in which it is assumed that the underground economy did not exist (or was a negligible proportion of national income). The choice is arbitrary; in many empirical studies, the base period is simply taken to be the first year or quarter in the sample of time-series data. Changing the base year can produce quite dramatic effects on the estimated size of the underground economy. For example, Matthews (1983) assumed that the underground economy in the United Kingdom was about 0.5% of GDP before 1971. In a later study, Matthews and Rastogi (1985) changed the base year to 1960, with the result that they estimated the underground economy to be nearly 12% of GDP in 1969 (see Thomas, 1988).

A fifth problem is the need to assume that the velocity of circulation of money in the overground economy is the same as the velocity of circulation of cash in the underground economy, an assumption that is completely untestable with the available data.

The sixth is a particular problem in applying the method to the United States, namely, the assumption that all U.S. dollars in cash are held in the United States and hence that those dollars not being used in the overground economy are lubricating the underground economy. As Tanzi (1982) points out, there is much evidence that U.S. dollars, particularly large-denomination bills, are held outside the United States and hence are irrelevant to the growth of the U.S. underground economy. Given this fact, it is hard to know what figure should be entered for cash in the cash-deposit ratio. This is likely to affect this method when applied to any country with a hard currency, and the same objection has been raised in its use with Swiss data (Weck-Hannemann & Frey, 1985).

Finally, for some countries, the assumption that transactions in the underground economy are carried out using only cash may not be valid. For example, Contini (1981a) pointed out that in Italy, because the disclosure of information concerning bank accounts is precluded by law, there would be no need to use only cash in underground economy transactions.

The other monetary approach is able to meet this objection, because Feige proposed it after producing microeconomic evidence that checks as well as cash were used in the underground economy in the United States.

The Monetary Transactions Approach

Feige's method starts from the quantity theory of money relationship among money, transactions, and income, but, apart from this, the steps in the procedure are similar to those in the cash-deposit ratio and the reader should consult Feige (1989) for technical details. It is open to the same criticisms as the cash-deposit ratio method, plus a problem of double counting. In constructing measures of national income, care is taken to avoid the double counting of the value of intermediate transactions and only the value added in each sector is included. To match transactions to income consistently, it is necessary to exclude intermediate transactions. Unless this is done, the income corresponding to a given volume of transactions will be overestimated. Boeschoten and Fase (1984) used data for the Netherlands to show that ignoring this problem may produce serious upward bias in the size of the underground economy calculated by this method.

This method was applied to data for the United States by Feige (1979) and for Canada by Mirus and Smith (1981) and is notable for producing much higher estimates of the size of the underground economy than those produced by other approaches (see Tanzi, 1982, pp. 72-74).

On the basis of the criticisms discussed earlier, I would argue that, while the indirect methods proposed by economists are ingenious, they are flawed in fundamental ways and do not provide reliable measures of the size of the underground economy.[2] Research continues in this area and, with the development of the relevant macroeconomic theories, it is possible that the use of latent variable models may provide improved indirect measures (see Frey & Weck-Hannemann, 1984; Helberger & Knepel, 1985).

While the size of the underground economy is an interesting issue, there are other questions concerning its structure that are important and, for information relevant to these questions, one must turn to microeconomic data.

Microeconomic Evidence Concerning the Underground Economy

Microeconomic data on the underground economy have been obtained from three main sources: (a) income tax audits, (b) labor market surveys, and (c) household surveys.

Information Obtained From Income Tax Audits

As Frey and Pommerehne (1982) reported, the extent to which tax auditing is used differs considerably between countries, with France, for example, having devised various programs to obtain information on the underreporting of income (such as random samples of tax returns in various departments and the use of discriminant analysis in the selection of taxpayers who are likely to be worth investigating).

One of the major attempts to extrapolate the tax audit results to the whole economy, however, was made in the United States, motivated in part as a response by the U.S. Congress to public reaction to the estimates of the underground economy's size as given by Peter Gutmann (discussed earlier). In 1979, the Internal Revenue Service (IRS) reported the results of a study that had submitted a probability sample of about 50,000 tax returns to a thorough audit, which included matching the files with data available from the Social Security Administration and the Bureau of Economic Analysis. The results suggested that, in terms of the amount of income reported on the tax return as a percentage of the amount of reportable income (shown in parentheses), the major underreporting involved the self-employed (60%-64%) and rent and dividends (50%-65%) as compared with wages and salaries (97%-98%; see Kenadjian, 1982).

The tax audit has considerable potential as a source of information on tax evasion, at least in principle, as long as the sampling frame includes nonfilers as well as those who file income tax returns. In practice, however, the potential depends on the powers of the authorities to carry out tax audits. In some countries, such as the United Kingdom, there are strict controls over the use that may be made of individual tax returns, and many voters might feel that extending the investigative powers of government is a high price to pay for better information on the underground economy. As a result, it is unlikely that the tax audit will provide more than occasional checks on the scale of underground economic activity in many countries.

Labor Market Studies

Evidence for the involvement of workers in the underground economy is seen by many in the fact that participation rates in the formal labor market have fallen over time in a number of countries, while output has increased faster than could be accounted for by increased productivity. For example, in Italy, the participation rate—measured as the ratio of the labor force to the total population—fell from 44% in 1959 to 34% in 1977 (Contini, 1981b, p. 404), while, in West Germany, the male participation rate—measured as the percentage of the group between age 15 and 65—fell from 94.9% in 1960 to 83.2% in 1978 (Frey, Weck, & Pommerehne, 1982, p. 507).

Informal activities in the labor market may take one of a number of forms. First, there may be workers who have a regular job for which income is reported but who work at a second job for which income is not reported (i.e., "moonlighting"). Second, there may be workers, usually self-employed, who have a full-time job but whose income is not reported; in U.K. tax circles, such individuals who have dropped out of the system are known as "ghosts." In some countries, illegal immigrants may be particularly important in this kind of labor activity. Third, there may be cases of unemployed workers who are in fact working but not reporting the resulting income so as to avoid losing unemployment benefits.

The type of data collected varies across studies (for an overview, see International Labour Organisation, 1987), with some researchers investigating moonlighting (see Alden & Saha, 1978), while other surveys collected data on those who admit to working in (or, more frequently, admit to making use of the services of individuals known, or suspected, to be working in) the informal labor market (see Smith, 1985). Given that the activities being investigated are often illegal, some commentators have questioned whether respondents are likely to tell the truth in such surveys. Gutmann (1985) pointed out that about two thirds of the interviews in U.S. Census Bureau household surveys are conducted by telephone and doubted that respondents would be likely to discuss illegal activities with an unknown person over the telephone.[3]

Langfeldt (1985) suggested that respondents at best are unlikely to reveal the full extent of their involvement in the informal labor market and that nonrespondents are probably more involved. Certainly, response rates seem low in some of these studies. Isachsen, Klovland, and Strom (1982) reported a 70% response rate in some Norwegian surveys, with an overrepresentation of women and people age 60 and over among the nonrespondents.

While there are many differences between the countries studied, the general conclusions that emerge are (a) that it is mainly small firms and the self-employed who operate in the informal labor market and (b) that construction and the retail and service industries offer the greatest scope for such activities.

Household Surveys

The Family Expenditure Survey (FES) in the United Kingdom has been used as a source of information on the underground economy

(Dilnot & Morris, 1981; O'Higgins, 1980). The FES is a sample survey of the household, or noninstitutional, population of the United Kingdom. Interviewers visit about 11,000 addresses during a 12-month period, and usually about 7,000 households (spread over the year) take part in the survey by keeping a diary of all expenditures for a 14-day period as well as supplying data on income and various socioeconomic characteristics. A comparison of household expenditures and income reveals cases where the former exceeds the latter. Allowance has to be made for the fact that the 14-day period is very short, so that the purchase of a major durable good may distort the normal relationship between income and expenditure, and there are timing problems in matching income to expenditure.

The nonresponse rate of about 30% in the FES has been analyzed (Atkinson & Micklewright, 1983; Kemsley, Redpath, & Holmes, 1980), and the high proportion of self-employed persons among the nonrespondents casts some doubts on the reliability of results based on this survey.

Obviously, economists are not the only social scientists to use household surveys that shed some light on the underground economy. In the United Kingdom, there have been some notable studies of the effects of unemployment in various regions. For example, sociologists at the University of Canterbury studied the Isle of Sheppey in Kent (Pahl, 1984, 1985; Pahl & Wallace, 1985a, 1985b). Others at the University College of Swansea studied the effects of redundancies at the British Steel Corporation's works at Port Talbot (Fevre, 1986; Harris, Lee, & Morris, 1985; Lee, 1985; Lee & Harris, 1985; Morris, 1984, 1985). There have been studies of the unemployed in Belfast (Howe, 1988; Trew & Kilpatrick, 1984), and in Cauldmoss, Scotland (Turner, Bostyn, & Wight, 1985), and of youth unemployment in County Durham (Coffield, Borrill, & Marshall, 1983, 1986).

Unfortunately, the primary concerns of these studies were not with the size and the nature of the underground economy. While they did provide important information on "off the books" working and contracting out (for a summary, see Thomas, 1988), they left unanswered the questions of interest to economists. There are, however, some important lessons for economists to learn from such studies and the approach of other social scientists.

Some Possibilities for an
Interdisciplinary Approach

In working with survey data, economists have either made use of existing statistical material collected for other purposes, such as the FES, or attempted to collect information on the underground economy directly using conventional survey techniques, without making any concessions to the fact that the data being collected were of a sensitive nature. Other social scientists have studied deviant behavior, and their experiences in collecting information on such sensitive topics as the incidence of abortion (in some communities), illegitimate births, racial discrimination, drug abuse (among both civilians and military personnel), and a range of criminal activities are relevant, as are their deliberations on the ethical problems of respecting the privacy and protecting the anonymity of respondents (see Bulmer, 1982).

One method of collecting sensitive information that has been used by sociologists but not as yet by economists is the randomized response technique (RRT). In its simplest form, this method is designed to provide an estimate of the proportion of respondents having a given characteristic without identifying which individuals have the characteristic.

An example of the RRT involves the respondent being given a die and a deck of playing cards and then being placed in a physical position where it is impossible for anyone to observe the results of throwing the die and drawing a card from the deck. The instructions given to the respondent are to throw the die and draw a card from the deck. If the score is 5 or 6, the respondent is to answer the first question; if the score if 4 or less, the respondent is to answer the second question. The questions to be answered might be these:

1. Do you evade paying your income taxes?
2. Was the card you just drew from the deck red?

Let m be the total number of "yes" answers in a sample of n; π, the probability that the first question is answered; and p_1 and p_2, the probabilities of a yes to questions 1 and 2, respectively. Then

$$m/n = \pi \cdot p_1 + (1 - \pi) \cdot p_2$$

and solving for p_1 we have

$$p_1 = [(m/n) - (1 - \pi) \cdot p_2]/\pi$$

In this example, because we observe m/n from the sample and know that $\pi = 1/3$ and $p_2 = 1/2$, we may evaluate p_1.

More elaborate versions of the RRT have been developed to collect quantitative information (see Fox & Tracy, 1986), so that, in principle, the amount of tax evasion could be investigated by this method. With the exception of one exploratory study (Lee, 1987), however, this technique has not been applied to the underground economy, and its development in this area provides an interesting opportunity for inter-disciplinary cooperation between economists and those having field experience with the RRT.

The microeconomic data collected by economists specifically to in-vestigate the underground economy have generally come from one-off surveys. In contrast, the sociologists' studies reported in the previous section involved working in and with communities for considerable periods of time. If such an approach were adopted by economists, would it make available any new methods of data collection that might be valuable? One great advantage of the protracted study is the possibility of "observing" the members of the sample in a range of situations that are not available in the context of the conventional interview.

Such observation could provide important additional information to test hypotheses generated by the indirect measures of the size of the underground economy. For example, using the monetary transactions approach, Feige (1981) estimated that, from a base percentage of zero in 1960, the underground economy in the United Kingdom grew from about 8% of GDP in 1971 to 22% in 1974 and then fell to about 14% of GDP in 1975. Feige commented that

> massive shifts between the observed and the unobserved sector which go un-noticed will give rise to governmental policies whose consequences might be quite different from their intent. . . . Social welfare policies which do not take adequate account of the redistributive impact of a sizable unobserved income may well lead to less equitable rather than more equitable distribution. (p. 212)

If movements into or out of the underground economy are as massive and rapid as Feige's estimates for the years 1971-1975 show, is it possible that they go unnoticed? Can they really be unobservable to trained social scientists? Reference to the studies cited in the previous section suggests that, if they exist, such movements could be observed and that the silence of the studies on this matter, while casting doubt on their existence, also reflects the fact that the studies were not focused on the underground economy. Collaboration between economists and other social scientists in future studies could provide this focus by formulating and testing hypotheses concerning the underground economy.

As examples of the kinds of questions that might be investigated in such studies, one might consider the following:

1. Economists have argued that the burden of taxation is the major reason for tax evasion, yet their estimates suggest that countries with the highest tax rates (e.g., Sweden) are not the countries with the largest underground economies (e.g., Italy). How do tax rates affect decisions with respect to the underground economy? What other factors influence these decisions? How does the growth in the proportion of self-employed workers relate to the growth in the underground economy?

2. Ghosts, moonlighters, and persons working while officially unemployed are all alleged to be operating in the underground economy, but what is the mixture? Are there regional differences in the mixture? Most of the sociological studies referred to earlier were conducted in areas of high unemployment. What is the mixture in areas of relative prosperity, such as the southeastern region of England?

3. Does the underground economy move procyclically or countercyclically with the overground economy? Is the relationship between the two economies competitive, symbiotic, or exploitative?

4. Smith (1987) presented evidence on the negative effects of unemployment on health. Are there negative effects of working in the underground economy? How do they compare with those of being unemployed?

Apart from information gathered through household or community studies, data may be collected through direct observation. Here, the techniques developed by social anthropologists and sociologists of participant observation, that is, by participation in the activities being studied, may be worth consideration by economists. Participant observation may be overt (i.e., carried out with the knowledge and agreement of those being observed) or covert, where the research is undertaken without the knowledge or consent of those under observation. In some instances, where organizations are being investigated, the participant observation may involve both elements, because the observer's role may be known to senior members of the organization, who have authorized the study, but not to those lower in the organization, who are being observed (see Jorgensen, 1989). Participant observation techniques raise ethical questions that are particularly acute on the issue of whether the study should be overt or covert, but the questions arise also because the activities being observed are likely to be criminal in nature (Bulmer, 1982; Jorgensen, 1989).

Given that persons operating in the underground economy are involved in criminal activities, they are unlikely to welcome overt participant observation, with the result that the technique may not seem appropriate for gathering information on this subject. This may be correct, but one would not wish to prejudge the issue without having an opportunity to consider the possibilities in more detail.

Covert participant observation would not be subject to this objection and the technique has been used to investigate various cases of industrial crime, such as customer "fiddling" among bread delivery workers (Ditton, 1977), pilferage in hotels (Mars, 1973) and among Canadian longshoremen (Mars, 1974), political corruption and bribery in Seattle (Chambliss, 1978) as well as drug dealing in California (Adler, 1985). Quite apart from the ethical questions it raises, the use of the covert participant observation technique to investigate the underground economy is likely to strike most economists as bizarre. While accepting that graduate students may have to take employment in their spare time to cover tutorial costs, the idea that serving in a bar or a shop might be a form of fieldwork for a thesis on the underground economy would be alien to most of the profession. The issues raised here are grave, and full consideration would require liaison between economists and other special scientists familiar with the use of participant observer techniques.

To summarize, economists have attempted to measure the size of the underground economy through indirect means but have not made much use of survey techniques to answer a range of questions concerning who is involved in the underground economy and how or why they operate. Other social scientists have developed techniques for studying deviant behavior, either directly or as a by-product of broader studies, but have not been concerned with questions of monetary magnitudes or economic modeling. This chapter has examined the possibility that an interdisciplinary approach involving economists and other social scientists might contribute to research on the underground economy. Given the positive conclusion reached, it is hoped that positive responses will be forthcoming, both from other social scientists and from research funding institutions.

Notes

1. Tanzi (1980) presented an approach using multiple regression analysis that allows for such effects and can avoid the arbitrary choice of a base year. See Thomas (1986, 1988) for a critique of this approach.

2. In addition, they have also been used by some economists to draw microeconomic conclusions that do not follow logically from their properties. Thus Gutmann (1985) calculated that the underground economy was 14% to 15% of measured GNP in the United States and suggested, largely on the basis of this figure, that from 5 to 6 million workers, who were officially unemployed, were in fact working full-time in illegal activities or in the underground economy, while a further 22 to 23 million workers in the overground economy were working "off the books" or were moonlighting in the underground economy. The problem is that knowledge of who is working in the underground economy requires information about the supply side of the economy, whereas the monetary methods are based on expenditures, which represent activities related to aggregate demand and tell us nothing about production or aggregate supply.

3. Economists have not investigated this assertion, but other social scientists have, and the National Academy of Sciences (1979) study showed a strong preference among respondents for personal interviews over mail shots or telephone interviews.

References

Adler, P. A. (1985). *Wheeling and dealing.* New York: Columbia University Press.

Alden, J. D., & Saha, S. K. (1978). An analysis of second jobholding in the EEC. *Regional Studies, 12,* 639-650.

Atkinson, A. B., & Micklewright, J. (1983). On the reliability of income data in the Family Expenditure Survey, 1970-1977. *Journal of the Royal Statistical Society, 146*(Series A), 33-61.

Becker, G. S. (1981). *A treatise on the family.* Cambridge, MA: Harvard University Press.

Blades, D. W. (1985). Crime: What should be recorded in the national accounts and what difference would it make? In W. Gaertner & A. Wenig (Eds.), *The economics of the shadow economy.* Berlin: Springer-Verlag.

Boeschoten, W. C., & Fase, M. M. G. (1984). *The volume of payment and the informal economy in the Netherlands, 1965-1982: An attempt at quantification.* Dordrecht: Martinus Nijhoff.

Bulmer, M. (1982). *Social research ethics.* London: Macmillan.

Cagan, P. (1958). The demand for currency relative to the total money supply. *Journal of Political Economy, 66,* 303-328.

Carter, M. (1984). Issues in the hidden economy: A survey. *Economic Record, 60,* 209-221.

Chambliss, W. J. (1978). *On the take: From petty crooks to presidents.* Bloomington: Indiana University Press.

Coffield, F., Borrill, C., & Marshall, S. (1983). How young people try to survive being unemployed. *New Society, 64,* 332-334.

Coffield, F., Borrill, C., & Marshall, S. (1986). *Growing up at the margins.* Milton Keynes, United Kingdom: Open University Press.

Contini, B. (1981a). The second economy in Italy. *Journal of Contemporary Studies, 4,* 199-208.

Contini, B. (1981b). Labour market segmentation and the development of the parallel economy: The Italian experience. *Oxford Economic Papers, 33,* 401-412.

Cowell, F. A. (1987). The economic analysis of tax evasion. In J. D. Hey & P. J. Lambert (Eds.), *Surveys in the economics of uncertainty.* London: Basil Blackwell.

Dilnot, A., & Morris, C. N. (1981). What do we know about the black economy in the United Kingdom? *Fiscal Studies, 2,* 163-179.

Ditton, J. (1977). *Part-time crime: An ethnography of fiddling and pilfering.* London: Macmillan.

Ehrlich, I. (1975). The deterrent effect of capital punishment: A question of life and death. *American Economic Review, 65,* 397-417.

Feige, E. L. (1979). How big is the irregular economy? *Challenge, 20,* 5-13.

Feige, E. L. (1981, July). The UK's unobserved economy: A preliminary assessment. *Journal of Economic Affairs, 1,* 205-212.

Feige, E. L. (1989). *The underground economies.* Cambridge: Cambridge University Press.

Fevre, R. (1986). Contract work in the recession. In K. Purcell, S. Wood, A. Waton, & S. Allen (Eds.), *The changing experience of employment.* London: Macmillan.

Fox, J. A., & Tracy, P. E. (1986). *Randomized response: A method for sensitive surveys.* Beverly Hills, CA: Sage.

Frey, B. S., & Pommerehne, W. W. (1982). Measuring the hidden economy: Though this be madness, there is method in it. In V. Tanzi (Ed.), *The underground economy in the United States and abroad.* Lexington, MA: Lexington.

Frey, B. S., & Weck-Hannemann, H. (1984, November/December). The hidden economy as an "unobservable variable." *European Economic Review, 26,* 33-53.

Frey, S. B., Weck, H., & Pommerehne, W. W. (1982). Has the shadow economy grown in Germany? *Weltwirtschaftliches Archiv, 118,* 490-524.

Gutmann, P. M. (1977). The subterranean economy. *Financial Analysts Journal, 34,* 24-27.

Gutmann, P. M. (1985). The subterranean economy, redux. In W. Gaertner & A. Wenig (Eds.), *The economics of the shadow economy.* Berlin: Springer-Verlag.

Harris, C. C., Lee, R. M., & Morris, L. D. (1985). Redundancy in steel: Labour market behaviour, local social networks and domestic organisation. In B. Roberts, R. Finnegan, & D. Gallie (Eds.), *New approaches to economic life.* Manchester: Manchester University Press.

Helberger, C., & Knepel, H. (1985). How big is the shadow economy? A re-analysis of the unobserved variable approach of B. S. Frey & H. Weck-Hannemann. *European Economic Review, 32,* 965-976.

Howe, L. E. A. (1988). Employment, doing the double and local labour markets in Belfast. In C. Curtin & T. Wilson (Eds.), *Ireland from below: Social change and local communities in modern Ireland.* Dublin: Gill & Macmillan.

International Labour Organisation. (1987). *Annotated bibliography on clandestine employment.* Geneva: International Labour Office.

Isachsen, A. J., Klovland, J. T., & Strom, S. (1982). The hidden economy in Norway. In V. Tanzi (Ed.), *The underground economy in the United States and abroad.* Lexington, MA: Lexington.

Jorgensen, D. L. (1989). *Participant observation: A methodology for human studies.* London: Sage.

Kemsley, W. F. F., Redpath, R. U., & Holmes, M. (1980). *Family Expenditure Survey Handbook.* London: Her Majesty's Stationery Office.

Kenadjian, B. (1982). The direct approach to measuring the underground economy in the United States: IRS estimates of unreported income. In V. Tanzi (Ed.), *The underground economy in the United States and abroad.* Lexington, MA: Lexington.

Langfeldt, E. (1985). Is a growing unobserved sector undermining monetary policy in the Federal Republic of Germany? In W. Gaertner & A. Wenig (Eds.), *The economics of the shadow economy.* Berlin: Springer-Verlag.

Lee, R. M. (1985). The entry to self-employment of redundant steel workers. *Industrial Relations Journal, 19,* 42-49.

Lee, R. M. (1987). *Methodological approaches to the study of the black economy: Final report.* Unpublished manuscript.

Lee, R. M., & Harris, C. C. (1985). Redundancy studies: Port Talbot and the future. *Quarterly Journal of Social Affairs, 1,* 20-27.

Machesich, G. (1962). Demand for currency and taxation in Canada. *Southern Economic Journal, 29,* 33-38.

Mars, G. (1973). Hotel pilferage: A case study in occupational theft. In M. Warner (Ed.), *The sociology of the work place.* London: Allen & Unwin.

Mars, G. (1974). Dock pilferage. In P. Rock & M. McIntosh (Eds.), *Deviance and social control.* London: Tavistock.

Matthews, K. (1983). National income and the black economy. *Economic Affairs, 3,* 261-267.

Matthews, K., & Rastogi, A. (1985). Little MO and the moonlighters: Another look at the black economy. *Quarterly Economic Bulletin, 6,* 21-24.

Mirus, R., & Smith, R. S. (1981). Canada's irregular economy. In V. Tanzi (Ed.), *The underground economy in the United States and abroad.* Lexington, MA: Lexington.

Morris, L. D. (1984). Patterns of social activity and post-redundancy labour market experience. *Sociology, 18,* 330-352.

Morris, L. D. (1985). Renegotiation of the domestic division of labour and the context of male redundancy. In B. Roberts, R. Finnegan, & D. Gallie (Eds.), *New approaches to economic life.* Manchester: Manchester University Press.

National Academy of Sciences. (1979). *Report of the panel on privacy and confidentiality as factors in survey response.* Washington, DC: Author.

O'Higgins, M. (1980). *Measuring the hidden economy: A review of evidence and methodologies.* London: Outer Circle Policy Unit.

Pahl, R. E. (1984). *Divisions of labour.* London: Basil Blackwell.

Pahl, R. E. (1985). The politics of work. *Political Quarterly, 56,* 331-345.

Pahl, R. E., & Wallace, C. (1985a). Household work strategies in economic recession. In N. Redclift & E. Mingione (Eds.), *Beyond employment: Household, gender, and subsistence.* London: Basil Blackwell.

Pahl, R. E., & Wallace, C. (1985b). Forms of work and privatization on the Isle of Sheppey. In B. Roberts, R. Finnegan, & D. Gallie (Eds.), *New approaches to economic life.* Manchester: Manchester University Press.

Reuter, P. (1982). The irregular economy and the quality of macroeconomic statistics. In V. Tanzi (Eds.), *The underground economy in the United States and abroad.* Lexington, MA: Lexington.

Smith, J. D. (1985). Market motives in the informal economy. In W. Gaertner & A. Wenig (Eds.), *The economics of the shadow economy.* Berlin: Springer-Verlag.

Smith, R. (1987). *Unemployment and health: A disaster and a challenge.* Oxford: Oxford University Press.

Smith, S. (1986). *Britain's shadow economy.* Oxford: Oxford University Press.

Tanzi, V. (1980). Underground economy and tax evasion in the United States: Estimates and implications. *Banca Nazionale del Lavoro Quarterly Review, 82,* 469-492.

Tanzi, V. (Ed.). (1982). *The underground economy in the United States and abroad.* Lexington, MA: Lexington.

Thomas, J. J. (1986). The underground economy in the United States: A further comment on Tanzi. *International Monetary Fund Staff Papers, 33.*

Thomas, J. J. (1988). The politics of the black economy. *Work, Employment and Society, 2,* 169-190.

Trew, K., & Kilpatrick, R. (1984). *The daily life of the unemployed: Social and psychological dimensions.* Unpublished manuscript.

Trundle, J. M. (1982). Recent changes in the use of cash. *Bank of England Quarterly Bulletin, 22,* 519-529.

Turner, R., Bostyn, A. M., & Wight, D. (1985). The work ethic in a Scottish town with declining employment. In B. Roberts, R. Finnegan, & D. Gallie (Eds.), *New approaches to economic life.* Manchester: Manchester University Press.

Weck-Hannemann, H., & Frey, B. S. (1985). Measuring the shadow economy: The case of Switzerland. In W. Gaertner & A. Wenig (Eds.), *The economics of the shadow economy.* Berlin: Springer-Verlag.

5

Doing Research in
Post-Tiananmen China

DANIEL J. CURRAN
SANDRA COOK

The 1980s was a decade of marked contrasts for scholars conducting sociological and legal research in the People's Republic of China. With the reestablishment of sociology and justice studies in 1979, open academic exchange was encouraged and the number of foreign experts involved in the analysis of Chinese society increased dramatically. For example, in the mid-1970s, there were no more than three English-speaking sociologists doing work in China but, by the mid-1980s, many organizations, such as the U.S. Fulbright program, supported sociologists, and numerous other scholars were involved in research with additional financial support coming from a variety of private sources. Collaborative studies were encouraged by both the Chinese and the foreign governments, and universities worldwide established ties with their Chinese counterparts.

As the social sciences were just reemerging as officially "sanctioned" disciplines in China, the challenges facing social researchers were many. At a technical level, the quality of social statistics released by Chinese officials was quite basic and availability was often an issue. Moreover, the data sets provided were often incomplete, which made longitudinal analyses difficult to conduct. As we will see, it was also necessary in some cases to question the validity of the data, that is, was it politically generated or edited? Still, during the early period of cooperation, foreign social researchers were granted access to data sets that allowed for preliminary research and were invited to participate in the development of more sophisticated survey instruments. The rapid acceleration of social science research was also due to the advocacy of Chinese scholars who had been exposed to such techniques while studying abroad and wished to implement the methods in their own country.

No doubt, though, the greatest challenge confronting social scientists in the 1990s has less to do with research design or the quality and quantity of data than with the skills of reading political signals being sent by researchers' own governments and that of China. More specifically, the suppression of the student democracy movement in the spring of 1989 had a significant impact on the progress that had been made. The fact that the initiators of the prodemocracy protest were from the universities led many of the more conservative governing cadre to call for stricter control of the curriculum. In particular, some officials pointed to the influence of "bourgeois" social sciences in the development of the student movement, arguing that research conducted by scholars in such disciplines focused on the gathering of information that identified negative social trends in China and that these findings fueled calls for reform. While informal measures were implemented immediately to limit the scope of sociological research, the first known official action was taken near the end of 1990 when the State Education Commission issued *Document Number 598*. Within this confidential communication, the State Education Commission prohibited Chinese universities and research institutes from providing or assisting in the collection of data for foreign scholars, especially data derived from social surveys of the Chinese population. This directive even included information gathered in jointly sponsored projects (WuDunn, 1991). According to several of the Chinese scholars interviewed for this chapter, other organizations, such as the Chinese Academy of Social Sciences, had or are drafting similar restrictions. Consequently, Chinese scholars already involved in research with foreign colleagues generally have found it necessary to limit the scope of projects and to have data from such research cleared by governmental officials prior to exchange or publication.

Another factor influencing the harsh reaction of the Chinese government was the perceived Western orientation of the democracy movement as well as the orchestrated efforts of the protesters to appeal to the foreign media. Consequently, action was quickly taken to curtail state-sponsored academic exchange. For example, the requirements for study abroad were made much more stringent, with one condition being that a student work for five years prior to departing. "Students who can afford to buy an exemption from the five-year work requirement may do so; the cost for each year overseas is US$550 for undergraduate studies, $870 for graduate studies, and $1,300 for doctoral research" (Committee on Scholarly Communication with the People's Republic of China, 1991, p. 31). In addition, as reported by one recently arrived Chinese scholar, some universities will also assess a monetary fee to those leaving professional positions to pursue advanced degrees.[1]

It has been argued by some Chinese officials that this decision was influenced by the failure of numerous Chinese students to return after foreign exchanges, but the fact is that the pattern of nonreturn had existed long before the Tiananmen incident and no restrictive mandate was issued. As we will discuss, the media exposure in the West of the student suppression also affected collaborative research because many private organizations became less willing to fund research projects in China and governmental support for new and existing programs was cut significantly. In the United States, the severe reduction in the number of Fulbright grants to China was a clear illustration.

This chapter presents two researchers' views on the impact of the Tiananmen Square incident on social research, in particular, that which examines China's justice system. As the Chinese government only began to reestablish a justice system in the Western sense in 1979, the same year that sociology was reintroduced in universities, the interest in law, criminal justice, and other forms of legal studies was great in the pre-Tiananmen period, and this environment provided for a variety of research possibilities. But the events of 1989 suddenly altered this open discourse. Doing research on the justice system became an extremely sensitive political issue and, as we will document, researchers generally had to adjust their approach in this changed environment. This chapter explores three general topics: first, the history of sociolegal research in China; second, conducting research in the People's Republic of China under new governmental restrictions; and, third, the problem of presenting data about China in a manner that protects Chinese colleagues without compromising the integrity of the research.[2]

Doing Sociolegal Research in China: A Brief History

There is no doubt that the actions taken on Tiananmen Square have severely hampered sociological research in China, but it is important to put the status of the social sciences into historical perspective. The value of sociological analyses has always been questioned by authorities in the People's Republic of China. Was such research of value and could it make a contribution to the socialist society, or was it a potential source of trouble? It could be argued that this debate was particularly true with regard to legal studies and criminology.

Prior to the establishment of the socialist government in 1949, the fields of sociology and law were quite advanced; in fact, some observers maintained that, outside of the United States and Western Europe, Chinese scholars were providing the most significant intellectual works in these disciplines. Exchange between the Chinese academic community and that of other nations was common and foreign scholars were even invited on occasion to consult with governmental agencies. For example, Roscoe Pound acted as an adviser to the Republic of China's Ministry of Administration and Justice prior to World War II (Li, 1989).

After the revolution, though, the socialist government eliminated what they considered to be Western-influenced law and justice. The existing court structure was replaced by a people's court with an emphasis on communal law and conflict resolution. Obviously, under these conditions, there was no perceived need for law programs.

At the same time, sociology and related studies came under scrutiny and were eventually deemed incompatible with the country's socialist agenda. Oddly, sociology was perceived in China much as it is in Western capitalist societies, that is, as an "oppositional science." The obvious difference is that sociology in Western nations frequently offers a liberal or leftist critique of a conservative capitalist regime, whereas, in China, both in the late 1940s and today, sociology is viewed as dangerous by a conservative socialist hierarchy. Indeed, as Shils (1985) comments, there may be reason for those in power to be concerned because sociology has "almost always been associated with movements for the reform of society" (p. 175). Another less ideological dimension of the sociological threat is its use of statistics to critically analyze social reality. The governmental ban on sociology and law-related studies meant that, outside of official self-examinations, empirical research on the justice system was virtually nonexistent for almost three decades.

The liberalization of the 1970s, however, brought about a rapid change in this situation. First, the opening of the economy demanded that China's legal system be more compatible with that of the world community. For example, to deal with multinational corporations, China needed lawyers who possessed an understanding of business-related law. To accelerate the development of this newly reestablished profession, Chinese universities primarily turned to legal scholars from the industrialized nations with whom they hoped to trade.

Simultaneously, many universities reintroduced sociology and other social sciences, and many scholars were encouraged to focus their research on the law and the justice system. Again, it could be argued that this emphasis on sociolegal studies was the by-product of economic reforms, given that the economic transition has resulted in a rise in the volume of crime throughout the nation.

Still, although there was an acceptance of sociological analyses, it was an uneasy one. As Li, a Research Fellow of the Institute of Comparative Law and Sociology of Law at Beijing University, wrote shortly before the Tiananmen incident, research methodology remained a concern:

> In the Chinese academic world, library research has been traditionally the only form of research, and even today when someone speaks of empirical research, many people think of a busybody with a clipboard, on the streets and lanes, asking women if they would like to be divorced. Moreover, government officials and lawyers often keep a wary eye on investigations that attempt to get to the bottom of things. Despite the unfavorable circumstances, some young researchers have gone beyond their studies and have earnestly practiced the fieldwork that they had advocated. (1989, p. 907)

Several of these efforts investigated social attitudes toward the legal system, and often they arrived at politically unacceptable conclusions. As we will discuss shortly, even survey research conducted by governmental agencies was deemed unacceptable and often hidden by labeling the findings "classified." Moreover, as one Chinese scholar interviewed for this study stated, the Spiritual Pollution Campaign of 1983 and 1984 actually limited research options although "at that time there was no kind of publicly stated limits or conditions upon research, but within the research institutes and among scholars there was definitely much suppressed" (personal interview, 1991). In addition to the methodological issue, many Chinese scholars began to employ Western theories to explain the rising incidence of crime. Often, these explanations pointed to the failure of the socialist government and the legal system to address the basic needs of the people in this time of rapid modernization.

In light of this environment, it was not surprising to those involved in research in China that, after Tiananmen Square, the government moved quickly to limit such sociological analyses. As stated earlier, *Document No. 598*, issued by the State Education Commission, barred Chinese institutions from collaborating with foreign counterparts on "sociological surveys in the form of public-opinion polls or written questionnaires." The mandate stated:

> In the current international situation, with political and ideological struggles being especially sharp, hostile forces in Western countries are constantly trying to overthrow, penetrate, or peacefully change our country. . . . Although not all data from surveys of social trends are confidential . . . according to the principle of distinguishing between internal and external matters, we cannot share such data with foreigners—nor, especially, can we send such data abroad for analysis. (quoted in Jacobson, 1991, pp. A1, A27)

In domestic media statements of late 1991, Chinese leaders increasingly warned their people that the West was involved in a "peaceful evolution" aimed at subverting the socialist structure.[3] As Li Zhun, an official in the Communist party Propaganda Department, stated in the *People's Daily*: "With the dramatic changes in the international situation, Western hostile forces have not only accelerated the pace of the peaceful evolution against socialist states, but have increasingly regarded China as the main stumbling block to their pursuit of power politics and defeat of socialism" (as quoted in Kristof, 1991, p. A7).

In Beijing, Li Ximing, a hard-line Communist party leader, summoned university administrators to an assembly where he firmly suggested that academic institutions take additional measures to control their students and form "a Great Wall against the peaceful evolution." In a Hubei Province newspaper, it was reported that Western powers were meeting "to study new methods in effecting the peaceful evolution of socialist countries" and that two of the main tactics of the West were academic exchanges and scholarly research (quoted in Kristof, 1991, p. A7). In sum, one might say that research, always considered politically sensitive by Chinese authorities, was now labeled subversive. What remains to be discussed is the impact of these pronouncements on research.

Controlling Research

The effect of post-Tiananmen restrictions on Chinese social scientists was immediate. The first action was increased control of what could be published. As one Chinese scholar stated:

After the Tiananmen Square incident, a whole host of probably the most important newspapers and journals in the country actually had changes in staff and personnel. . . . As a result of that it was quite evident that there was an increased level of censorship and you can say that the Communist Party's control over these outlets was made doubly strict. . . . The publishing houses in China are in fact governmental ministries, so the author or writer has to go through the process of having it approved by the publishing house, or the university if it is a university publication. The conditions are principally political or social. Basically the conditions are that you can't oppose the Communist Party, you can't oppose the leadership of the Party, and you can't promote bourgeois liberalization. So if one argued that crime had gone up in the post-Tiananmen period and you were trying to make a connection in some sort of way, well then you would have trouble in being able to get that published. (personal interview, 1991)

Often, even though social research is judged as "too sensitive" by censors, and therefore unpublishable, it still will be circulated among governmental departments. One Chinese scholar based in Beijing forwarded the following example:

Beijing [officials] last year [1990] approved a social report [to be conducted] at Beijing University in the sociology department. The research topic was "The Communist Party and Socialism: Do People Believe In It?" The research report discovered that in fact a fairly sizable number of people didn't believe at all. Obviously in relation to that report it can't possibly be published. But that type of report would go straight to the central committee or to various political committees or the Politburo. That kind of report and that treatment as it were is pretty standard. (personal interview, 1991)

Another dimension of control over research is the surveillance of domestic and foreign scholars. The most obvious effect of the observation is that Chinese scholars are quite fearful of speaking to foreigners. As one Chinese researcher stated, "People who come to China [must realize] that people have definite limits on what they would say to a foreigner. If I were giving my opinion to foreigners, for instance, I would not tell them anything that in any way questions government policy" (personal interview, 1991). Meetings are now more structured and observation by government officials standard. Notably, while the main focus has been on Western visitors, all scholars appear to be considered potentially negative influences and therefore warrant observation. For example, one person spoke of a group from Russia:

In August or September of 1989, a delegation from the Moscow Republic visited China and their specializations were politics and sociology. When they arrived in China, there were investigations carried out by the Bureau of State Security and they were also supervised, that is, tabs were kept on them, because a number of the members of the delegation were also believed to be high ranking members of the government. (personal interview, 1991)

Another form of control is the heightened restrictions on travel by Chinese scholars. One method of travel control is the withholding of the academic's travel documents. For instance, an organizer of a panel on China at an international symposium reported: "The Chinese government held the invited participant's passport until the day before the conference making the individual's participation impossible" (personal interview, 1991).

Obviously, such practices have curtailed open exchange, but it is important to realize that Western nations' reactions to the Tiananmen incident also played a role in the Chinese government's willingness to suppress academic programs. As one interviewee pointed out, "The fact that there was a reduction of international funding of academic projects and the curtailment of exchanges after the events of 1989, but continued trade activity, sent a clear message to those in Beijing. And since the social sciences are not viewed as critical to the continued development of the economy why not limit them" (personal interview, 1991). Indeed, another Chinese respondent indicated that, if the United States had, for example, refused to renew China's most favored nation status, the Chinese would have retaliated much more harshly.

Obstacles, Misunderstandings, and Criticisms: Justifying Research in China

Barriers to foreign researchers have also increased. Letters of invitation are more difficult to secure, and there is clearly an effort on the part of the Chinese authorities to screen projects and to gain more control over existing research efforts. Independent study is limited, and most researchers must be cleared by governmental agencies. But the obstacles established by the Chinese government are only one part of the problem; the other dimension is that research in China is also politically sensitive at home.

The encouragement and excitement expressed in Western academic circles and by funding agencies about conducting research in China prior to the Tiananmen incident have been replaced by extreme caution and, on occasion, even outright condemnation. Funding opportunities, both public and private, have been reduced; universities have shied away from joint programs; and existing projects were cut or eliminated. Individuals and organizations supportive in the past now talk about the human rights record of the People's Republic as being problematic. No doubt, we agree that the actions of the Chinese regime violated the participants' basic rights, but reacting by reducing support for sociolegal and other social science research represents a misunderstanding of the past and a shortchanging of the future.

First, it is inaccurate to portray the human rights issue as a new issue because even in the early 1980s, when enthusiasm for collaborative research was at its peak, there were severe human rights problems, especially in Tibet. Second, the social sciences brought to light many basic social inequalities in China; a reduced commitment to this type of research will only allow these problems to return to obscurity. Moreover, reducing funding for sociolegal research while allowing programs in the hard sciences to continue only rewards the actions of Tiananmen and reinforces the position of the governing cadre. Third, it is clear that China will play an increasingly significant role in the world community and that academic exchanges and research will provide both parties with a better understanding of each other. The key to success is improving the process, but, as one U.S. scholar stated: "How, of course, is the problem. Perhaps one way would be to guard against over-politization of programs, attaching too many 'strings.' At the same time it seems we should be increasingly stringent that the PRC meet the same standards for academic reciprocity as they expect of us or other nations do" (Strevy, 1990, p. 75).

Beyond the reduced support for research, the individual who has conducted research in China is confronted with problems due to another dimension of the sensitive nature of the research. First is the ethical issue of the protection of human subjects. As Michael Oksenberg, a professor of political science at the University of Michigan points out, "This document [No. 598] makes clear that cooperative research in China could place one's Chinese colleagues or the respondents to question-naires at risk" (quoted in Jacobson, 1991, p. A27). One cannot simply publish findings because it could mean the end of another academic career or the punishment of respondents.

This leads us to a second point, that is, the lack of awareness of other scholars of the ramifications of publicly exposing sources or openly attacking official policy. If one has worked or developed relationships with Chinese scholars, it would be irresponsible to endanger others with controversial statements. This is not to say that one should withhold the data or information but, instead, that one may have to hold back and let others more critically examine the data. For example, after the presentation of a paper on the Chinese justice system, it was implied that the two authors were naive about China because of their failure to expose the repressive nature of the system. One of the authors replied, "If being labeled naive is the price I have to pay to protect Chinese colleagues and continue our research, it's a price I will gladly pay" (personal communication, 1991).

Notes

1. Contrary to popular belief, in 1991 there was actually an increase in the number of Chinese studying abroad relative to previous years. While new regulation has reduced the number of government-sponsored scholars, the decline has been offset by the large number of self-sponsored students who have fulfilled the five-year requirement (Committee on Scholarly Communication with the People's Republic of China, 1991).

2. The interviews presented in this chapter were conducted in late 1991. Because the majority of those who agreed to participate desired to remain anonymous, we have withheld the names of all persons interviewed.

3. Chinese authorities stated that "peaceful evolution" is a strategy that was developed by the United States in the late 1940s. Comments made in the 1950s by Secretary of State John Foster Dulles about the "evolutionary change" of communist nations over time are often cited as evidence of this policy.

References

Committee on Scholarly Communication with the People's Republic of China. (1991). Newsbriefs. *China Exchange News, 19*(3, 4), 31.

Jacobson, R. L. (1991, June 19). Universities in China are told not to cooperate in social research projects with "hostile" West. *The Chronicle of Higher Education,* pp. A1, A27.

Kristof, N. D. (1991, September 19). Changes in China stir U.S. *New York Times,* p. A7.

Li, W. (1989). The sociology of law in China: Overview and trends. *Law and Society Review, 23,* 903-914.

Shils, E. (1985). On the eve: A prospect of retrospect. In M. Bulmer (Ed.), *Essays in the history of British sociological research.* Cambridge: Cambridge University Press.

Strevy, C. (1990). *Current status of academic and cultural exchanges between us and PRC institutions a year after Tiananmen.* New York: Institute of International Education Clearinghouse on Chinese Student/Scholar Needs.

WuDunn, S. (1991, June 25). China said to curb foreign research. *New York Times,* p. A8.

6

Developing a Community Sample of Gay Men for an Epidemiological Study of AIDS

JOHN L. MARTIN[1]
LAURA DEAN

By 1982, it was established that, in the United States, an epidemic of acquired immunodeficiency syndrome (AIDS) was afflicting homosexual men (Centers for Disease Control [CDC], 1981a, 1981b, 1982a, 1982b; Fauci, 1982; Follansbee et al., 1982; Friedman-Kien, 1981; Gottlieb, Schroff, & Schanker, 1981; Siegal, Lopez, & Hammer, 1981). Within a short time, it appeared likely that transmission of the disease in this population was associated with sexual activity and possibly illicit drug use (CDC, 1982c; Dowdle, 1983; Jaffe et al., 1983; Marmor et al., 1982). Large biomedical epidemiological studies (e.g., Chmiel et al., 1987; Mayer et al., 1986; Moss et al., 1987; Stevens et al., 1986; Winkelstein, Lyman, & Padian, 1987) were needed to determine patterns of AIDS within the affected population, establish risk factors for the disease, and elucidate the full spectrum of its natural history and manifestations. In addition,

AUTHORS' NOTE: An earlier version of this chapter was originally published in the *American Behavioral Scientist, 33,* 546-561. This research was supported by the National Institute of Mental Health (R01 MH39557) and by the New York City Department of Health. We are deeply grateful to the leaders of gay organizations who helped us recruit men, to those members of our study group who recruited others, and to all the men who took part in this research.

psychosocial epidemiological studies of the homosexual population were required to determine specific sexual behaviors associated with AIDS transmission, knowledge and attitudes about the disease, approaches taken to prevent infection and illness, and methods of coping with the increasing frequency of personal illness and bereavement (e.g., Joseph et al., 1987; Martin, 1987, 1988; Martin, Dean, Garcia, & Hall, 1989; Martin, Garcia, & Beatrice, 1989; McKusick, Horstman, & Coates, 1985). While the populations of interest and topics of inquiry were fairly self-evident to those interested in conducting this research, the appropriate methodology for generating useful samples and probing highly sensitive topics was, and continues to be, open to debate.

Kinsey's work (Kinsey, Pomeroy, & Martin, 1948) clearly demonstrated that any large-scale research involving sexual behavior was highly sensitive and difficult to execute. Because homosexuality and drug use involve not only private behaviors but behaviors that are widely condemned and frequently carry serious social and legal ramifications, epidemiological research on AIDS is particularly sensitive and problematic. Not only is the relevant information delicate in nature, but the target populations are hidden ones: No census-based sampling frame nor any other reliable source is available to define and randomly sample subsets for study. In light of the complex nature of sexuality, which involves thoughts and feelings as well as behaviors, the development of a complete sampling frame of homosexual males is difficult to conceive, because it is unlikely that a consensus among experts could be achieved regarding the boundaries of homosexuality.

It should also be noted that the geometric increase in cases of AIDS that occurred during the first three years of the epidemic (CDC, 1983) lent great urgency to research efforts in this area. (There were more than 120,000 U.S. cases in gay and bisexual men reported to the CDC as of January 1992.) Studies had to be mounted quickly, with little time to consider and experiment with various probability sampling options or screening procedures. Even in the absence of this time urgency, federal research funds from the U.S. Public Health Service for AIDS were so limited during the first few years of the epidemic (Office of Technology Assessment, 1985) that the development of a national or citywide sampling frame of any segment of the homosexual population using conventional telephone or face-to-face screening procedures was highly impractical for researchers dependent on public funds.

The problem of sampling unenumerated populations using nonprobability methods, however, is not new in social science research. While nonprobability sampling approaches have traditionally been used in qualitative research (Patton, 1987), they have also been successfully employed in quantitative research efforts. For example, Himmelfarb and his colleagues (Himmelfarb, Loar, & Mott, 1983) have demonstrated the accuracy of sampling the Jewish population using a list of 35 distinctive Jewish surnames. Rothbart and his colleagues (Rothbart, Fine, & Sudman, 1982) have developed and evaluated the use of multiplicity sampling of kin networks in their studies of Vietnam veterans. Biernacki and Waldorf (1981) relied heavily on snowball sampling and chain referrals to locate and interview untreated ex-heroin addicts. Their work is particularly noteworthy in the current context of AIDS research and sensitive topics because these researchers were attempting to study illegal, widely condemned behavior among members of a hidden, difficult-to-define population.

Recently, Sudman and Kalton (1986) have described a number of alternative methods for sampling special populations. It is clear from this work that the use of special sampling techniques can lead to substantial and quantifiable savings of time and money. In addition, the use of certain types of nonprobability samples does not preclude the estimate of population parameters. Progress is being made toward accurate estimates of biases (Sudman & Kalton, 1986, pp. 402-405) associated with various alternative sampling approaches, and it is likely that statistical refinements will develop.

This progress is important because, with a few notable exceptions, nonprobability sampling is characteristic of all epidemiological research on homosexual men and AIDS conducted to date in the United States. Furthermore, it is the findings from this research that form the basis for public health policy, service planning, and resource allocation (Turner, Miller, & Moses, 1989). Thus it may be useful to begin to examine various approaches that have been taken to developing samples of populations at risk for AIDS so as to begin to estimate the generalizability of findings from any one study or set of studies to the larger population from which research participants have been drawn.

This chapter describes our efforts to develop a community-based sample of gay men living in New York City. Our primary goal was to evaluate over time the impact of the AIDS epidemic on the emotional and behavioral functioning of gay men, using an epidemiological cohort study design. Ideally, such a study would include all types of homosexual men, ranging from those most open about their sexuality to those who do not consider themselves to be homosexual but who nevertheless engage in sex with other men (or another man). Because we did not have resources or time to generate a population-based sample from which to select individuals from the continuum of homosexuality (Kinsey, Pomeroy, & Martin, 1948), however, a minimum requirement for inclusion in the sample was the private recognition that one was a homosexual or bisexual man. This criterion of homosexual or bisexual self-identification was the basis for defining the target "gay community" of this study. No other shared characteristic of members of the sample was implied or assumed by the term *community*.

Rationale and Methods

An initial sample size of at least 700 was required. Three sampling options were considered: (a) to conduct an enumeration of the gay male population of either New York City as a whole, or a specific section or neighborhood of the city, thereby developing a sampling frame from which respondents could be randomly drawn; (b) to draw respondents from a number of different sources, recognizing that the resulting sample would not be random but might include diverse segments of the gay population; (c) to draw from narrow or singular samples of convenience easily and cheaply available that were neither random nor representative.

The drawbacks of the third approach caused us to reject it (see Sudman & Kalton, 1986), because it was important to strive for diversity. Choosing between the first and second approaches, however, involved weighing the costs and benefits of each, with reference to time, effort, practicality, and the scientific goals of the study. In the end, the enumeration approach was rejected because it entailed built-in limitations that detracted from the ability to yield a representative sample of the gay population. Given the stigma attached to homosexuality and the increasing rate of antigay harassment and violence (Dean, Wu, & Martin, 1992), it was assumed that only a very select type of gay man would be willing to state his sexual preference or describe his sexual behavior during a brief screening interview conducted either by phone or in person. Thus developing a sampling frame based on responses to screening questions would very likely include only gay men who were the most confident and "out" about their sexual preference.

The door-to-door method, such as would be used in household sampling, even in a neighborhood with many homosexual residents, was also rejected because of both logistical problems and anticipated biases.

For example, although it is sometimes compared with San Francisco's Castro district, New York's Greenwich Village may not be comparable in terms of the density of gay men. Even if it were feasible to gain access to apartment buildings of village residents, the cost of a door-to-door enumeration of this area would have been prohibitive due to the sheer numbers of people it would have been necessary to screen. Had we opted for this approach, we still would have been left with the question, "Are Greenwich Village gay men representative of New York City gay men?" Because the village is a predominantly white, high-rent district, in which openly gay men tend to live, the answer to that question was no. A sampling frame derived solely from this geographic area, or any particular geographic area of the city for that matter, would not be representative of the broad spectrum of individuals composing New York's gay population. This problem was particularly serious with regard to recruiting men in the sample who did not view themselves as part of the "gay community" despite acknowledging that they had sexual encounters with other men.

The approach we adopted employed a combination of (a) *recruitment from diverse sources* and (b) *personal referral* into the sample by those individuals recruited through these sources. The rationale for using this combination of methods was that recruitment from a variety of sources would help to ensure a broad cross section of respondents, while personal referrals provided by the numerous individuals recruited through these different sources would give us a more diverse sample. To establish one segment of the sample as a probability sample, in the traditional statistical sense, gay organizations were selected as one of the recruitment sources, because a reasonably complete sampling frame of gay organization members could be constructed.

Five Recruitment Sources

Gay Organization Members

The first recruitment source was gay organizations. Men drawn from this source make up a two-stage stratified probability sample of gay organization members. More than 150 New York City organizations, whose memberships consisted primarily of homosexual and bisexual individuals, were canvassed by telephone in March 1985 to determine the size of their membership and the ratio of men to women. A special effort was made to locate and include in the sampling frame any gay groups composed primarily of ethnic minorities, because African American and Hispanic men are not represented in studies on AIDS in proportions similar to their representation in the general population. From this survey, a master list was compiled of 90 New York City gay organizations eligible for inclusion. The groups were stratified by size of membership (small, 5 to 25; medium, 26 to 50; large, 51 or more) and by type (political, religious, professional, social, and college based). Within each stratum, a random half of all organizations was formally approached for assistance in recruiting subjects into the study. Out of 52 groups from whom assistance was requested, 92% (48) agreed to participate.

Once cooperation was obtained from a group, the leader was instructed in the random selection of five men to whom invitational materials should be sent. The invitational materials, compiled in the research office and delivered to the groups' leaders, consisted of four items: (a) a cover letter from the organization describing the random method of selection and assuring the recipient that we, the researchers, had no knowledge of his identity; (b) a letter from the research group describing the nature and goals of the study; (c) a brief screening form with 10 demographic questions and a space to indicate willingness to participate; and (d) a stamped, addressed envelope to return the screening form to the research unit.

After adjusting for ineligible individuals (defined as those living outside the city, those with a diagnosis of AIDS, and those under 18 years of age), our final response rate (defined by the completion of a baseline interview) for this organizational sample was 72%. A total of 131 men were interviewed from this source.

Unsolicited Volunteers

Although study participants were never solicited through newspaper print ads, a number of men who read news reports about the study in *The Advocate, New York Native, Gay Men's Health Crisis Newsletter #5,* and *The New York Times* contacted the research unit to enroll. Because a number of studies of gay men and AIDS had employed samples consisting primarily of volunteers recruited through advertisements, we opted to enroll these highly motivated volunteers in the cohort for comparison with other subgroups enrolled through other sources; 41 unsolicited volunteers were interviewed.

Pilot Sample Referrals

The third sample source was personal referrals from participants in the pilot study; 26 men, chosen for their diversity, were enrolled as pilot subjects for the penultimate version of the interview procedures. These procedures included the systematic request for personal referrals of gay male friends into the study. Having generated a pool of these referrals through the pilot interviews, we included them in our cohort for comparison purposes; 32 pilot sample referrals were interviewed.

Gay Pride Festival Participants

The fourth sample source was the 1985 Christopher Street Festival and Gay Pride Parade. Men from this source were recruited on June 30, 1985, in face-to-face requests, at the annual street festival commemorating the Stonewall riots of 1967; 72 men were interviewed from this source.

Sexually Transmitted Disease Clinic Clients

The fifth source of recruitment was a New York City public health clinic located on the west side of Manhattan. Counselors responsible for conducting exit interviews with all clients were instructed to briefly describe the study and provide each man, regardless of sexual orientation, with an invitational letter, brief screening form, and self-addressed, stamped envelope to return to the research unit to enroll in the study. This source was of particular interest to us because it represented a potential means of access to men who were least likely to view themselves as connected to, or part of, the gay community but who participated in sexual activity with other men. After intensive efforts over a six-week period, only 15 men from the clinic were interviewed.

A total of 291 respondents were recruited through these five sources. We refer to this group of men as "generation zero" because they formed the initial group of respondents who would act to generate sources for the remainder of the sample.

Snowball Sampling:
Generations One Through Five

At the conclusion of each interview, respondents were given three packets of invitational enrollment materials and instructed to send a packet to three friends. These friends had to be gay, be aged 18 or over, reside in New York City, and not have a diagnosis of AIDS. As with the materials sent by group leaders to members of organizations, packets sent by a respondent to his friends were addressed from the respondent and contained a cover letter signed by the respondent indicating that he had taken part in the study and that he was inviting others to participate to help the researchers conduct the work. The letter emphasized the fact that the researchers did not know the friend's identity, which could only be revealed by that individual if he chose to return the form indicating his interest in being interviewed. (This issue is described in detail by Biernacki & Waldorf, 1981.)

Our primary concern about the snowball sampling procedure with regard to selection bias was that respondents would influence friends' willingness to participate. In an attempt to reduce any biases, interviewers instructed respondents to avoid "prescreening" selected friends, emphasizing the importance of letting each friend read the material describing the study on his own so that he could decide privately about his participation. While we fully expected respondents to discuss the study with friends to whom they sent materials, our goal was to keep this discussion to a minimum. Thus even those respondents who found the interview stressful or unpleasant would at least provide friends with the opportunity to learn about the study. Similarly, even friends of respondents who would tend to decline a verbal request to receive invitational materials would have the opportunity to read about the study prior to making a final decision.

The snowball referral procedure was built into every interview conducted, and we interviewed men up to five generations removed from respondents in generation zero. The number of men interviewed in each generation, broken down by sample source, is shown in Table 6.1. It can be seen that the reproductive rate diminished: Generation one was 71% the size of generation zero (207/291); generation two was 67% the size of generation one (137/206); generation three was 59% the size of generation two (81/137); generation four was 28% the size of generation three (23/81); and generation five was 30% the size of generation four (7/23).

Because each interview included a section that elicited the first names or initials of members of respondents' social networks (Fischer et al., 1977), we attempted to keep track of the number of friends invited into the study by asking respondents to indicate network members to whom they intended to send invitational materials. Although this approach to

Table 6.1 Distribution of the Sample by Recruitment Source and Generation

Generation	Organizations	Volunteers	Sample Source Pilot Networks	Gay Festival	Clinic	Total
0	131	41	32	72	15	291 (39%)
1	112	40	22	30	2	207 (28%)
2	90	18	11	18	0	137 (18%)
3	63	10	3	5	0	81 (11%)
4	18	5	0	0	0	23 (3%)
5	7	0	0	0	0	7 (1%)
Total	421	114	68	125	17	746
	(57%)	(15%)	(9%)	(17%)	(2%)	(100%)

establishing a valid denominator for calculating response rates was attractive in theory, it did not work in practice. Through follow-up phone calls made to each respondent, we found much variation in willingness and interest to recruit friends into the study. This was true despite stated willingness by most respondents at the time of the interview to recruit friends. While some respondents mailed all three packets to friends they had selected from their social network roster, many other respondents failed to send some or all of the materials or mailed the materials to ineligible individuals. Because resources were limited with regard to the number of follow-up telephone calls we could make, it was not possible to determine the number of invitations that were actually received by eligible social network members of those who had been interviewed. Thus we could not estimate a valid response rate for our snowball sampling efforts. We know only that, over a period of three months, 585 men returned screening forms to the research unit, indicating an interest in being interviewed. A total of 455 of these men were included in the baseline sample interviewed in 1985. The remaining 130 men were placed on a waiting list and contacted to be interviewed for the first time in the following year during our second wave of data collection.

Results

Our initial interest was in determining the extent to which the *source* of recruitment led to differences in the sample composition. These results are shown in Table 6.2. The most striking difference is between the group of respondents recruited from the public health clinic compared with the respondents recruited from the other sources. As a group, these 15 men were younger, were less educated, had lower annual incomes, and were primarily African American or Hispanic. In addition, compared with men recruited from the other sources, those recruited from the clinic were less likely to be coupled with a lover, less likely to reside in Manhattan, less likely to be a member of a gay group or organization, and less likely to have contact with a person with AIDS through paid or volunteer work. These differences indicate that the population of gay men we accessed through the public health clinic was quite different than the population accessed through the other sources.

In fact, the differences among the other four sources tend to be small. There are, however, two differences that should be noted. First, the sample drawn from gay organizations is composed of 2.5 to 6 times more African

Table 6.2 Characteristics of Respondents Recruited Through Five Sources

Characteristic	Organizations (n = 131)	Volunteers (n = 41)	Sample Source Pilot Networks (n = 32)	Gay Festival (n = 72)	Clinic (n = 15)	Total (N = 291)
Mean age	37	38	36	36	29	36
Mean years education	17	16	16	16	14	16
Median income	$25,000	$25,000	$25,000	$25,000	$15,000	$25,000
Black or Hispanic	18%	7%	3%	7%	73%	15%
Manhattan resident	77%	93%	91%	70%	53%	78%
Coupled[a]	43%	41%	28%	43%	20%	40%
Gay group member[b]	91%	51%	41%	60%	20%	68%
Mostly "out"	69%	82%	91%	76%	60%	75%

a. A respondent qualified as being coupled with a male lover if (a) he said he had a lover, (b) his lover viewed him as his lover (reciprocity), (c) friends viewed the two as a couple (public recognition), and (d) the relationship was extant for six months or more (duration).
b. Of gay group members, 9% did not consider themselves a member of a group at the time we interviewed them.

American or Hispanic respondents (18%) compared with groups drawn from unsolicited volunteers (7%), pilot networks (3%), and the gay pride festival (7%). Second, the sample drawn from gay organizations and from the gay pride festival are each composed of more men from New York City boroughs other than Manhattan (23% and 30%, respectively) compared with the groups drawn from the unsolicited volunteers (7%) and pilot sample networks (9%).

Our next question concerned differences in sample composition that may be due to the snowball method of recruitment compared with the respondents recruited from the primary sources. To evaluate these effects, we compared demographic characteristics of generation zero with the characteristics of generation one and generations two through five, combined.

The snowball sampling method led us to groups of men with a lower median income, fewer of whom were coupled with a lover, fewer of whom where African American or Hispanic, and more of whom resided in Manhattan than in one of the other boroughs of the city. It is interesting to note that snowball sampling did not lead to groups of men who were markedly different with respect to age or education.

Comparisons With Random Probability Samples

In evaluating the results of our sampling approach, we compared our New York City sample with two samples of gay men drawn in San Francisco at approximately the same time—1984 to 1985. The first of these samples, developed by the Research and Decisions Corporation for the San Francisco AIDS Foundation (Research and Decisions Corporation, 1984), employed citywide random digit dialing methods to conduct a telephone survey of gay men regarding knowledge about AIDS and behavior changes occurring because of AIDS. The sample size was 500 and the response rate for the initial screening questions regarding sexual orientation was reported to be 97%. The second sample, developed by the Center for Survey Research for the San Francisco Men's Health Study (Winkelstein et al., 1987), employed a cluster probability sample of households in the 19 census tracts constituting the Castro District of San Francisco to conduct a cohort study of the natural history of AIDS among gay men using face-to-face interview methods and blood tests. The sample size was 823 and the response rate for completing the initial testing and interview was 59%.

Table 6.3 Comparison of a New York City Sample With Two San
Francisco Samples

| | | San Francisco | |
Characteristic	New York City (N = 746) (percent)	R & D Corporation[a] (N = 500) (percent)	SFMHS[b] (N = 823) (percent)
Race			
white	87	87	92
black	6	4	4
other	7	9	4
Education			
high school or less	6	12	10
some college	17	31	36
college graduate or more	77	57	54
Age			
34 or younger	52	46	59
35-44	35	34	28
45 or older	13	20	13
Degree of closetedness			
completely out	42	49	na
mostly out	38	34	na
half out	17	14	na
mostly not out	3	3	na

a. Data from a Research and Decisions Corporation report (December 3, 1984).
b. Data from the San Francisco Men's Health Study (courtesy of Jim Wiley, Ph.D., June 1986).

The comparisons between our New York City sample and the two San
Francisco samples on race, education, age, and degree of being "out of
the closet" regarding one's homosexuality are shown in Table 6.3. It can
be seen that, despite the diverse approaches to sampling, the composition of the three groups with respect to race and age are quite similar.
Approximately 90% of all three groups were white; approximately 50%
of all three groups were aged 34 or younger, while approximately 30%
in each group were aged 35 to 44. In addition, the New York sample and
the Research and Decisions sample are very similar with respect to
degree of being "out of the closet."

Education was the variable on which the New York City group appears to contrast most strongly with the two San Francisco samples. Of
the former, 77% had completed a four-year college degree or more education, while just over half of each of the San Francisco samples had
done so. On the other hand, considering the low end of the education

distribution, none of the three groups contained large proportions of men with only a high school education or less; from 6% to 12% fell into the lowest category of educational attainment.

Discussion and Conclusion

Based on indicators of central tendency, the sample we drew in 1985 using multiple methods resulted in a group that was primarily white, well educated, and the majority of whom resided in Manhattan. The average age of the group was 36, and their median income bracket in 1984 was from $25,000 to $30,000. The majority of these men were single, belonged to at least one gay organization, and considered themselves to be completely or mostly "out of the closet" about their homosexuality. There was also much diversity among members of the sample, as indicated by measures of variability and binomial distributions: 13% were either African American or Hispanic, 6% had only a high school education or less, 18% resided in a New York City borough other than Manhattan, 37% were coupled with a lover, 42% had no affiliation with a gay group or organization, and 16% considered themselves to be in the closet at least half of the time. Ages ranged from 20 to 70 (SD = 8.50 years) and annual income ranged from under $3,000 per year to more than $100,000 per year (SD = $12,000).

A key question, however, was whether the distributions on these variables reflected the distribution in the larger population of gay men living in New York City who did not have AIDS. Because no random sample of gay men had been drawn in New York City, it was necessary to consider samples of gay men drawn from San Francisco, where at least two groups had been randomly drawn using conventional probability sampling methods. While the comparisons we have conducted are quite rough, it appears that the New York City sample we drew using a combination of methods is similar to the two randomly drawn San Francisco samples, particularly with regard to race, age, and the degree of being out of the closet. In addition, the samples are similar with regard to the low end of the educational distribution. These results suggest that we were able to assemble a reasonably representative group of gay men in New York City in the absence of a citywide sampling frame, a door-to-door enumeration, or a random digit dialing screening procedure.

One limitation of the comparative analysis lies with the San Francisco samples: Not only do both of those samples have built-in limitations but the composition of the gay population of San Francisco may be somewhat different than the composition of the New York City gay population. Indeed, the higher rates of education found in the New York sample may reflect a true difference between the two cities: New York being a magnet for highly educated ambitious individuals aiming for the top of their fields, and San Francisco being a magnet for individuals aiming for a more relaxed life-style in a physically attractive geographic area. At this time, we have no means of assessing the extent to which this may be true. There is little doubt, however, that the most serious bias present in our sample involves the rate of inclusion of African American, Hispanic, and Asian gay men. With New York City census figures indicating that from 25% to more than 50% of males aged 15 to 75 are African American or Hispanic, it is unlikely that our proportion of 13% comes close to representing the size of the nonwhite gay population of New York City. Our inability to recruit larger numbers of minority gay men into our study even with special efforts indicates the importance of this problem.

A key point made by Sudman and Kalton (1986) throughout their discussion of alternative sampling methods is that the "range of alternative sampling procedures for special populations should be carefully considered before resorting to ad hoc convenience samples, especially if one wishes to generalize to the total special population" (p. 427). We believe that this point is well supported by the results presented here of our efforts to assemble a sample of gay men using a number of different sampling approaches, each carefully and systematically executed. Not only have we shown that men drawn through nonprobability sampling methods can be quite similar, as a group, to those drawn from a defined sampling frame of gay organization members but, taken together, the total group closely resembles two independent samples selected through probability sampling strategies. It is unlikely that the evidence would have supported this conclusion had we simply advertised for volunteers, relied on a single recruitment strategy, or recruited men solely from bars, bathhouses, or clinics.

It is important to note that the effort we expended to assemble the sample as described here is having a significant influence on the picture portrayed of the gay community in a number of areas. For example, there has been widespread belief that alcohol abuse and problems due to excessive drinking afflict in excess of 30% of all homosexuals at any given time (Ziebold & Mongeon, 1982). This figure, however, was derived primarily from ad hoc convenience samples of gay individuals seeking treatment. In contrast, based on the sample we have described here, we estimate that from 9% to 12% of the male homosexual population has severe drinking problems involving abuse and dependence (Martin, 1990). We have also shown (Martin, Garcia, & Beatrice, 1989) that the estimate of the prevalence of human immunodeficiency virus (HIV; the virus that causes AIDS) is substantially lower in our sample (36% as of 1986), compared with estimates ranging from 44% to 67% based on ad hoc samples of homosexual men drawn from health clinics and hepatitis B cohort studies (Curran et al., 1985; Stevens et al., 1986).

There is no doubt that sample selection using conventional probability techniques should be the method of choice when conducting quantitative epidemiological research. When the lack of time, resources, or an adequate sampling frame do not permit the use of such methods, however, alternative approaches are available that are superior to ad hoc convenience samples. These alternative methods, many of which are outlined by Sudman and Kalton (1986), can result in samples that approach representativeness of the population of interest and can be considered scientifically valid by virtue of their explicitness and replicability.

Note

1. John L. Martin, the principal investigator of the landmark psychological study that forms the basis of this chapter, died of AIDS on January 17, 1992.

References

Biernacki, P., & Waldorf, D. (1981). Snowball sampling: Problems and techniques of chain referral sampling. *Sociological Methods and Research, 10,* 141-163.

Centers for Disease Control (CDC). (1981a). Kaposi's sarcoma and *Pneumocystis* pneumonia among homosexual men: New York City and California. *MMWR, 30,* 305-308.

Centers for Disease Control (CDC). (1981b). *Pneumocystis* pneumonia: Los Angeles. *MMWR, 30,* 250-252.

Centers for Disease Control (CDC). (1982a). Persistent, generalized lymphadenopathy among homosexual males. *MMWR, 31,* 249-251.

Centers for Disease Control (CDC). (1982b). Diffuse, undifferentiated non-Hodgkins lymphoma among homosexual males: United States. *MMWR, 31,* 277-279.

Centers for Disease Control (CDC). (1982c). A cluster of Kaposi's sarcoma and *pneumocystis carinii* pneumonia among homosexual male residents of Los Angeles and Orange Counties. *MMWR, 31,* 305-307.

Centers for Disease Control (CDC). (1983). Update: Acquired immune deficiency syndrome (AIDS)—United States. *MMWR, 32,* 465-467.

Chmiel, J. S., Detels, R., Kaslow, R. A., Van Raden, M., Kingsley, L. A., & Brookmeyer, R. (1987). Factors associated with prevalent human immunodeficiency virus (HIV) infection in the Multicenter AIDS cohort study. *American Journal of Epidemiology, 126,* 568-577.

Curran, J. W., Morgan, W. M., Hardy, A. M., Jaffe, H. W., Darrow, W. W., & Dowdle, W. R. (1985). The epidemiology of AIDS: Current status and future prospects. *Science, 229,* 1352-1357.

Dean, L., Wu, S., & Martin, J. L. (1992). Trends in violence and discrimination against gay men in New York City: 1984 to 1990. In G. M. Herek & K. Berrill (Eds.), *Hate crimes: Understanding and responding to anti-gay violence.* Newbury Park, CA: Sage.

Dowdle, W. R. (1983). The epidemiology of AIDS. *Public Health Reports, 98,* 308-312.

Fauci, A. S. (1982). The syndrome of Kaposi's sarcoma and opportunistic infections: An epidemiologically restricted disorder of immunoregulation. *Annals of Internal Medicine, 96,* 777-779.

Fischer, C. S., Jackson, R. M., Stueve, C. A., Gerson, K., Jones, L. M., & Baldessare, M. (1977). *Networks and places: Social relations in the urban setting.* New York: Free Press.

Follansbee, S. E., Busch, D. F., Wofsy, C. B., Coleman, D. L., Gullet, J., Aurigemma, G. P., Ross, T., Hadley, W. K., & Draw, L. (1982). An outbreak of *Pneumocystis carinii* pneumonia in homosexual men. *Annals of Internal Medicine, 96,* 705-713.

Friedman-Kien, A. E. (1981). Disseminated Kaposi's sarcoma syndrome in young homosexual men. *American Academy of Dermatology, 5,* 468-471.

Gottlieb, M. S., Schroff, R., & Schanker, H. M. (1981). *Pneumocystis carinii* pneumonia and mucosal candidiasis in previously healthy homosexual men. *New England Journal of Medicine, 305,* 1425-1431.

Himmelfarb, H. S., Loar, R. M., & Mott, S. H. (1983). Sampling by ethnic surnames: The case of American Jews. *Public Opinion Quarterly, 47,* 247-260.

Jaffe, H. W., Choi, K., Thomas, P. D., et al. (1983). National case-control study of Kaposi's sarcoma and *Pneumocystis carinii* pneumonia in homosexual men: Part 1, epidemiologic results. *Annals of Internal Medicine, 99,* 145-151.

Joseph, J. G., Montgomery, S. B., Emmons, C. A., Kessler, R. C., Ostrow, D. G., Wortman, C. B., O'Brien, K., Eller, M., & Eshleman, S. (1987). Magnitude and determinants of risk reduction: Longitudinal analysis of a cohort at risk for AIDS. *Psychological Health, 1,* 73-96.

Kinsey, A. C., Pomeroy, W. B., & Martin, C. E. (1948). *Sexual behavior in the human male.* Philadelphia: W. B. Saunders.

Marmor, M., Laubenstein, L., William, D. C., Friedman-Kien, A. E., Byrum, R. D., D'Onofrio, S., & Dubin, N. (1982, May 15). Risk factors for Kaposi's sarcoma in homosexual men. *Lancet,* pp. 1083-1087.

Martin, J. L. (1987). The impact of AIDS on gay male sexual behavior patterns in New York City. *American Journal of Public Health, 77,* 578-581.

Martin, J. L. (1988). Psychological consequences of AIDS-related bereavement among gay men. *Journal of Consulting and Clinical Psychology, 56,* 856-862.

Martin, J. L. (1990). Drinking patterns and drinking problems in a community sample of gay men. In D. Seminara & A. Pawlowski (Eds.), *Alcohol, immunomodulation and AIDS*. New York: Alan R. Liss.

Martin, J. L., Dean, L., Garcia, M. A., & Hall, W. (1989). The impact of AIDS on a gay community: Changes in sexual behavior, substance use, and mental health. *American Journal of Community Psychology, 17,* 269-293.

Martin, J. L., Garcia, M. A., & Beatrice, S. (1989). Sexual behavior changes and HIV antibody in a cohort of New York City gay men. *American Journal of Public Health, 79,* 501-503.

Mayer, K. H., Ayotte, D., Groopman, J. E., Stoddard, A., Sarngadharan, M., & Gallo, R. (1986). Association of human T-lymphotropic virus type III antibodies with sexual and other behaviors in a cohort of homosexual men from Boston with and without generalized lymphadenopathy. *American Journal of Medicine, 80,* 357-363.

McKusick, L., Horstman, W., & Coates, T. J. (1985). AIDS and sexual behavior reported by gay men in San Francisco. *American Journal of Public Health, 75,* 493-496.

Moss, A. R., Osmond, D., Bacchetti, P., Chermann, J. C., Barre-Sinoussi, F., & Carlson, J. (1987). Risk factors for AIDS and HIV seropositivity in homosexual men. *American Journal of Epidemiology, 125,* 1035-1047.

Office of Technology Assessment. (1985, February). *Review of the Public Health Service's response to AIDS: A technical memorandum* (OTA-TM-H-24). Washington, DC: U.S. Congress.

Patton, M. Q. (1987). *How to use qualitative methods in evaluation.* Beverly Hills, CA: Sage.

Research and Decisions Corporation. (1984). *Designing an effective AIDS prevention campaign strategy for San Francisco.* San Francisco: San Francisco AIDS Foundation.

Rothbart, G. S., Fine, M., & Sudman, S. (1982). On finding and interviewing the needles in the haystack: The use of multiplicity sampling. *Public Opinion Quarterly, 46,* 408-421.

Siegal, F. P., Lopez, C., & Hammer, G. S. (1981). Severe acquired immunodeficiency in male homosexuals, manifested by chronic perianal ulcerative herpes simplex lesions. *New England Journal of Medicine, 305,* 1439-1444.

Stevens, C. E., Taylor, P. E., Zang, E. A., Morrison, J. M., Harley, E. J., de Cordoba, S. R., Bacino, C., Ting, R. C. Y., Bodner, A. J., Sarngadharan, M. G., Gallo, R. C., & Rubinstein, P. (1986). Human T-cell lymphotropic virus type III infection in a cohort of homosexual men in New York City. *Journal of the American Medical Association, 265,* 2267-2272.

Sudman, S., & Kalton, G. (1986). New developments in the sampling of special populations. *Annual Review of Sociology, 12,* 401-429.

Turner, C. F., Miller, H. G., & Moses, L. E. (1989). *AIDS: Sexual behavior and intravenous drug use.* Washington, DC: National Academy Press.

Winkelstein, W., Jr., Lyman, D. M., & Padian, N. S. (1987). Sexual practices and risk of infection by the AIDS-associated retrovirus: The San Francisco Men's Health Study. *Journal of the American Medical Association, 257,* 321-325.

Ziebold, T. O., & Mongeon, J. E. (1982). Alcoholism and the homosexual community. *Journal of Homosexuality, 7,* 3-7.

PART III

Sensitivity in Field Research

Field research using participant observation, depth interviewing, and the like has often seemed like an ideal way of studying sensitive topics. The researcher who uses such methods relies on sustained or intensive interactions with those studied as a way of establishing trustful relations between researcher and researched. In these circumstances, it is assumed, barriers to the researcher's presence are eventually removed to reveal the hidden, the deviant, or the tabooed. Yet the establishment of trustful relations is never easy. In many situations, researchers face hostility and sometimes danger. It is not unusual for the powerless or the disadvantaged to treat the researcher with skepticism, fearing that cooperation will bring in its wake only their further exploitation.

Getting close to those one studies also carries the risk of one's becoming an accomplice or an apologist. Although she discusses the problems of sampling and some of the legal issues raised by research on new religious movements or "cults," the primary focus of Marybeth Ayella's chapter in this part is with the process of gaining entry to the group or setting one wants to study. (In field research, concerns over sampling traditionally have been superseded by a preoccupation with problems of access.) Although there is a general assumption that deviant groups are difficult to study, Ayella points out that gaining initial access to some groups may be relatively easy but that, once inside, access may be difficult to sustain. Some cults, for instance, may welcome the researcher at first, perceiving him or her as an interested newcomer and potential convert. When conversion does not appear within a given period of time, however, the researcher may be ejected from the group and denied further access.

Ayella notes that some researchers are able to maintain access by establishing a unique role or special category of membership for themselves, such as "fringe devotee." Others apparently handle this problem successfully by honestly expressing their disagreements with the group and by stressing their role as researcher rather than as member. Still others negotiate access by establishing a reciprocal relationship with the group. For example, the researcher may, in effect, lend legitimacy or respectability to the group in exchange for access, although Ayella rightly warns of the dangers of co-optation of the researcher in such situations. In line with Johnson (1975), who argued that access is not an initial phase of entry to the setting around which a bargain can be struck but a continuing process of negotiation and renegotiation, Ayella advises researchers not to allow the groups they wish to study to set the research agenda for them.

Ayella examines a number of other problems, such as culture shock and handling one's emotional responses to stressful research situations, that are related to sustaining a research project on deviant groups. John Brewer, in his chapter in this part, elaborates on many of the points raised by Ayella. He discusses the difficulties of conducting research in a setting—Northern Ireland—that is politically, psychologically, and physically threatening to both researchers and study participants. One of the most significant aspects of Brewer's chapter is that it highlights the contextual nature of sensitive research. Although other field studies of police officers demonstrate that the police in general are a difficult group to study (Fielding, this volume; Hunt, 1984; Klockars, 1985; Van Maanen, 1988), the politically charged and conflict-ridden atmosphere of Northern Ireland renders a study of the police force there especially sensitive.

To conduct research on the Royal Ulster Constabulary (RUC), Brewer first had to obtain permission from the chief constable. This had the potential for severely restricting the research, because "gatekeepers" frequently impose explicit conditions on the way in which research may be conducted as well as on how the findings may be disseminated. Although this did not happen in Brewer's case, obtaining permission from the chief constable created other problems, not the least of which was the suspicion it produced among ordinary police officers about the researchers' and police managers' objectives and motives.

In short, although gaining initial access to the RUC proved fairly straightforward, Brewer and his research assistant had to pass through a second set of gatekeepers, the ordinary police officers. Given that, as in organizational contexts generally, the RUC is characterized by what Dingwall (1980) called a "hierarchy of consent," it was assumed that superiors have the right to permit subordinates to be studied. This does not, however, ensure that the subordinates will be cooperative. As Brewer and others have discovered, people in research situations may intentionally undermine the research through obfuscation and deception. In addition, researchers may be subjected to repeated "trust tests" that force them to legitimate themselves in the eyes of study participants and, like some of the researchers cited by Ayella, they may have to construct or capitalize on a special identity.

During the research, the identity of Brewer's research assistant proved to be an important factor. She was a Catholic studying mostly Protestants, an innocuous element in other contexts, but, in the context of Northern Ireland, it prompted the researchers to try (unsuccessfully) to conceal her religious identity from those studied. As the research proceeded, the field-worker found herself being "culturally contextualized" (Warren, 1988) in terms of both her religion and her sex (see also Edwards, this volume, on "placement" of the researcher by research participants).

As other female field-workers have noted, women researchers may become "encapsulated in the stereotypical [gender] role designated by subjects" and consequently have limited access to data, especially data in such male-dominated groups as the police (Hunt, 1984, p. 286). Warren (1988), however, maintained that gender itself is a negotiated rather than an ascribed status in the field. Furthermore, she pointed out that researchers may be able to capitalize on the sexism of study participants. For instance, while doing fieldwork in a drug rehabilitation center, Warren discovered that she had relatively free access to areas usually off limits to outsiders and could even investigate the contents of file drawers because the male staff at the center often viewed themselves as too engaged in "important business" to worry about a harmless female (p. 18). Brewer's research assistant encountered a similar attitude among some RUC officers. Of course, Warren also noted that this trade-off of accepting sexism to obtain information often is both personally and politically repugnant to female researchers. In addition, she showed that, while gender issues in the field have usually been most problematic for women, male researchers must deal with them at times. Johnson (1986), for instance, reported that he encountered considerable resistance to his presence from the female elementary school teachers he was observing because these women typically had their professionalism and authority

undercut by their male colleagues and supervisors. As Johnson interpreted it, the teachers needed to determine whether he, as a man, could
be trusted.

Brewer's chapter also raises the issue of the researcher's personal
security. In the context of the kind of violent social conflict found in
Northern Ireland, research can be a dangerous activity (Burton, 1978;
Lee, 1981). Indeed, at various times, researchers have been forced into
hiding or have had to leave Northern Ireland due to fears (apparently
unfounded, it should be said) that research materials were finding their
way to the security forces (Taylor, 1988). While many researchers are
unlikely to face the stresses produced by research in a violent social
situation, it should also be borne in mind that "researcher jeopardy" can
take a number of forms. As we noted earlier, work with deviant groups
also can lead to unwelcome consequences for researchers who may find
themselves subject to "stigma contagion." This seems to be particularly
true of research on human sexuality. Those involved in the study of
sexual deviance or sexual variation have frequently remarked on their
stigmatization by colleagues, university administrators, and students
(Plummer, 1983; Troiden, 1987; Weinberg & Williams, 1972). In a similar
way, research in controversial areas that produces findings unpopular
among colleagues can lead to negative consequences for the researcher
(Sieber & Stanley, 1988).

Blauner and Wellman (1982) note the complaint of ghetto residents
in some U.S. cities that they have put dozens of students through graduate school. This wry comment reflects the perception in minority communities that researchers come into the community, take what they can
get out of it, and are never seen again. Such concerns have prompted
calls for a more expressly collaborative or participatory research style
through the use of "research communes" or "community review boards"
(Hessler & New, 1972; Hessler, New, & May, 1980; Kelman, 1972;
Schensul, 1980; see also Blauner & Wellman, 1982; Vargus, 1971; for
similar concerns voiced by feminist writers, see Finch, 1984; Oakley,
1981).

Two chapters in this part explore ways of establishing collaborative
research with research participants in field research. Fielding, a crimi-
nologist, is critical, on one hand, of the naturalistic approach to field
research. This approach advocates that the researcher should take an
"appreciative" stance (Matza, 1969) toward his or her informants and
their accounts of events and behavior. Naturalism stresses rapport and
empathic relations with informants in the field. Fielding notes that this

is easier to accomplish in studies of nonthreatening or nonthreatened groups than in those of "unloved" groups, such as the police. Moreover, the naturalistic approach establishes a false dichotomy in relation to the accounts of the research given by those involved: Those of the study participants are viewed as complete and accurate, while those of the researcher are viewed as partial and flawed.

An alternative approach to research based on the appreciative stance involves "investigative research" or the use of "conflict methodologies" (Douglas, 1976; Galliher, 1973). Such approaches—involving the use of covert research, the analysis of publicly available data, the seeking out of, for example, dissatisfied former employees as informants, and so on—have an advantage in that they do not require the cooperation of powerful subjects. Fielding, however, is critical of the assertive skeptical role embodied in this kind of research, for he sees a danger in that the researcher may become manipulative and deceitful with informants or that skepticism may turn into cynicism that prevents informants' accounts from being taken seriously by the researcher.

Instead, Fielding calls for field researchers to take an "intercalary role" in relation to study participants, an approach not unlike Maguire's (1987) participatory research model or the collaborative research style favored by Bowser and Sieber (this volume). Taking an intercalary role places the field researcher in a position between passive recipient of informants' accounts and skeptical investigator. In this model, the field-worker and study participants are simultaneously inquirers into the group's culture and educators of one another with respect to that culture. In this way, the researcher and the researched coproduce fieldwork. Fielding skillfully demonstrates the usefulness of the intercalary role for studying sensitive topics and groups through his discussion of an incident that occurred during his own field research on the criteria of competence in urban policing. One particularly valuable outcome of adopting the intercalary role is that it presents an opportunity to understand the issue of sensitivity from the point of view of the study participants rather than solely from the perspective of the researcher.

Fielding's emphasis on a collaborative research style is echoed in Bowser and Sieber's chapter in this part. Bowser and Sieber set out with admirable clarity the challenges raised by AIDS prevention research. In particular, they focus on the risk that a developing research community around issues of AIDS prevention could become inward looking and self-perpetuating. To avoid this danger, they argue, researchers need to work *with* at-risk groups rather than *on* them. Moreover, researchers need to give attention to the meanings risk-takers give to their behavior for more structured approaches like surveys and experiments to be used effectively.

Bowser and Sieber carried out their research in an economically marginal urban area with a high proportion of the population at risk of HIV infection. To promote a collaborative style of working, Bowser and Sieber adapted the focus group to the needs of AIDS prevention research. More traditionally used by market researchers, focus groups have the advantage of requiring active group participation and are ideal for exploring the meanings that underpin behavior. Bowser and Sieber argue that the approach they adopted had important benefits for the people they studied. Focus group participants, who were members of social groups traditionally suspicious of research, were able to build trustful relations with the researcher because the group provided a forum in which they could develop and express their own agendas as well as challenging that of the researcher. Participation also provided them with an opportunity to make a contribution to the wider community.

Following the experiences of urban anthropologists in the 1970s, work in a collaborative style with research participants has not been without its critics. Some writers (e.g., Goudy & Richards, 1973) have argued that collaborative researchers have sometimes been too ready to assume consensus within local communities. They have thus ignored the extent to which apparently homogeneous groups may be internally differentiated on the basis of a plurality of competing interests. While this danger needs to be borne in mind, collaborative approaches, whatever their ethical basis, seem to have methodological advantages in the study of sensitive topics (see also Edwards, this volume; Kennedy Bergen, this volume).

References

Blauner, B., & Wellman, D. (1982). The researcher and the researched: Decolonizing social research. In R. B. Smith & P. K. Manning (Eds.), *A handbook of social science methods: Vol. 2. Qualitative methods.* Cambridge, MA: Ballinger.

Burton, F. (1978). *The politics of legitimacy: Struggles in a Belfast community.* London: Routledge & Kegan Paul.

Dingwall, R. G. (1980). Ethics and ethnography. *Sociological Review, 28,* 871-891.

Douglas, J. D. (1976). *Investigative social research.* Beverly Hills, CA: Sage.

Finch, J. (1984). "It's great to have someone to talk to": The ethics and politics of interviewing women. In C. Bell & H. Roberts (Eds.), *Social researching: Politics, problems, and practice.* London: Routledge & Kegan Paul.

Galliher, J. F. (1973). The protection of human subjects: A reexamination of the Professional Code of Ethics. *American Sociologist, 9,* 93-100.

Goudy, W. J., & Richards, R. O. (1973). On resistance to community surveys: Who puts the bite on whom? *Social Problems, 20,* 400-401.

Hessler, R. M., & New, P. K. (1972). Toward a research commune? *Human Organization, 31,* 449-451.

Hessler, R. M., New, P. K., & May, J. T. (1980). Conflict, consensus, and exchange. *Social Problems, 27,* 320-329.

Hunt, J. (1984). The development of rapport through the negotiation of gender in field work among police. *Human Organization, 43,* 283-296.

Johnson, J. M. (1975). *Doing field research.* New York: Free Press.

Johnson, N. B. (1986). Ethnographic research and rites of incorporation: A sex- and gender-based comparison. In T. L. Whitehead & M. E. Conway (Eds.), *Self, sex, and gender in cross-cultural fieldwork.* Urbana: University of Illinois Press.

Kelman, H. C. (1972). The rights of the subject in social research: An analysis in terms of relative power and legitimacy. *American Psychologist, 27,* 989-1016.

Klockars, C. (1985). *The idea of police.* Beverly Hills, CA: Sage.

Lee, R. M. (1981). *Interreligious courtship and marriage in Northern Ireland.* Unpublished doctoral dissertation, University of Edinburgh.

Maguire, P. (1987). *Doing participatory research: A feminist approach.* Amherst: University of Massachusetts, Center for International Education.

Matza, D. (1969). *Becoming deviant.* Englewood Cliffs, NJ: Prentice-Hall.

Oakley, A. (1981). Interviewing women: A contradiction in terms. In H. Roberts (Ed.), *Doing feminist research.* London: Routledge & Kegan Paul.

Plummer, K. (1983). *Documents of life: An introduction to the problems and literature of a humanistic method.* London: Allen & Unwin.

Schensul, S. L. (1980). Anthropological fieldwork and sociopolitical change. *Social Problems, 27,* 309-319.

Sieber, J. E., & Stanley, B. (1988). Ethical and professional dimensions of socially sensitive research. *American Psychologist, 43,* 49-55.

Taylor, R. (1988). Social scientific research on the "troubles" in Northern Ireland. *Economic and Social Review, 19,* 123-145.

Troiden, R. R. (1987). Walking the line: The personal and professional risks of sex education and research. *Teaching Sociology, 15,* 241-249.

Van Maanen, J. (1988). *Tales of the field.* Chicago: University of Chicago Press.

Vargus, B. S. (1971). On sociological exploitation: Why the guinea-pig sometimes bites. *Social Problems, 19,* 238-248.

Warren, C. A. B. (1988). *Gender issues in field research.* Newbury Park, CA: Sage.

Weinberg, M., & Williams, C. J. (1972). Fieldwork among deviants: Social relations with subjects and others. In J. D. Douglas (Ed.), *Research on deviance.* New York: Random House.

7

"They Must Be Crazy"

Some of the Difficulties
in Researching "Cults"

MARYBETH AYELLA

This chapter examines some of the methodological difficulties encountered in researching "cults." The last 10 years have seen an enormous amount of research and writing on groups known variously as *cults, new religious movements, charismatic groups,* or *world rejecting groups,* to name some of the most commonly used terms.[1]

In this chapter, I use the word *cult.* What I am interested in exploring is how one does research on groups popularly labeled as "cults." This labeling of a group as a cult makes this a sensitive topic to study, for, given the public's predominantly negative assessment of cults,[2] one is researching a group considered by many to be deviant.

I will discuss some of the methodological problems that I think are particularly vexing in the study of cults, and I will point to some solutions suggested by researchers. My examination will be limited to one kind of research done by sociologists: field research.[3] I focus on this type of research because it seems to have been stimulated by cults. Robbins (1988) pointed to a virtual explosion of anthropological-like

AUTHOR'S NOTE: This chapter originally appeared in the *American Behavioral Scientist,* 33, 562-577.

studies by sociologists of religion. Field research seems to be an attempt to get behind the strangeness and controversial aspects of cults. This method provides the closest look at cult groups, and it thus has the potential to provide in-depth understanding of the group examined as well as the group's self-understanding. This research has as its strong point debunking overly psychiatric or psychological "brainwashing" perspectives, in showing the interactional aspect of becoming and remaining a cult member. This humanizes cult members—they are portrayed as more than crackpots, psychological basket cases, or brainwashed robots.

Gaining Access

Contingencies of Research

Mitchell, Mitchell, and Ofshe (1980, chap. 9), Wallis (1977a, 1977b), Bromley and Shupe (1979; Shupe & Bromley, 1980), and Barker's (1984, chap. 1) discussions of their research on Synanon, Scientology, and the Unification Church highlight the contingencies of research, which are those aspects of research over which the researcher has little or no control. One very important contingency is the group's current social reputation.

Richard Ofshe's research on Synanon began in the summer of 1972 with a chance visit to Synanon's Tomales Bay facilities. Ofshe's neighbor, a marine biologist, was asked by Synanon for help in setting up a lab for a sewage-treatment system. Ofshe accompanied his neighbor on a visit and was given a trail-bike tour of the ranching facility. After the visit, Ofshe asked the ranch director if he could come back to do research. During the next year, Ofshe paid over 50 visits, during which he did participant observation, to the ranch and Synanon facilities in Oakland, San Francisco, and Santa Monica. In addition, five of his students did research on Synanon over a three-month period, joining the Oakland "game club" and participating in games and in Synanon community life to varying degrees. Ofshe's and the students' professional interests and intentions to observe and analyze were made known to management and community members from the initial contact. Ofshe's entry was welcomed. Two aspects of Synanon's history seem important in explaining his welcome: (a) In 1972, Synanon considered itself a social movement and an alternative society, and it welcomed middle-class professionals, hoping to recruit them as members; and (b) Ofshe followed three researchers who had visited Synanon and written books favorable to the organization. Synanon's openness seemed based on its changing self-conception and its good reputation, which grew largely out of its claims of the unprecedented effectiveness of its drug rehabilitation.

Roy Wallis offers a contrasting example. He presented himself at an introductory "Communications Course" in Scientology as an interested newcomer. He wanted "to learn how 'anyman' coming in off the street would be received, not how a visiting sociologist doing a thesis on Scientology would be treated" (Wallis, 1977b, p. 155). He arranged to stay in a Scientology "boarding house" during this course. Wallis left after two days because he found it too difficult to continue. He felt he would have been able to stay only if he were in agreement with what he was officially learning. Not feeling this agreement, Wallis felt it would have been dishonest to indicate agreement. When Wallis later officially requested help from the movement's leaders, this earlier abrupt exit, as well as the movement's knowledge that Wallis had surveyed (with a questionnaire) current and ex-members, needed to be explained. Scientologist David Gaiman commented in an appendix to Wallis's article that he "could not understand at that time, and still do not understand, the ethics of his failing to declare this to me in his initial approach" (Wallis, 1977b, p. 169).

Wallis had initially thought to do covert participant observation, because he anticipated a hostile reaction to an open request from a sociologist, given previous, critical investigations by the Food and Drug Administration (FDA) in the United States and government bodies in Australia and New Zealand, and because he thought "that approaching the leaders and officials of such a public-relations-conscious social movement directly, for assistance with my research, was simply to invite public relations" (Wallis, 1977b, p. 152).

David Bromley and Anson Shupe's simultaneous participant observation of the Unification Church (UC) and the "anticult" movement seemingly originated in two chance events. While writing a conference paper on the enormous negative media coverage of the Unification Church, they requested information from the headquarters for the National Ad Hoc Committee-Citizens Engaged in Freeing Minds (CEFM) and discovered that it was based in a nearby metropolitan area. At the same time, two high-ranking and 50 rank-and-file members of the Unification Church arrived in the area, seeking to recruit university students. One of the researchers was acting chair of his university's sociology department and he agreed, "on civil libertarian principles," to be faculty sponsor for a UC campus student organization. In exchange, Bromley and Shupe were permitted in-depth interviews and were allowed to observe the group.

Eileen Barker's research on the Unification Church is unique in that, after two years of negotiating with the church to do research on her terms (e.g., receiving a list of all members, so that she might draw a random sample to interview), she seemed to have been granted relatively free access to the group. She did not, however, search out the Unification Church; rather, she was in the favorable position of being sought out by the church to do research on it. Being sought out may have put her in a more powerful position to negotiate for a favorable research "bargain."

The UC apparently sought her out as an established sociologist of religion. She had participated in one conference that the UC sponsored and in a "series of three residential weekend 'Roundtables on Science and Religion' " (Barker, 1984, p. 13) held at the UC's national headquarters in London before she was asked if she would like to write about the church. A Moonie she knew sought her out because he was worried about a sociologist of religion doing research on the group, based on negative reports. Barker replied it was "hardly surprising that he had to rely on negative reports, as it was well-nigh impossible to get any other kind of information" (p. 14). She later found out that the UC agreed to let her do her research because she "had been prepared to listen to their side of the argument, and they could not believe that anyone who did that could write anything worse than what was already being published by people who had not come to find out for themselves" (p. 15). They felt she was open-minded enough to present a fair picture of them. This seeking her out, and her negotiating for certain conditions of research, allowed her free and long-term access to the group.

There are several points worth noting from these brief descriptions of extant research on cults. Most important, the researcher should be critical of access, asking the question of why the group has allowed the researcher in, looking at the recent history of the group and its current self-understanding in answering this question. One should question the kind of access one is being given, ever conscious of the possibility of sanitization or impression management. The researcher should not simply assume the group he or she is studying understands and agrees with the pursuit of unfettered scientific inquiry. The researcher should learn as much as he or she can about the group—through newspaper/ media accounts, public relations materials, or efforts such as open houses and interviews with ex-members or current members—before undertaking field research. These actions, however, may have unforeseen consequences.

Researcher as Person

Downes and Rock (1982, p. 30), in discussing research on deviance, made the point that "one will not be at ease everywhere. There are always likely to be certain social groups who defy research by certain sociologists. . . . Many of the barriers which divide people from one another in everyday life also keep the sociologist at bay." Field research highlights the researcher. Some researchers, like informants, are simply better able to establish rapport and to feel at ease in a new, let alone strange, setting. Wallis (1977b, p. 155) said of himself in his brief participant observation on Scientology:

> Good participant observation required a particular personality or discipline which I did not possess. Outside a "mass" context I felt uncomfortable in my role. It felt like spying and a little dishonest. In general, I tried to shift the situation to an "open" interaction context as quickly as possible.

Among the problems relating to the researcher are culture shock, handling emotional responses to the group (the chief difficulty here is that overrapport may hinder objectivity), handling conversion attempts of the group, and the stigma of investigating a group considered by many to be deviant.

Balch (1985, p. 24) emphasized that the authoritarian social worlds of cults may rub against the grain of researchers' views of reality, because researchers tend to be humanists. In addition, there is the question of dealing with bizarre behaviors. Balch stated his first reaction to the UFO cult that he and Taylor studied: "My gut reaction to this message was something like: 'They look normal to me, so how can they possibly believe this nonsense?' " (p. 24). Continued interaction with the group overcame these responses, in a way similar to anthropologists' dealing with culture shock.

Whose Perspective? Sampling Members

In researching any group, the question arises immediately as to who and what to sample. The problem of sampling interacts with that of brief field research. That is, if one is going to observe a group for a very short time, the question of who one interviews becomes more important. With longer time in the group, one can make efforts to gain a sampling of members to represent the various viewpoints that are present in the group.

Drawing a representative, random sample of a cult or of ex-cult members (of one group or of all groups) is very difficult. If the group presents a sample of members to a researcher, how does the researcher know if these members are representative? Perhaps they are more intelligent, more likely to be "true believers," or those thought more likely to present the group in a good light than other members. How does the researcher determine how they were selected? Given the high turnover in most cults, longitudinal analysis of a sample of members is also difficult, and such longitudinal analyses of conversion are few (Balch, 1985).

Different understandings within a group are a fact of life. These differences of perspective are the result of one's role and status in the group, one's length of time in the group, and one's analytical abilities, among other things. In studying any group, the researcher needs to get a sampling of views from all factions to come up with a complete picture of the "reality" of the group. One problem in identifying these factions is that cults often are precisely those organizations that brook no public dissent, so that the only view expressed is the official view. That is, the group presents the appearance of unanimous agreement to outsiders and insiders. Factions do not emerge as organized entities with a recognized different point of view. Individuals remain in a state of pluralistic ignorance of discontent and doubt or criticism of the group. They do not know others share doubts; they feel only they have doubts (Ayella, 1985; Bainbridge & Stark, 1980).

Yet, here too, "politics" are a fact of life, and it is important for the researcher to assume that members experience the group differently, even when confronted by apparent unanimity. As Rochford (1985, p. 42) concluded from his study of the Hare Krishnas, "First, many, if not most settings are characterized by local politics. To take on a membership role necessarily involves making choices about what sort of member the researcher wants to be." This role will then influence how other members treat the researcher. The researcher would be wise to accept Downes and Rock's (1982, p. 27) advice on researching deviant behavior: "It is only by taking a jaundiced perspective on the world that its disreputable life becomes apparent. Surfaces reveal little. They certainly do not point one at deviant populations." The deviance to be searched for here is doubt, uncertainty, and less than total commitment to the official group ideology.

An additional aspect of sampling remains. New religious movements (NRM) researchers have often described leavers of cult groups as "apostates," and they discount their accounts (of their entry, life, and exit from the group) as being valid sources of data on the group, as being biased—as being no more than "atrocity tales" cultivated in deprogramming sessions. On the other hand, they often accept accounts from current members as being acceptable sources of information on the group. Beckford (1985) is one NRM researcher who has criticized this approach to ex-members' accounts, asserting the desirability of taking ex-members' testimony as seriously as that of current members and rejecting "the idea that ex-members' accounts can all be subsumed under the heading of 'atrocity tales' " (p. 146). Having made this statement, Beckford felt compelled to defend himself from the assumption that he is anticultist (1985, pp. 146-147).

If one sees only ex-members, one's sample is likely to be of people who were unhappy enough with the group to leave on their own or people who were deprogrammed. The methodological question is how one interprets these ex-members' versions of the group and its effect on them. One way is to recognize the contextual construction of individual accounts of participation and leave taking—that is, the fact that such accounts are strongly shaped by individuals' current reference groups. Thus a current member's account is shaped by other members' views, including the desirability of presenting the appearance of complete commitment.

Beckford (1978) and Rochford (1985) both emphasized how the group's ideology presents itself as a "screen" by which members can reinterpret their past and present. Balch (1985) also emphasized how retrospective reinterpretation needs to be taken into account in interviewing both members and ex-members. Recognizing that neither group, current members nor ex-members, can express the complete "truth" is a step toward resolving this problem. In addition, Wright (1987) and Solomon's (1981) research showed that individuals' modes of leaving the group shape their evaluation of the group. Solomon's questionnaire study of ex-Moonies suggested differences in adjustment between ex-cultists who have been deprogrammed and those who have not. She emphasized that we cannot generalize to all members or ex-members of cults from samples of ex-cultists who seek therapy, because we do not know how they compare with ex-cultists who do not seek therapy.

Maintaining Access

Access Easy, Maintenance Difficult

Conversion-oriented groups provide a paradoxical research setting where access may be easy but continued presence or interaction is more difficult. This is the result of their expectation that one should accept the group's perspective—and convert—within some specified time period. This carries with it the expectation that one's behavior should change to reflect this conversion or commitment (e.g., living with the group and giving up previous ties or jobs).

John Lofland, in his now classic (and disguised) study of the early Unification Church, "assumed the standard seeker's posture, namely, interested and sympathetic but undecided" after he and two fellow graduate students decided in 1962 to study the group (Lofland, 1966, pp. 270-271). The group pressured the three to commit themselves to serious study of the Divine Principle (the group's theology) and to move in with the group. Lofland then expressed interest in doing a sociological study of the group and met with enthusiastic approval from the group's leader. For 11 months, he did participant observation on the group: From February through October of 1962, he spent about 15 hours a week with the group; and, from November 1962 through January 1963, he lived in the center four days a week. During this time, Lofland thought there was a shared understanding of his interest in the group: "I was personally sympathetic to, and accepting of, them and desired to understand their endeavors, but I was not likely to be a convert" (p. 274). In January 1963, the leader told Lofland "that she was tired of playing the 'studying the movement' game" (p. 274). Given his apparent unlikeliness to convert, the leader saw no further reason for his presence, and Lofland left the group. A sociology undergraduate student who feigned conversion and joined the group, however, provided information to Lofland until June 1963.

Lofland's experience highlights the problem of adopting a long-term participant observer stance with a conversion-oriented group. What happens if one does not convert after what the group considers a reasonable time? Robbins, Anthony, and Curtis (1973) also illustrated an unsuccessful resolution of this dilemma in Anthony's participant observation study of a Jesus Freaks group. When confronted by questions as to his religious beliefs, Anthony refused to discuss them, feeling that the religious beliefs he held would alienate group members and end his observation. This response brought strenuous pressure from the group on him to convert. Anthony responded to the pressure by gradual withdrawal.

Richardson, Stewart, and Simmonds (1979) suggest that this outcome of ejection from the group (in their cases, that of a fundamentalist commune) may be averted by the expression of honest difference of opinion, admitting that one is aware of the necessity to be "saved" but that one rejects it. This strategy apparently was successful, for they had maintained a relationship with the group for almost seven years at the time of publication of their article. Gordon (1987), too, found this strategy to be successful in his research on two fundamentalist Jesus groups. He suggested that researchers in these groups cultivate distance in the interaction. Two methods of doing this are to be forthright about one's own, differing beliefs and to emphasize one's research role. Doing so did not alienate members of the group he studied; paradoxically, he felt a sense of greater rapport. Gordon theorized that this open discussion and emphasized researcher role kept the group from feeling their persuasion efforts had failed.

Shupe and Bromley's (1980; Bromley & Shupe, 1979) articles describing their research on both the Unification Church and the anticult movement also illustrated initially easy access and difficulty as interaction continued. Their role as sociologists was important in two ways in reducing the barriers between themselves and the groups: The role itself "carried a certain degree of legitimacy," and "each group was seeking some type of legitimation to which it was perceived we might contribute" (1980, p. 8). Underpinning both groups' welcome of the researchers was the understanding that "to 'really know' their respective positions was to come to believe in them" (1980, p. 12). The difficulties arose when greater knowledge of the groups did not generate belief.

Each group knew that Bromley and Shupe were investigating both groups, and this presented one of the difficulties they faced. Neither group could understand why the researchers needed information from the other group, and Bromley and Shupe were continually forced to explain each interaction with the other group. When time passed and it was clear the researchers were no longer ignorant of the other group, members of each group pressured them to take a public stand in support of their respective group, in advocating for the group in the media and to other interest groups. Their delicate solution to this persistent dilemma was to "avoid interviews that seemed superficial, highly partisan, or exploitative" (1980, p. 13) and to present each group in its complexity when doing an interview or giving a public talk.

As their research proceeded, Bromley and Shupe sought more extensive and more sensitive information. In attempting to visit the UC's seminary, they became involved in a lengthy negotiation process. They feared this access would not be granted because "the authors' published work was perceived as not sufficiently 'objective' and sensitive to the uses to which the information might be put by others" (1980, p. 9). The UC scrutinized their written work, requested a list of the questions they wanted to ask, and a seminary faculty member visited their campus to "test fully our good will, honesty, and neutrality" (1980, p. 14). Part of the UC's concern stemmed from the fact they were unable to locate Bromley and Shupe on a supporter/opponent continuum, and they felt they had been harmed by previous researchers to whom they had granted access.

How can researchers cope with the pressures to adopt the group's perspective, to become a committed participant instead of a researcher concerned with objectivity? Richardson et al. (1979) emphasizes the importance of maintaining a base camp at the research site to daily reinforce, through conversation with coworkers, one's alternative (to the group's) reality. This may facilitate the handling of culture shock and prevent researcher conversion, but it also helps the researcher in other ways. Two (or more) researchers can share the moral dilemmas encountered during the research; they can correct each other's biases (Stone, 1978); and they can alleviate the loneliness of the "professional stranger" role. Barker (1984, pp. 21-22) described her reaction to a BBC producer who

> spent some time with me doing "joint participant observation" in preparation for the filming. Each time we ended a visit I would thrust a tape recorder into her hands and beg her to pour out whatever occurred to her. The fact that her impressions largely coincided with my own did not, of course, prove that we were right and everyone else wrong, but it was enormously reassuring to learn that I was not totally idiosyncratic.

The Researcher's Role in the Group

Groups vary in the kind of access they allow: "potential convert" may be the only way they conceptualize outsiders, in spite of the researcher's identification of self as researcher. In my 3 week participant observation of the Unification Church (Ayella, 1977), I identified myself as a researcher from the start. I was told I could observe the group, but I was treated throughout more as a "potential convert" than as a researcher. When attempting to get background information on members or newcomers, I was repeatedly interrupted and asked to do something else. One night, when I chose to skip a lecture (I had learned that that week's set of lectures was virtually identical to the set of lectures given the previous week) to read and take notes, I was confronted with repeated requests from other members to attend. Finally, I decided to do so, thinking that the members would simply stay with me and request my presence until the lecture was over. When I returned to the trailer in which I was staying, the article I had been reading (on Synanon) was gone, as were some notes. No one remembered seeing the article when I questioned members; neither article nor notes ever turned up. This incident was one of the events that destroyed my trust—I doubted the group really meant for me to do research. The consequence was that I stopped taking notes to the degree that I had previously.

In contrast, Rochford (1985) mentioned that, at the time of his research on the Hare Krishnas, the movement was changing from an exclusionist group to more of an inclusionist group. As an exclusionist group, one was either an insider or an outsider. At the time of Rochford's research, the movement was developing a role for less committed individuals: that of movement sympathizer. This allowed him to continue participant observation beyond the stage allowed for in the "potential convert" role. This also illustrates some of the contingencies of research. That is, Rochford was in the right place at the right time to do long-term participant observation.

Rochford's reflections (1985, chap. 2) on his research on the Hare Krishna group also highlight the difficulties of long-term participant observation. The Hare Krishnas demanded high commitment and belief from members, so one problem was how much to participate in the group's activities. As Rochford stated, "Because of strong pressures to participate in the activities of the group, it often becomes difficult to work out a role that is acceptable both to the researcher and to those under study" (1985, p. 22). Rochford's role in the group evolved over the 7 years of his research. After the first year, he became a "fringe" member of the group, and he was able to maintain this "fringe" devotee role in the group's Los Angeles community for the next several years. This status enabled him to research ISKCON (International Society for

Krishna Consciousness) communities in other parts of the country: "I sent each of these communities a letter from a well-known and respected devotee, who showed his support for my research and pointed out my general sympathies toward Krishna Consciousness and ISKCON" (1985, p. 29). In his own letter of request, Rochford emphasized his 5 years' involvement, his interest both sociological and spiritual, and his involvement in the community school and the "bhakta" program for newcomers. He gained stronger support for his research in the form of a higher rate of questionnaire completion from the other communities. In his own (Los Angeles) community, however, Rochford's fringe devotee status resulted in the lowest rate of questionnaire completion.

Rochford pointed out other instances in which his being a fringe member made research personally difficult; for example, at times he was shown to be an "incompetent" member of the group by his repeated ignorance of Sanskrit. Reflecting on this, he realized that learning the language was of lesser importance to him than were other research occupations. In addition, he had "little or no access to the dynamics of recruitment," and he avoided asking questions when he was not sure of something, because he was "very sensitive not to appear ignorant in the eyes of devotees" (1985, p. 31).

Leaving the Field

After successfully gaining access to a group and studying it in depth, several important questions confront the researcher: What, if anything, can one generalize from one's research? How representative of the group are one's observations? How representative of cults is this group? While field research may substantially increase our understanding of a particular group, it certainly complicates generalization.

The longer one is with the group, the more confident one may be that one has (a) pierced the public front of the group; (b) gained the trust of members, which often precedes the researcher's entry to back regions of a group; and (c) seen the difference between attitude and behavior. Cults, as social movements, change continually in response to both internal (e.g., in response to a charismatic leader's desires) and external (e.g., a spate of negative media publicity) events; thus "snapshots" of the group may soon be outdated. Knowledge of the long-term development of the group may help to establish how representative a snapshot of the group is, but the difficulty is that one does not know at times whether one is at the beginning, middle, or end of the group's history. Lofland's (1966) *Doomsday Cult* portrayal of the early Unification church would not have led one to predict its evolution into a larger and more successful group.

Very few researchers are going to be able to do much different in-depth research—for example, Barker had been studying the Moonies for 6 years when she published *The Making of a Moonie* (1984). At the time of publication of "Researching a Fundamentalist Commune" (1979), Richardson et al. had been doing research for almost 7 years on this group. Rochford had studied the Hare Krishnas for about 8 years before his *Hare Krishna in America* was published in 1985. Compounding the difficulty, Balch (1985, p. 24) argued that one cannot compare groups using other people's research, for "any secondary analysis of the current research is apt to get bogged down by ambiguous terms, incomplete data, and idiosyncratic research methods."

In addition to the question of what the researcher can generalize to after doing field research, there is the difficulty of getting published. Cults may attempt to prevent critical research from being published or may respond to published critical research by litigation. Both Beckford (1983) and Horowitz (1981) pointed to the Unification Church's efforts to prevent their research from being published and distributed. Wallis's (1977b) account of his difficulty in getting his research on Scientology published is daunting. Synanon responded to the publication of Mitchell et al.'s (1980) book, *The Light on Synanon,* with libel suits, necessitating countersuits by the defendants that dragged on for years.

Conclusion

If politics are present at the level of the individual researcher and cult, they are also present at the level of scientific community and society. Jonestown seems to have been a watershed event in terms of public awareness and evaluation of cults. This event was widely publicized, and, in its wake, greater credibility was given to those critical of cults, stimulating government investigations and legislation to regulate cult practices (Barker, 1986). As Barker (1986, p. 332) saw it:

> After Jonestown they tended to be all lumped together under the now highly derogatory label "cult." Despite pleas from the movements themselves . . . all the new religions were contaminated by association, the worst (most "sinister" and "bizarre") features of each belonging, by implication, to them all.

Applying Schur's (1980) concept of "deviantizing," cults are engaged in "stigma contests," or battles over the right to define what shall be termed *deviant*. The outcome of deviantization is the loss of moral standing in the eyes of other members of society. A negative assessment of a group by a researcher may be used in this stigma contest and may change public opinion significantly, making it more difficult for the group to mobilize resources of people and money to accomplish its goals. Conversely, a positive assessment may assist the cult in countering accusations of deviance (e.g., being labeled as an "unauthentic" religion). In Schur's analysis of the politics of deviance, the more powerful group usually has the edge in stigma contests. In this instance, the more powerful cults have the resources to use the courts to assert their rights. Robbins (1988, p. 181) described cults' reaction to the "anticult" movement: "However, the latter, buoyed by their initial 'institutionalized freedom' and insulation from routinized controls, stridently affirms their 'rights,' which are interpreted as granting to 'churches' freedom from all interference."

If the group studied is powerful, it can use its resources to hinder critical evaluations from being published. Scientology's wealth enabled it to successfully insist on changes in Wallis's manuscript, using the threat of an expensive libel suit, which neither Wallis nor his publisher wanted. Synanon is another group that used its considerable resources —the unpaid labor of its many lawyer members—to discourage journalists and other observers from making critical public comments. The group's use of lawsuits charging libel and seeking multimillion-dollar damages so deterred large newspapers and news magazines that the small newspaper, the *Point Reyes Light,* was the one paper willing to publish the negative reports of Synanon (Mitchell et al., 1980).

Co-optation of the researcher can be a major problem for the unwary researcher, because he or she can become, without intent, a "counter" in the ongoing stigma contest between cult and anticult. Openness to social scientists (with their relativizing, "debunking" perspective) can be used as evidence to counter accusations of extreme authoritarianism or totalism of belief and practice. The researchers' participation in cult-sponsored conferences and publication in cult-printed publications can lend the prestige of social science to the group, fostering social respectability. Perhaps the most noteworthy example of this is the Unification Church's sponsorship of conferences and publication of the conference proceedings. The journal *Sociological Analysis* devoted a 1983 issue to discussion of a conference on the propriety of participation in such proceedings. Beckford (1983) emphasized that individual participation may have long-term "transindividual" negative consequences for social scientists specializing in the study of new religious movements. In this instance, Beckford worried that UC sponsorship of conferences and publications would restrict publication to those approved of by the UC and divide the academic specialist community.

The point here is that research has consequences: to generate favorable or unfavorable publicity, an increase or a loss of social prestige, funding or financial support or its loss, or an increase or loss of moral standing (in the case of people considered to be "cultists," they are not just regarded as less prestigious people but as different kinds of people —as "nuts" or "crackpots"). The fact that many of the groups referred to as cults are social movements, which need an ongoing relationship with the society outside their doors to survive and to grow, means that they are particularly sensitive to public opinion. In the wake of Jonestown, however, I am arguing that "stigma contests" increased, making cults even more sensitive to public opinion.

Stigma contests over what is acceptable behavior continue to be fought by cults. It is inevitable that researchers will be caught up in these contests, because concerns with respectability and social power are ever-present concerns of cults, given the widespread perception of them as deviant. This fact of stigma contests can influence the researchers' gaining and maintaining access, their analysis of research, and their perceived credibility. The important point to emphasize here is that the researcher should not let his or her research agenda be set by the movement. Maintaining one's own agenda will no doubt cause various problems, not all of which can be determined in advance.

Notes

1. It is impossible to explore here the range of theoretical and methodological issues involved in this research. Whichever term we use, these groups have been very controversial, and this is also true of the research done on the groups. The two predominant theoretical positions are those of the "new religious movements" and the "destructive cult" researchers. For the uninformed reader, I would recommend Robbins's *Cults, Converts, and Charisma* (1988) for the most comprehensive and well-balanced analysis of the research. Beckford's *Cult Controversies* (1985) provides a compelling analysis of the controversiality of cults. Both of these are from the perspective of "new religious movements" researchers. For a statement of the issues from "destructive cult" researchers, I

suggest Clark, Langone, Schecter, and Daly's *Destructive Cult Conversion: Theory, Research, and Treatment* (1981).

2. Barker (1984, p. 2) illustrated widespread public awareness and negative assessment of these groups and events by referring to a late 1970s survey in which "a thousand Americans born between 1940 and 1952 were given a list of 155 names and asked how they felt about each of them. Only 3 per cent of the respondents had not heard of the Reverend Moon. Only 1 per cent admitted to admiring him. The owner of no other name on the list elicited less admiration, and the only person whom a higher percentage of respondents did not admire was the ritual killer Charles Manson." Elsewhere, Barker (1986, p. 330) referred to a December 1978 Gallup Poll, which found that "98% of the US public had heard or read about the People's Temple and the Guyana massacre—a level of awareness matched in the pollsters' experience only by the attack on Pearl Harbor and the explosion of the atom bomb."

3. I suggest the collection of papers edited by Brock K. Kilbourne, *Scientific Research and New Religions: Divergent Perspectives* (1985), as the single best source of information on this research. Both "new religious movements" and "destructive cult" researchers are represented, so that one obtains a sampling of both perspectives as they influence analyses of research.

References

Ayella, M. (1977). *An analysis of current conversion practices of followers of Reverend Sun Myung Moon.* Unpublished manuscript.

Ayella, M. (1985). *Insane therapy: Case study of the social organization of a psychotherapy cult.* Unpublished doctoral dissertation, University of California, Berkeley.

Bainbridge, W. S., & Stark, R. (1980). Scientology: To be perfectly clear. *Sociological Analysis, 41,* 128-136.

Balch, R. W. (1985). What's wrong with the study of new religions and what we can do about it. In B. K. Kilbourne (Ed.), *Scientific research and new religions: Divergent perspectives.* San Francisco: American Association for the Advancement of Science.

Barker, E. (1983). Supping with the devil: How long a spoon does the sociologist need? *Sociological Analysis, 44,* 197-206.

Barker, E. (1984). *The making of a Moonie.* New York: Basil Blackwell.

Barker, E. (1986). Religious movements: Cult and anticult since Jonestown. *Annual Review of Sociology, 12,* 329-346.

Beckford, J. A. (1978). Accounting for conversion. *British Journal of Sociology, 29,* 249-262.

Beckford, J. A. (1983). Some questions about the relationship between scholars and the new religious movements. *Sociological Analysis, 44,* 189-196.

Beckford, J. A. (1985). *Cult controversies.* New York: Tavistock.

Bromley, D. G., & Shupe, A. D., Jr. (1979). Evolving foci in participant observation: Research as an emergent process. In W. Shaffir, A. Turowitz, & R. Stebbins (Eds.), *Fieldwork experience: Qualitative approaches to social research.* New York: St. Martin's.

Clark, J. G., Jr., Langone, M. D., Schecter, R. E., & Daly, R. C. B. (1981). *Destructive cult conversion: Theory, research, and treatment.* Weston, MA: American Family Foundation.

Downes, D., & Rock, P. (1982). *Understanding deviance.* New York: Oxford University Press.

Gordon, D. (1987, August). *Getting close by staying distant: Field work on conversion-oriented groups.* Paper presented at the annual meeting of the American Sociological Association, New York.

Horowitz, I. (1981). The politics of new cults. In T. Robbins & D. Anthony (Eds.), *In gods we trust.* New Brunswick, NJ: Transaction.

Kilbourne, B. K. (Ed.). (1985). *Scientific research and new religions: Divergent perspectives.* San Francisco: American Association for the Advancement of Science, Pacific Division.

Lofland, J. (1966). *Doomsday cult.* Englewood Cliffs, NJ: Prentice-Hall.

Mitchell, D., Mitchell, C., & Ofshe, R. (1980). *The light on Synanon.* New York: Seaview.

Richardson, J. T., Stewart, M. W., & Simmonds, R. B. (1979). Researching a fundamentalist commune. In J. Needleman & G. Baker, (Eds.), *Understanding the new religions.* New York: Seabury.

Robbins, T. (1988). *Cults, converts, and charisma.* Newbury Park, CA: Sage.

Robbins, T., Anthony, D., & Curtis, T. (1973). The limits of symbolic realism: Problems of empathetic field observation in a sectarian context. *Journal for the Scientific Study of Religion, 12,* 259-272.

Rochford, E. B. (1985). *Hare Krishna in America.* New Brunswick, NJ: Rutgers University Press.

Schur, E. M. (1980). *The politics of deviance.* Englewood Cliffs, NJ: Prentice-Hall.

Shupe, A. D., Jr., & Bromley, D. G. (1980). Walking a tightrope: Dilemmas of participant observation of groups in conflict. *Qualitative Sociology, 2,* 3-21.

Solomon, T. (1981). Integrating the "Moonie" experience: A survey of ex-members of the Unification Church. In T. Robbins & D. Anthony (Eds.), *In gods we trust.* New Brunswick, NJ: Transaction.

Stone, D. (1978). On knowing how we know about the new religions. In J. Needleman & G. Baker (Eds.), *Understanding the new religions.* New York: Seabury.

Wallis, R. (1977a). *The road to total freedom.* New York: Columbia University Press.

Wallis, R. (1977b). The moral career of a research project. In C. Bell & H. Newby (Eds.), *Doing sociological research.* London: Allen & Unwin.

Wright, S. (1987). *Leaving cults: The dynamics of defection* (Monograph No. 7). Washington, DC: Society for the Scientific Study of Religion.

8

Sensitivity as a Problem in Field Research

A Study of Routine Policing in Northern Ireland

JOHN D. BREWER

Textbooks on research methods rarely mention the problems that arise when undertaking research on controversial topics or conducting it in sensitive locations. When the question of sensitivity is considered, it is usually approached from the perspective of ethics (e.g., Rainwater & Pittman, 1966). Comments range from the naive to the prosaic, so there is little textbook advice on which to draw. Therefore the issues raised by it can only be addressed in the context of specific studies where this was a problem. For example, Punch (1989) has recently reflected on his study of police corruption in Amsterdam and noted how the sensitivity of the topic caused several personal and professional difficulties. The catalyst here is the author's ethnographic study of routine police work by the Royal Ulster Constabulary (RUC) in East Belfast, Northern Ireland (see Brewer, 1991a).[1]

AUTHOR'S NOTE: An earlier version of this chapter was published in the *American Behavioral Scientist, 33,* 578-593. Earlier versions were also presented to the ESRC Fieldwork Methods Seminar at the University of Edinburgh, September 1987, and the conference, Contemporary Issues in Criminal Justice, organized by the University of Surrey, November 1988.

The interest that the RUC has as a police force derives entirely from the political and social context in which it operates. The RUC has been forced to adopt a high political profile in its attempts to contain Northern Ireland's social and political divisions, resulting in controversy but also professional expertise in security policing (on the RUC, see Brewer, Guelke, Hume, Moxon-Browne, & Wilford, 1988; Weitzer, 1985). But this context is both a spur and a hindrance to the researcher. Policing in Northern Ireland is an emotive topic in a sensitive environment, and this sensitivity has implications for the research, especially its design and location, and the validity and reliability of the results. In documenting these effects, this chapter will provide more than the usual anecdotal confessions of a researcher. If reflexivity on the part of authors is a vital quality in helping others understand how social scientific knowledge is produced, as Woolgar has recently claimed (1988), these reflections are important to demonstrate some of the social processes lying behind and operating upon this study.

In the past, many researchers have tended to underscore the problems that arose in the process of research in case they affected how the results were evaluated, although there have been a few ex post facto disclosures in books intended to show social research as an often messy enterprise (Bell & Newby, 1977; Bell & Roberts, 1984). In particular, ethnographers of the police have largely been silent on the difficulties they encountered, implying that their entry into the field and relations with police officers were unproblematic. The only issues to be explored systematically are those of negotiating access (e.g., Fox & Lundman, 1974; Holdaway, 1982) and the effects of gender on practice in the field (e.g., Easterday, Papademas, Schorr, & Valentine, 1977; Hunt, 1984; Warren, 1988; Warren & Rasmussen, 1977). Until very recently, however, the leading ethnographers of the police in Great Britain and the United States made few disclosures. Although often studying less controversial forces than the RUC, their almost Panglossian portrayal had to be disbelieved, especially as they often indicated in an occasional footnote, revealing preface, or aside remark that they faced difficulties in the field (Holdaway, 1982, 1983; Van Maanen, 1981, 1982; Westley, 1970). An increasing awareness of this omission, however, has led some specialists in the area of ethnographic work on the police to address systematically the problems they encountered in the field (see Punch, 1989; Van Maanen, 1988). In the case of the RUC, it is essential to reflect on the problems that arose in the research, and the following is an account of the difficulties that were encountered and the solutions devised. The chapter will suggest that researchers need to address more directly the negative effects of sensitivity and that they should be aware that it requires them to make a number of pragmatic compromises that depart from the textbook portrayal of ideal research practice.

Sensitivity as a Problem

Five types of problems were encountered in studying the RUC—problems of *technique, methodology, ethics, social context,* and *personal security.* These terms will become clearer upon discussion of the specific problems that arose in each type. Briefly, however, *technical* problems are problems of technique and practice; *methodological* problems describe the broader theoretical and epistemological issues raised by one's technique and practice; while *ethical* problems describe the moral dilemmas raised by the research. These three types are common to all research of whatever kind, topic, or location. The last two are more closely associated with research in sensitive settings or on controversial topics. *Contextual* problems are those that arise from the social, political, and economic environment within which the research takes place; while problems of *personal security* are self-explanatory and refer to the researcher's physical safety.

Clearly, these problems are not restricted to sensitive research. No research takes place in a vacuum and this context can have a bearing upon it, whether in terms of the nonavailability of funds, the ease of access, or public reception of the findings. The point is merely that these contextual problems are more severe when dealing with sensitive topics or working in sensitive locations. They become a prominent feature of the research design and fieldwork, having to be continually borne in mind by the researcher at all stages of the research rather than just contemplated as a vague possibility or a theoretical truism once fieldwork is completed. Similarly, it is possible to have one's physical safety threatened during any research. But mostly the danger arises from the everyday life activities required in the research and is quite incidental to the topic and geographic location of the research itself. It is also so unlikely to occur that it is not a major element of the researcher's thoughts. By the very sensitivity of their topic or location, however, some pieces of research make the danger less incidental and more real.

In the research discussed here, problems of context and security are integrally linked: Indeed, in studying the RUC in Northern Ireland, problems of personal security are a direct consequence of the context within which the research occurs. But the reason they have been distinguished is because these two types of problems do not necessarily go together. Problems of personal security can be quite real and paramount without there being any serious contextual problems, and vice versa. For example, an ethnographic study of a sensitive topic, such as organized crime in the United States, might cause one or two problems of personal security for the researcher, but the social and political context of the research adds few special problems.

What is important to emphasize is that, while only problems of context and security are directly associated with sensitive research, they have ramifications for, and complicate, the more general types of problems. Just as sensitivity is involved in more than one type of problem, it affects all the different processes that constitute the research enterprise. Research is not a unitary or homogeneous activity but breaks into discrete stages, such as planning, obtaining access, fieldwork, and the dissemination of results. These stages are important junctures when discussing sensitivity, for its effects vary as research proceeds. The categorizations of research stages and types of problems offer a useful framework for examining the effects of sensitivity on our study, as represented in Table 8.1.

Studying the RUC

Anyone planning research on the RUC has first to confront the major contextual problem that the research will end up in the public and not just the academic domain. This causes problems of personal security because researchers may become seen as endorsing the force or be intimidated into passing on information that would threaten the personal security of respondents. These were intractable problems and had to be lived with if the sensitivity of the topic was not to lead to the abandonment of the research at the very beginning. Once adapted to, a technical issue was then faced. The chief constable's permission for the research was necessary if the researchers were not to be morally responsible for getting those policemen and women who talked to us privately sacked because they had done so without the chief constable's permission. Members of the force over whom this threat does not hang or by whom it is treated lightly, such as ex-policemen and women or disgruntled members of the force, are too unrepresentative to give a balanced view

Table 8.1 Types of Problems

Stages of Research	Technical	Methodological	Ethical	Context	Security
Planning	Permission of CC	Which style of research?	Threaten job prospects	High public profile	Association with force, intimidation of respondents
	How to get permission? Time Distance from field	Team ethnography	Someone else shares danger	Overcome police resistance	
Access	Presentation of research		Gatekeeper	Gatekeeper is involved with conflict	Associated with force
			Gatekeeper's motives RA faces most danger	Security checks Religion of RA, consequences of being Catholic	Visits/files Risks on patrol, and so on
Fieldwork	Winning trust Recording notes	Is it possible?	Secretive recording		
Dissemination of results	Withdrawal Concealment of information		Lack of control	High public profile	Political slant

CC = chief constable; RA = research assistant.

129

of policing. Therefore it was necessary to undertake an overt study and to obtain permission for the research from the chief constable.

Many different kinds of research require the permission of a gate-keeper, including all overt police research, which is the reason Holdaway chose to undertake his research covertly (see Holdaway, 1982). If the research is overt, the reliability of the data depends upon what control the gatekeeper demands, something Douglas calls retrenchment from the front (Douglas, 1972), and the integrity of the researcher in withstanding such pressure. Research on policing in divided societies is especially likely to provoke suspicion about its reliability for these reasons. Hence it is worth explaining that, once permission was granted, no limits were laid down by senior officers and no censorship role was retained by the RUC. The field-worker, or research assistant, was able to spend as much time in the field as the principal investigator thought necessary. No restrictions were placed on her going out on patrol, traveling in vehicles, or going to incidents of routine police duty. The particular section[2] upon whom we came to focus attention was decided by us, not the police management. Visits were allowed to other stations, including, on three occasions, those in areas of high tension in West and North Belfast. We also visited the Women's Police Unit, which deals entirely with sex crimes.

Given that the permission of a gatekeeper was necessary, there was a further technical problem of how to design the research so that the suspicion of outsiders could be overcome. Suspicion is a trait of all police officers but was a particular contextual problem in Northern Ireland because of the extra security risks the RUC face in opening up their leviathan to strangers. A technical problem such as this raises interesting methodological questions because it forces researchers to ask which style of research is better suited to overcoming respondents' resistance. It was thought that a questionnaire that asked police officers about controversial issues, especially when put by a total stranger, would be unreliable because of the reluctance of respondents to give truthful answers. Research on the police that has used mailed questionnaires has suffered from a low response rate (e.g., Policy Studies Institute, 1983). Ethnographic research has special qualities suited to dealing with controversial topics in sensitive locations. It entails a gradual and progressive contact with respondents, which is sustained over a long period, allowing rapport to be established slowly with respondents over time. It also allows researchers to participate in the full range of experiences involved in the topic. This is why a great deal of the best police research is based on the ethnographic method and why members of several other unusual, offbeat, difficult, or demanding occupations have been studied in this way, such as truck drivers (Hollowell, 1968), traffic wardens (Richman, 1983), cocktail waitresses (Spradley & Mann, 1975), and prison wardens (Jacobs & Retsky, 1975).

To be successful, however, ethnographic research demands a considerable time commitment. This is true especially with sensitive topics where the researcher's penetration into the field takes longer and, once successful, continually needs to be reinforced by intensive contact. This time factor created a technical problem that was overcome by employing a research assistant to be responsible for data collection. There are methodological limitations to team ethnography of this sort, however, that constitute another implication of sensitivity for methodology and technique. It was the research assistant who participated in the field while the principal investigator remained distant from it, and it is impossible to know how much of the research assistant's experiences in the field were lost when writing up the notes secondhand for the principal investigator. Team ethnography is more feasible, however, if principal investigators can overcome a further technical problem and design the research in such a way as to compensate for their distance from the field. This can be done by giving the research assistant a special role not restricted to data collection, especially in writing up the research. The reliance on a research assistant was not an easy solution to the time problem, for it created an insurmountable ethical problem, in that the research assistant also faced problems of personal security.

At the stage of obtaining access, new problems arose and old ones reappeared. A major technical problem was for the research to be presented to the gatekeeper in such a way that permission would be given, something that the chief constable had never before done. On the assumption that the chief constable considered certain topics to be too sensitive, the researchers needed to be careful in how they designed and presented the research. The key to this no doubt lay in the attraction to the RUC of the idea of research on how routine policing is affected by Northern Ireland's security situation and the appeal of giving ordinary policemen and women an opportunity to express their views about policing. The experience of other police forces who had granted researchers permission illustrated that no great difficulties were created as a result, and permitting the research is in accord with the professionalism that is the core value of senior officers in the RUC. It is worth noting here that this topic has less attraction for ordinary policemen and women. Although they might take pleasure in thinking someone is interested in what their views are, it is they who run the risks associated with answering someone's questions and from being observed while doing their job. This is what Fox and Lundman (1974, p. 53) mean when they say that there are two gates within police organizations that affect access—winning the support of both senior managers and the ordinary members of the force who are the subjects of the research. This point will be returned to later, for the caution and suspicion of ordinary policemen and women created numerous technical problems at the stage of data collection.

The strategy of carefully presenting and designing the research with the central gatekeeper's permission in mind constituted an important compromise. The interests of a gatekeeper were allowed to affect *some* of the conduct of the researchers—a topic was chosen by us that we thought the chief constable would grant permission to undertake (and we were right). The Northern Ireland context makes this compromise an especially sensitive issue, for the gatekeeper is directly involved in the conflict over the state's legitimacy, intensifying the risks to the researchers' personal security. Another contextual problem arising from seeking this particular gatekeeper's permission is the certainty that a security check was run on the researchers, which is probably permanently on file. Our selection of the topic in this way is not, however, as unethical as it looks. Once in the field, all manner of issues were raised with the respondents, and we faced no restrictions by senior officers after permission was granted. In return, however, the gatekeeper probably had interests in granting permission of which the researchers were unaware. This compromise with the gatekeeper might lead some people to abandon the research, but, without making it, researchers would be unable to study the RUC empirically.

Because of the nature of the Northern Ireland context, religion is a major means by which people assess identity and political attitudes. The research assistant was Catholic, presenting the problem of whether or not to reveal this fact to the largely Protestant respondents—something that would not have been a problem in most other contexts. It was initially decided to conceal her religion because we thought it would be a sensitive matter for respondents and might make penetration into the field harder. People in Northern Ireland are very skilled in telling identity (Burton, 1979), however, and it was quite easily uncovered. It is difficult to estimate precisely how sensitive this proved to be for respondents, although, as we shall argue shortly, there are grounds for our claim that it was not a source of systematic bias. The field-worker's religion was, however, useful in automatically placing on the agenda the issue of police attitudes toward Catholics, as was her sex in relation to sexism within the force.

It is well known that the personal characteristics of a participant observer affect his or her research practice (see Hunt, 1984; Warren, 1988; Warren & Rasmussen, 1977; Wax, 1979) and that being female brings its own problems in the field. In this regard, the field-worker's experiences with the RUC are similar to those of other young female researchers, in being subject to sexual hustling, fraternity, and paternalistic attitudes from male respondents (see Easterday, Papademas, Shorr, & Valentine, 1977). There also are, however, advantages to being female. Young female researchers may be treated as "acceptable incompetents" (Lofland, 1971, p. 100) and perceived as nonthreatening (Easterday et al., 1977, p. 344; Warren & Rasmussen, 1977, pp. 360-361). As Jennifer Hunt (1984) showed in respect to her work on the police, these qualities can increase a female researcher's penetration in the field and facilitate the development of rapport.

The major technical problem in all ethnographic fieldwork is that of engendering the trust of respondents, but this was of unusual importance in Northern Ireland because of the religion of the research assistant. Methodologically, it is impossible to be absolutely sure ethnographers have gained trust. In our case, it was never a simple matter of trust once having been won being forgotten about, as most textbooks suggest, although this was true for some respondents. Most policemen and women periodically sought reassurance from the researcher about the purpose of the research, what was being written down about them, who would have access to the material, and what the researcher's politics and allegiances were. The field-worker's legitimacy had to be earned continually and skillfully, and trust was gained as a result of a progressive series of negotiations. As Johnson puts it (1975), trust is not a "one-shot agreement" but is continually negotiated during fieldwork (see also Emerson, 1983, p. 176).

The permission of the chief constable was also a disadvantage in the field because it raised doubts among respondents about the purpose of the researcher's questions over and above those that naturally arise from the political situation in Northern Ireland. The almost inherent suspicion the police have of strangers was in the RUC's case added to by worries about whether their personal security would be compromised and concern over the intentions of the police management.

It is worth outlining the ways we attempted to resolve these problems to allow readers to assess whether or not they were overcome. To help engender trust and familiarity, the field-worker's contact in the station was restricted at the beginning to a few hours a shift once a week, gradually being built up to a full shift, including nights, twice a week. Fieldwork took place over a 12-month period between 1987 and 1988 and was sufficiently prolonged to avoid the criticism that brief "smash and grab" ethnographies often deserve. Initially, the field-worker's relations with respondents in the field were especially and unusually effusive, which runs counter to the norm in ethnographic research. She was seen as a light relief from the boredom or demands of the shift, and, as a female, she was treated as a "pretty face" in a working environment that is heavily masculine (for similar experiences, see Easterday et al., 1977; Hunt, 1984; Warren & Rasmussen, 1977). As contact in the field increased, and the presence of the field-worker became routine, her treatment by respondents likewise became routine. It was only at that point that we felt confident that the field-worker was being talked to by respondents as a person rather than as some novel sex object, and the veracity of what they said could be treated by us with more confidence. We therefore dispute Van Maanen's (1981, p. 480) view that researchers on the police have to be male to be able to participate fully in the occupational culture of the police (for the difficulties in establishing rapport experienced by a male researcher on the police, see Warren & Rasmussen, 1977, p. 358).

What is more important than gender is the personality and skill of the field-worker in overcoming the feelings of suspicion the police have of all outsiders, especially in the more enclosed and threatened world of the RUC. In our case, the field-worker's sex seemed no bar to her obtaining access to the masculine canteen culture of policemen or to participating in conversations on the topics that are popular in that culture. Given the men's conventional views of gender roles, being female actually facilitated the introduction of topics of a more emotional kind in which women are commonsensically thought to be more interested. Respondents therefore talked freely about stress, death, the paramilitary threat and its effect on the family. These are particularly pertinent in Northern Ireland's police force (for a discussion of respondents' feelings about being in danger, see Brewer, 1990). Moreover, it also allowed entry into the policewomen's world, which, using Van Maanen's logic, would have been denied a male field-worker.

While no researcher, irrespective of his or her sex, can ever be totally sure that respondents are being truthful, our research design compensated for this. It is difficult to sustain untruths and false masks over 12 months of contact in the field, particularly when this contact involves sharing very private moments with respondents, such as those provided when in the canteen, or during the quiet hours of the night shift, when riding in the back of a vehicle, or accompanying them in the guard post on sentry duty. After several months of working full eight-hour shifts, the constables frequently forgot that an outsider was present, or no longer cared, and the field-worker experienced moments when it would have been difficult to maintain a front. While a few policemen tried to the bitter end to avoid conversations with the field-worker, sufficient rapport was established over time for the majority to talk quite openly to her about what are highly sensitive and controversial topics in a Northern Ireland context. It is for this reason that data mostly comprise accounts and verbatim records of spontaneous conversations in natural situations.[3]

As one further measure of the rapport that was established, most respondents eventually became assured enough in her presence to express their feelings about being the subject of research. Over a 12-month period, a field-worker's persistent inquisitiveness is bound to become something of an irritant, and Van Maanen notes how field-workers cannot expect to be liked by all respondents (1982, p. 111). But, leaving aside instances of momentary irritation, of which there were many, most respondents became confident enough in the field-worker's presence to express what were no doubt widely held fears about the research. Sometimes these concerns were expressed through humor and ribaldry. The field-worker became known among some policemen as "old nosebag," and there were long-running jokes about spelling people's names correctly in Sinn Fein's *Republican News,* the party newspaper of the Irish Republican Army (IRA). On one occasion, the concerns were expressed through anger. Toward the end of a long and tiring night shift, when news was coming through of the murder of another member of the RUC, one policeman in particular decided to put the field-worker through a test of trust:

Police Constable 1:   Look, just hold on a wee minute. What gives you the right to come here and start asking us these personal questions about our families and that. . . . You're not going to learn anything about the police while you're here. They're not going to tell you anything. . . . And you know why? Because you're always walking around with that bloody notebook writing everything down, and you're not getting anywhere near the truth. . . . Like what use is this research you're doing anyway? Is it going to do me or my mates any good? What you doing it for? 'Cos let me tell you, the only people who are going to be interested in your bloody research are the authorities.

Woman Police Constable: Can't you see that? They're just using you . . .

Police Constable 1:   See this research, as far as I'm concerned you'll learn nothing. It's a waste of time. To be honest, I couldn't give a monkey's fart about your research. If you really want to learn something you should have started at the top. It's them you need to be looking at. They don't care about the family man getting shot, they don't care about the families. The guy shot tonight will be forgotten about in another few weeks. It's them you should be talking to. The so-called big men up at the top don't care about us.

Woman Police Constable: But it's us who are getting shot and blown up.

Police Constable 2:   I'll tell you this. See when I come in here on a night, it's not the IRA I'm worried about, it's them upstairs.

Police Constable 1:   I don't care what you're writing down, just as long as I don't see it in *Republican News.* Maybe the police has made me this way, but do you not see that if you're going to come in here asking me questions about my family, if you're going to want to know all these things, I've got to be able to trust you. Like after this tonight, I'd let you come out in a vehicle with me. (Field notes [FN], 30/8/87, pp. 33-45)

This extract is useful to illustrate how the field-worker, in the one policeman's own admission, both needed to be tested and was successful in passing. There were many different sorts of trials set for the field-worker,[4] and the apologies other members of the section afterward gave her because of this policeman's conduct is proof that they too were successfully passed. But this particular extract is useful for another reason in that it shows, through the subplots that appear within it, the range of issues provoked by the research about which respondents were sensitive. Some of these are worth highlighting in greater detail as a means of contextualizing the data and illustrating the contingencies operating upon them.

One of the consequences of the RUC's dual role is that it has features typical of most police forces and also qualities special to it. This is reflected in the respondents' sensitivity toward the police management, an enduring theme in the conversations of ordinary policemen and women in any force and toward the paramilitary threat. The latter makes what is already an internally homogeneous organization even more enclosed and protective. As one constable put it, "I don't mind you being here, I don't mind you taking notes. I don't mind you at all, but the boys they'd be suspicious of anyone who's not a member of the police force, and that's how people see you: you're not a member of the force" (FN, 23/10/87, p. 20). Establishing a research role was therefore always going to be a task of Sisyphean labor, but the sensitivity of the topic and location made it more difficult than is usual in ethnographic research.

The issues about which respondents expressed concern included the use made of the results by, variously, the police authorities and the IRA, and the associated question of whether the field-worker was a spy for the authorities or the Republican paramilitaries (being perceived as spies is common to field-workers; see Ericson, 1981, p. 31; Hunt, 1984, pp. 288-289; Manning, 1972, p. 248). Other issues about which the policemen and women were sensitive included the obtrusiveness of the ethnographer's ubiquitous notepad, worries over the field-worker's religion, and the whole focus and topic of the investigation. Concern about our motives in doing the research was combined with a feeling that it would do those participating in it little good but would certainly benefit those in the police management and outside who wanted to do them harm. Variations on the fears expressed below appear throughout the field notes.

The way we look at it is, there's people out there want to kill me and the authorities let you in here and give you access to more than we will probably ever get. It's OK for the authorities because it's not them you're looking at, you won't be walking the beat with them. It's not them you're writing about. It mightn't be a bad idea if it was. The way some people look at it is, why should I let you write a book that won't do me any good but might do me some harm? Like the men who won't talk to you think they're just protecting themselves. Something you write could lose somebody their job . . . it might be the authorities who give you permission but when it comes to the bit it's the ordinary policeman who's getting shot. By letting you do this research they're putting an additional risk on us. . . . But like most people here accept you. For goodness sake, there's some peelers [members of the police] they never accept. (FN, 19/9/87, pp. 12, 15)

Well like, I can remember when the word went round that someone was coming to do research on the RUC. Like, you just think for yourself; look at the IRA's intelligence network. . . . I've seen how they recruit young girls. (FN, 2/3/87, pp. 9-10)

It was easy to anticipate that respondents would be sensitive about such matters, and it was our general tolerance of such fears that continually led us to try to pacify and reassure respondents. This, in large part, won, in return, their acquiescence in the research, at least for the majority. Their enthusiasm for the research increased after the policemen and women had reassured themselves about the field-worker's religion, sensitivity toward which was initially intensified by the commonsense view among some ordinary constables that Queen's University of Belfast is a Republican stronghold. Some respondents knew from the beginning that she was Catholic, and those who did not soon learned about it. It is impossible to know the extent to which this knowledge had a reactive effect in the field, although the research was designed in such a way as to try and establish, as best as one could, whether there was a mask behind which respondents were concealing their true behavior and feelings. Nonetheless, our judgment is that this knowledge did not have the reactive effect that the sensitive nature of the issue might suggest. On one level, it did not prevent some respondents from expressing disparaging remarks about Catholics or dissuade them from giving opinions on controversial political issues. On a deeper level, however, the identity category "Catholic" is, for the majority of policemen and women, not an all-inclusive typification in which every Catholic is categorized alike (on police typifications generally, see Holdaway, 1983; Manning, 1977). Most members of the RUC we encountered used an interpretive process that contains a set of typifications for distinguishing between "decent" Catholics and the minority who are involved in political violence, either as gunmen or as their supporters. Once the field-worker was categorized as conforming to their typification of "decent" Catholic, then her religion was no longer as important as it might appear at first sight, although the extent to which it had a residual effect is impossible to estimate. It seemed to remain of crucial importance only to a small minority of bigoted constables who classify all Catholics as equally evil and nefarious. We suspect, therefore, that this knowledge had a markedly distorting effect only among a minority of respondents.

It is this more subtle classification system that explains why policemen and women were so concerned from the very beginning with the field-worker's background, schooling, area of residence, affiliations, and political opinions, even though it was already known that she was Catholic. Further, in the area where the fieldwork was based, there is very little "troubles"-related crime, so that the police do not develop the attitude that law and order is a battle between the RUC and Catholics. This encourages a balanced view of the Catholic community, something that can be absent among some policemen and women beleaguered behind their reinforced stations in areas of high tension and conflict.

There are other technical problems in data collection. The research assistant needed to overcome the problem of how to ask questions on topics the researchers anticipated would be sensitive. Westley explains how he made sure he stayed around long enough that his respondents had to talk, because of the difficulty people have of remaining silent for long (1970, p. viii). Our research was also designed to ensure that the field-worker was around a great deal, and she was stubborn in exploiting the naturally occurring situations of privacy. Where natural conversation is inevitable because it is interactionally difficult to abstain from it—such as when in the back of vehicles, while on guard duty, relaxing in many of the recreational rooms, or off duty. Of course, some policemen and women, at the other extreme, welcomed the research as an opportunity to talk about issues that are so often taken for granted among colleagues and family that they are not topics of conversation. Over lunch in the canteen, very early in the fieldwork, the conversation turned to stress and the danger members of the RUC face, and one constable said, "Why didn't you get a bit of discussion going like this before? I think it's a great. I find all this dead interesting. This is the sort of stuff you should be asking us" (FN, 16/3/87, p. 18). Many also saw it as a means of informing the authorities of their grievances.

Further, a study of policing in Northern Ireland is aided by the fact that conversation and social context are so interrelated. Sensitive and controversial topics often occur naturally in conversation, or can be introduced in what appears a casual manner, because the social context encourages this. Events seen on the television the night before, read about in the day's newspaper, or relayed as they happen to police stations throughout the province facilitate natural talk on sensitive topics or can be used as contextually related props to achieve the same end.

Another technical problem of great significance at the stage of data collection is that of recording data (see Van Maanen, 1982). The ethnographer's conventional notepad can be obtrusive, yet, when the time in the field extends to a full eight-hour shift, it is impossible to do without this aid. One way of allaying fears is by taking notes in as unobtrusive a manner as possible. This is done by reducing the visibility of the pad and the physical activity of note taking; occasionally foregoing it when the situation seemed appropriate, as in the canteen or recreation and television rooms; and emphasizing that the notebooks were not secret. We reiterated this from time to time by showing them pages from the field notes and extracts from the data. Methodologically, however, it is impossible to know the reactive effects of this obtrusive form of recording data. But, in the context of Northern Ireland, where police officers are so sensitive about security, it would have been even more suspicious and disruptive if the research assistant had taken frequent and lengthy absences to surreptitiously record data.

Inasmuch as most of the data collection was done by the research assistant, the principal investigator had to face the moral problem that the bulk of the physical danger at this juncture was borne by someone else. In Northern Ireland, people become inured to such risks, but, even so, the fieldwork was based in East Belfast, where the specific risks associated with fieldwork were negligible. Yet the fact still remained it was not the principal investigator who ran them.

Before moving to the final research stage of dissemination of results, it is worth noting a significant difference between our experience in data collection and usual police research: namely, the reversal in the process of retrenchment. Many studies describe a retrenchment from the front (Douglas, 1972) that occurred as police management sought to control or influence the research design and practice. What retrenchment we experienced was from below and occurred during data collection, which illustrates that working daily with the field-worker was a source of greater sensitivity to ordinary policemen and women than was the idea of research to senior officers (for similar experiences, see Punch, 1989). The techniques by which a minority of respondents sought to impose limits from below included direct refusals to answer questions "for security reasons," occasional resorts to lying, and frequent use of coded conversations in which the meaning was concealed by maintaining a protective hold on the background knowledge to the conversation and the meaning of phrases. Sometimes they would drive off in their vehicle without the field-worker. On one occasion, they locked her in the car when they went to a call, and sometimes they wound down the window to prevent her overhearing. Once, upon getting out of the car, they deliberately maneuvered the vehicle so as to trap the field-worker to prevent her accompanying them. Dodges like this immediately make one suspicious about what they had to hide, and they tended to occur when they were wishing to do some personal business while on duty or simply avoid work. Such techniques were therefore popular among the lazy. These were the sorts of respondents who nicknamed the field-worker "tell her nothin" and "nosebag" and tried to assert informal checks on colleagues who were conversing with the field-worker by reminding them of the notepad and that she writes everything down.

At the final stage of research, there was the technical problem of withdrawing from the field and publishing in such a way that the chief constable would not deny future researchers the opportunity to obtain permission. It was easy to anticipate that, in the Northern Ireland context, the results would have, temporarily at least, a high public profile, and, as researchers, we needed to be sensitive to the fact that the results might have been given a political slant, leading to further problems of personal security. Rainwater and Pittman's (1966) reflection on their study of a controversial housing development project identifies publication of the results as an acute problem. People's bigotry can be inflamed by what they read, and the results can be interpreted by members of the public in whatever way they want. Careful use of prose was therefore important. Agonizing over prose was also necessary to avoid revealing information that might be used to threaten the physical safety of respondents. There is a more intractable ethical issue behind these difficulties, for researchers have no control over the ideological use to which the data might be put.

We tried to deal with some of the problems at the publication stage by doing our utmost to restrict publicity to the academic domain, such as by refusing appearances on local radio and television as well as interviews with the press. But our efforts were defeated by the publisher, who agreed to serialization in a Northern Ireland Sunday newspaper against our advice; and no author has control over journalists' definitions of what constitutes news (see Channels, this volume). The public reactions to the book are thus worth noting because they relate to the issue of sensitivity.

Although the book dealt with a whole range of issues in policing in Northern Ireland beyond those that are associated in the public mind with the controversial image of the RUC, journalists and reviewers picked up on two features that bear most on this image: that of how the police handle danger and the threat from the paramilitary organization, and wider police professionalism and impartiality. Other arguments were simply ignored. It was on the last of these two issues that most public comment had dwelt, and, in disputing our claim that the RUC's sectarianism tends to be localized, journalists and reviewers have questioned the method that underlies and supports our claims. They doubt the capacity of the ethnographic method to support contentious arguments, but on the whole they have been too ready to focus on the weaknesses of ethnographic data without recognizing that they also simultaneously have strengths (on these issues, see Brewer, 1991b).

The police, however, also dislike the book, seeing other features of it as sensitive, and I have been refused permission to undertake further research on the RUC. The chief constable who gave permission for the study has since retired, and the new chief constable seems to have a different agenda. The new management dislikes the idea that policemen and women are ordinary human beings who have not been brutalized by their paramilitary role; instead, they like to think of the police as superhuman, extraordinary, and unlike the rest of us (thus also unbrutalized, but for different reasons). The book displays that policemen drink and that policewomen fart in public, for example, therefore cutting against this superman-superwoman view, threatening the RUC's unrealistic image of itself.

Yet, if we had given in to problems like these, we would have allowed the sensitivity of the topic to defeat us. Punch (1989) notes how important it is for researchers on controversial topics not to become oversensitive so as to avoid dubbing the setting or topic virtually unresearchable. Our study of the RUC confirms that tenacity, toughness, and single-mindedness are important when undertaking sensitive research —so is the possession of a certain balance and pragmatism that helps researchers avoid overreaction to specific problems at the time; the travails can be worth it in the end.

Conclusion

On the whole, researching the RUC has been more difficult than seems to have been the case in most other studies in the sociology of policing, precisely because of the sensitivity of the topic in its social

context. This bears directly on the question of the sociological definition of *sensitivity*. Three general lessons arise from this research. First,
the issue of sensitivity needs to emerge from the shadows and be
recognized as an important problem in research, so that social researchers can give more attention to its negative effects. Sensitivity creates
problems of its own, ranging from those connected with the social
context of the research to the personal security of the researchers. But
it also intensifies the more usual problems found in all research, beyond
those of ethics, for it can affect research design, methodology, and data
collection. Some of the problems caused by sensitivity are easily solved,
while others are intractable. Because the research methods literature
largely ignores the problems raised by sensitivity, there is little textbook
advice on which to draw in solving them: Solutions are devised in an
ad hoc fashion on the basis of common sense and experience. Therefore
the solutions adopted in this study might not have general appeal but
might be useful as a catalyst for debate.

Second, since the publication of several books that recount the personal experiences of researchers involved in major projects, students of
research are now familiar with the idea that in the real world researchers
often have to make pragmatic compromises that depart from the textbook portrayal of research practice. This study of the RUC suggests that,
when the research involves sensitive locations or topics, the pragmatic
compromises tend to increase in number and in the magnitude of their
departure from ideal practice.

Finally, our research shows sensitivity to be highly situational. Implicit in the above account is a definition not only of what has become
sensitive to police officers in the context of Northern Ireland's divided
society but what the researchers considered to be sensitive when studying the topic. This suggests that sensitivity is a social construction, the
meaning of which is indexical, for what is sensitive changes relative to
the circumstances of the research and the biographical experiences of
the people involved. Consequently, textbooks can be of very little use,
so that at the planning stage researchers themselves need to give serious
attention not only to what *they* believe to be controversial and sensitive
but also to what their respondents, potential gatekeepers, and the community at large might consider to be sensitive about the research.

Notes

1. The research reported here was funded by the ESRC on grant number E 00232246. I also wish to acknowledge the assistance of Kathleen Magee in data collection.

2. A "section" is an administrative unit comprising the group of policemen and women on duty for the shift. In other forces, it is usually referred to as a "relief." A section numbers about 20 constables plus a small number of officers. Each section has at least one policewoman.

3. Van Maanen has argued that most ethnographic data are talk based (1982, p. 140).

4. Other researchers have noted the trials and tests to which they have been put by subjects in the field (see Douglas, 1972; Van Maanen, 1982).

References

Bell, C., & Newby, H. (1977). *Doing sociological research.* London: Allen & Unwin

Bell, C., & Roberts, H. (1984). *Social researching.* London: Routledge & Kegan Paul.

Brewer, J. D. (1990). Talking about danger: The RUC and the paramilitary threat. *Sociology, 24,* 657-674.

Brewer, J. D. (1991a). *Inside the RUC: Routine policing in a divided society.* Oxford: Oxford University Press.

Brewer, J. D. (1991b). *The ethnographic critique of ethnography—or how sectarian is the RUC?* Paper presented at the conference, Systematic Aspects of Qualitative Research, University of Surrey.

Brewer, J. D., Guelke, A., Hume, I., Moxon-Browne, E., & Wilford, R. (1988). *Police, public order and the state.* London: Macmillan.

Burton, F. (1979). *Politics of legitimacy.* London: Routledge & Kegan Paul.

Douglas, J. D. (1972). Managing fronts in observing deviance. In J. D. Douglas (Ed.), *Observing deviance.* New York: Random House.

Easterday, L., Papademas, D., Schorr, L., & Valentine, C. (1977). The making of a female researcher. *Urban Life, 6,* 333-348.

Emerson, R. (1983). *Contemporary field research.* Boston: Little, Brown.

Ericson, R. V. (1981). *Making crime.* Toronto: Butterworth.

Fox, J. C., & Lundman, R. (1974). Problems and strategies in gaining access in police organizations. *Criminology, 12,* 52-69.

Holdaway, S. (1982). An insider job: A case study of covert research. In M. Bulmer (Ed.), *Social research ethics.* London: Macmillan.

Holdaway, S. (1983). *Inside the British police.* Oxford: Basil Blackwell.

Hollowell, P. (1968). *The lorry driver.* London: Routledge & Kegan Paul.

Hunt, J. (1984). The development of rapport through the negotiation of gender in field-work among the police. *Human Organization, 43,* 283-296.

Jacobs, J., & Retsky, H. (1975). Prison guards. *Urban Life and Culture, 4,* 5-29.

Johnson, J. (1975). *Doing field research.* New York: Free Press.

Lofland, J. (1971). *Analyzing social settings.* Belmont, CA: Wadsworth.

Manning, P. K. (1972). Observing the police. In J. D. Douglas (Ed.), *Research on deviance.* New York: Random House.

Manning, P. K. (1977). *Police work.* Cambridge: MIT Press.

Policy Studies Institute. (1983). *Police and people in London: A survey of police officers.* London: Policy Studies Institute.

Punch, M. (1989). Researching police deviance. *British Journal of Sociology, 40,* 177-204.

Rainwater, L., & Pittman, D. (1966). Ethical problems in studying a politically sensitive and deviant community. *Social Problems, 14,* 357-366.

Richman, J. (1983). *Traffic wardens.* Manchester: Manchester University Press.

Spradley, J., & Mann, B. (1975). *The cocktail waitress.* New York: John Wiley.

Van Maanen, J. (1981). The informant game: Selected aspects of ethnographic research in police organizations. *Urban Life, 9,* 469-494.

Van Maanen, J. (1982). Fieldwork on the beat. In J. Van Maanen (Ed.), *Varieties of qualitative research.* Beverly Hills, CA: Sage.

Van Maanen, J. (1988). *Tales of the field.* Chicago: University of Chicago Press.

Warren, C. A. B. (1988). *Gender issues in field research.* Newbury Park, CA: Sage.

Warren, C. A. B., & Rasmussen, P. (1977). Sex and gender in field research. *Urban Life, 6,* 349-369.

Wax, R. H. (1979). Gender and age in fieldwork and fieldwork education. *Social Problems, 26,* 509-522.

Weitzer, R. (1985). Policing a divided society. *Social Problems, 33,* 41-55.

Westley, W. (1970). *Violence and the police.* Cambridge, MA: MIT Press.

Woolgar, S. (1988). *Knowledge and reflexivity.* London: Sage.

9

Mediating the Message

Affinity and Hostility in
Research on Sensitive Topics

NIGEL G. FIELDING

This chapter explores the field-worker's role in relation to social actors in qualitative research. It focuses on the various ways of eliciting members' accounts and the status to be accorded them. The chapter commends an approach based on Barnes's notion of the "intercalary role," which lies midway between the passive role encountered in conventional urban ethnography and the assertive, skeptical role exemplified by Douglas's "investigative" model. These matters are central to the validation of field data, a particular problem in research on sensitive topics. The "intercalary role" is illustrated by data collected in an observational study of urban policing. Until recently, the police world has been relatively closed to researchers, and police remain sensitive to the presence of observers. Policing is a sensitive matter in another way, in that much police work is conflictual, and, for some, the police are an "unloved" group from whom they wish to keep their distance. The chapter seeks to demonstrate the value of the "intercalary role" in such circumstances.

AUTHOR'S NOTE: An earlier version of this chapter was published in the *American Behavioral Scientist, 33,* 608-620.

Naturalist Conventions

Qualitative research, with its emphasis on intensive field experience and appreciative understanding, faces dilemmas in studying sensitive social phenomena. Its methods are particularly open to relativism, obliging practitioners to recognize that analysis is a matter of perspective. Yet, while perceiving that all analysis is partial, we seek to convince others that our own is compelling. Conventionally, analytic closure is achieved at a point of even balance between oneself as outsider (detached observer) and oneself as insider (participant in setting). To pass in an alien setting, one has ostensibly to believe in the false, setting-specific self one has created. Appreciation of the meaning of action to members is not gained simply by "telling it like it is" for them. One gains insight from appreciation of the separate assumptions about reality on which both selves are founded. Meaning emerges from experience of the tension between distinct and discordant selves (Glassner, 1980, p. 42).

Sharing in the actor's world, then, enhances insight into one's own perspective. While one's account may be public, the introspective knowledge is not. Practitioners have therefore pursued a principle of verifiability. The adept observer provides others with instructions on how to pass in the same setting. Following such recipes, one should ideally have similar experiences and hence personally appreciate the truth of the description. Subordinate to this is any member test of adequacy, either by direct feedback or by the procedures of "grounded theory" (Glaser & Strauss, 1967). While the more "objective" data can be checked by informants, and one may have the chance to indirectly gauge reaction to analyses of the sort one intends to make, this is as close as the conventional approach gets to the involvement of members in the construction and validation of analysis.

This limited involvement is advantageous to ethnographers, who avoid an informal challenge to their preferred schema. It is also advantageous in the special case of research on sensitive topics and on groups that are closed to overt research. Conventional naturalism is the approach that, in contrast to positivism's scientific model, accords primacy to subjective experience, is preoccupied by the multiplicity of perspectives, and is reluctant to aggregate data by quantification. Whether "appreciation," so closely tied to conventional naturalism, demands affinity for the research subjects is debatable. In practical terms, this is a matter of contentment with play-acting and deceit (Fielding, 1982), and it is revealing that one prominent participant observer was herself originally an actress (Barker, 1986). While the literature is replete with discussions of rapport and empathy, these are based on studies of groups that researchers found conducive, whimsical, or at least unthreatening. Less discussed are the problems in applying these methods to "unloved" groups and those hostile to research. The police are notoriously skeptical of outsiders and the research example below focuses on a common, conflictual incident about which they are particularly sensitive. The last word has not been said on the place of members in the account, but this discussion will be put aside momentarily to consider the critique of naturalism.

Naturalism's stress on trusting relations in the achievement of reliable, valid data is consistent with the primacy of introspection. The data must be trustworthy because, with the onset of analysis, field relations move off center stage and the analytic running is done by the researcher, alone in her or his study communing with "the data." The focus of the communion is the way the field-worker had to change to get by in the field. This enjoys an uncertain relation with the "principle of verifiability," with its antirelativist assumption that in any relationship what matters is that the actors know the "rules" (Hughes, 1976). Replication is, in any case, an uncomfortable companion for introspection, a means of analysis as ultimately inaccessible as the mental process of the researcher. Can we be certain that researchers comprehend their "self" enough to gauge whether it has changed to pass in the setting? If this were not a vexed question, existentialism would have no problematic.

Consequently, naturalism has fallen prey to the critique both of phenomenologists (some arguing the rightful focus of ethnography is the ethnographer) and to those such as Jack Douglas (1976), whose critique stems from dissatisfaction with the "small town Protestant do-gooder" mentality informing its early and dominant formulation. Douglas commends procedures involving attempts to catch the subjects out on the basis that they have to earn the researcher's trust too, and the way to find out if they merit it is to do such things as going for a massage to see if one is offered sex, having heard from one's sample of proprietors that there is no such naughtiness in their parlors (Douglas, 1976, pp. 146-147). This treatment of responses to the problem of validating analysis is hardly exhaustive, but the variety of responses at least suggests the need to move beyond simple regurgitation of members' accounts.

An Intercalary Role

The damage naturalism suffers from such critiques directly pertains to the practical matter of whether field relations should be informed by rapport or skepticism. In naturalism's "appreciative" stance, there is a fine line between analytic appreciation and field affinity; the latter may lead to overidentification with subjects, as the texts continually remind us. Should we be, or aim to become, fond of our subjects?

Barnes urges that "there must be some amount of compatibility between the values of the scientist and those of the citizens he [sic] studies" (1979, p. 116). While at first blush this suggests we should not do observational research on groups we find obnoxious, it is a coy formulation. Barnes's "amount of compatibility" may appear stringent, say, in demanding acceptance of "democracy" in the case of a political group, but what if the group espouses "mass democracy" or suffrage for racial elites but not minorities? Lofland goes further, suggesting we should "truly like" group members even if we disagree with their worldview (Lofland, 1971)—by all accounts, Hitler could be a charming salon conversationalist. The history of sexuality suggests that affective "liking" is a standard that can produce unstable matches. Good causes can be advanced by bad people or by good people for bad motives. Value compatibility would have us all researching those like ourselves. It would amplify subjectivity and corrupt any attempt at generalization.

The degree of compatibility necessary must be limited to sufficient common ground to engage in a sustained relationship for the instrumental purpose of collecting data. For example, it would be futile for a black researcher to undertake observational research on the British National Front (a white supremacist party that claims it would accept black members because, embracing party policy, they would repatriate themselves to Africa). But does the instrumental standard not drive the field relation back from "appreciation" to manipulation and deceit? This is the danger of Douglas's approach. Analysis will always be limited if it is informed first and last by skepticism. Skepticism, too, quickly becomes cynicism. If the fieldwork begins with an attempt to catch members out, rather than attempting to see why a worldview appeals to a particular group, the analysis will never be able to take members' beliefs seriously. While those confining themselves to reflecting the member's evocation of his or her experience produce accounts that excite suspicion of a loss of objectivity, field-workers wishing to produce an "objective," warts-and-all account deny the very power of the belief that makes adherence possible despite all the warts. And Douglas's field-workers still have to learn the culture before they can pursue leads enabling them to establish its true ambit.

This is where another part of Barnes's case is edifying. Ideally, Barnes thinks, sensitive fieldwork effects a process that expands the understanding of the *subject* group about *society*. The researcher occupies an "intercalary" role (Barnes, 1963, p. 127). By explicit discussion of how the culture varies from cultures with which the researcher is familiar, it is intended to heighten both the groups' understanding and the external audience's that theirs is but one part of a complex reality. Searching for an acceptable role in the unfamiliar setting initiates an educational process for both field-worker and members (an argument aligned with the radical participatory research of Latin America). If research aims to inform public debate, then this style of field relation is not just about methodological adequacy. As Phillipson put it, social research, "through its clarification of [human beings'] practical activities . . . can help the members of a society to pose their own dilemmas more clearly and acutely" (1971, p. 169; see also Becker, 1964; Rock, 1979). This ambitious role offers special promise in research on sensitive topics, not least the appreciation of what is "sensitive" to members.

Coproducing Fieldwork

A stance that puts researchers in a mediating role speaks directly to the feelings of guilt that profoundly inform our anxieties about sensitive fieldwork and invest debates over ethics with much of their heat. Is it really proposed that we add to the burden by trying to educate subjects, even making them effective at catching the public ear and thus transforming phenomena we set out to study in all humility? In fact, there is another reason for considering this tack. It is useful to set the stage by considering an incident recounted by Van Maanen.

Van Maanen (1982) notes that, because fieldwork is only rarely marked by noteworthy events, the interpretive work of members is generally implicit, as is the degree of trust they grant the researcher at any one time. But there is more to it than the researcher's problem. Members, too, have problems, not just in negotiating trust but in negotiating reality. Van Maanen takes a case where a young policeman talks about an incident that was unforgettable, dramatic, and "lost in an existential fog. . . . 'The guy . . . fired five times and I can't remember it and I can't remember my own gun firing. I just remember it kicking in my hands. It's very, . . . strangest thing I think I've ever. . . . Just unbelievably strange' " (p. 140).

Van Maanen dryly remarks that there is "obviously an essential ambiguity surrounding data of this type." Most researchers would probably discuss the experience with the officer; together, new understandings may emerge on both sides. What makes this so important is that this problem extends to all data that cannot be expressed as behavioral, concrete description. Not only are subjects as unsure and equivocal as we are some of the time, they are operating in a culture, and culture is itself an interpretation; it mediates their "objective" experience too. In the extreme case Van Maanen gives, simple humanity is probably enough to make us want to talk more with that young officer. We should recognize that the rewards of inquiring with subjects into their experience merit the effort much more often than in the dramatic circumstance. Its ramifications touch on ethnographic authority, methodological adequacy, and, ultimately, standards of "science."

Like Van Maanen, Sharrock and Anderson assert that the characterization of "culture" as designating some "integrated and discrete body of rules to which the native has privileged access" is erroneous (1980, p. iii). Where ethnography is depicted as the analysis of culture by the faithful representation of the native's perspective, its project is inherently impossible. The canon of sound analysis becomes descriptive adequacy rather than validity, a harsh criterion indeed. The difficulty is overcome if we argue that different societies display a range of cultural differences around a heuristically significant common core. This affords a base for cultural translation and offers the prospect of members being treated as inquirers into their culture alongside researchers; researchers and informants collaboratively make sense of ("coproduce") activities.

We can well understand much that members do because, particularly in research in our own society, we are presented with similar problems. What, then, about the residue of things predicated on beliefs we do not share? Sharrock and Anderson (1980) argue that "the requirement is not to excavate the meanings that members have for the actions they take, but to ensure that in our accounts we treat them as interpretive actors, *and only as interpretive actors,* until the cultural rules that are held to explicate their actions are demonstrated" (p. 20). This hinges on showing how mutual understanding and shared expectations are achieved, with the subject "making what he [or she] does accountable to the researcher, who in turn demonstrates his [or her] understanding, his [or her] account, by the things that he [or she] does" (p. 22). This obviously creates room for the researcher's forays into the process of the attribution of meaning and puts a new, less narcissistic cast on reflexivity.

An Example

The illustration I will use of the intercalary role arose in fieldwork on criteria of competence in urban policing.[1] A team of three observers accompanied patrol officers over a period of 18 months, documenting more than 1,400 policing incidents (Fielding, 1988). We emphasized that our interest was in *good* practice, because a highly critical report commissioned by the London police had made them even more sensitive than usual to evaluations of routine patrols. Senior officers quickly perceived, however, that we had not said we were not interested in bad practice, only that we were keenly interested in its opposite. What would we do if we encountered malpractice? We acknowledged that such an occurrence would be analytically useful but insisted we were not seeking evidence with which to lambast the police. Discussion thereafter concerned at what level of malpractice we would feel obliged to take action. This point was never reached, perhaps because our previous experience somewhat inured us to the indelicacy of police work.

The issue often recurred with officers new to our research, however. The pragmatic police perspective is that "competence" is anything not punished under discipline regulations. It is an understandable perspective, albeit one the police accept, when challenged, as not being the last word. Having reached this point in discussion with officers we were accompanying, we would acknowledge the implicit utility of bad practice for identifying standards. This having been aired, good relations generally prevailed, aided by our acceptance of the unsocial working arrangements the officers themselves tolerated. Versions of what we were doing, however, continued to be requested.

Our extended fieldwork sometimes afforded us better knowledge of incidents and policies than that of officers we accompanied. Gradual recognition of this, and the realization that the field notes were being recorded in detail, meant that we could be useful to officers. This could plainly be abused; it put us in a position to influence the standards we had come to observe. I shall indicate the opportunities and constraints of that influence by reference to a field example.

In April 1986, I accompanied "Dave," a tall gruff Scot in his late twenties. Married to a "care officer" in an old people's home, Dave claimed he could relate to youths on the public housing estates because "I was a bit of a yob when I was their age" and you had to be a fighter to survive a childhood on an estate. I spent several 1400-2200 shifts with Dave in a small one-officer car, during which the following incident occurred.

1400-1415. Canteen. . . . All settling with tea when a "shout" (officer in distress call) comes through; the ripple of officers responding works its way down the canteen in 20 seconds.

1415-1435. *Officer in distress.* . . . Dave is having trouble with his gear and is last away. Everyone hurtles down the two flights of stairs two at a time. Dave tears his trousers as he launches himself into the car and he's done a mile before he realizes he hasn't got his seat belt on. The call was from —Park, east entrance. On arrival the area car is up on the grass 100 yards inside the entrance, officers are running to it. As Dave and I get out the van cruises past us up onto the grass. The area car driver has hold of one arm of a violently struggling male black youth in black leather jacket and jeans, his other arm held by a young blond female. She is wearing a bomber jacket and slacks, and inside the jacket hangs a police radio, squawking. They wheel the youth around and the van operator joins them, steering the now physically-subdued but shouting youth into the back of the van. The doors bang shut behind him and three of the officers—the area car driver, van operator, and another officer. "I think they're helping him to his seat," an officer remarks as howls and banging emanate from the van. The van is rocking on its springs. But around its front all is tranquil, as officers discuss the turn-out. Dave chats with the blond. "All it was was a stop, but now it's an assault." The youth gave lip when she stopped him to search for car-breaking tools, then she sensed him getting seriously aggressive and issued the shout. She is part of the plain-clothes auto crime squad run from the uniform reliefs (in other words, less experienced than permanent detectives). Suddenly our talk is interrupted by another priority call. The burglar alarm at a sensitive address has gone off [at the home of a prominent politician]. It's only a block from the park and all cars respond. Dave sees a [community constable] he knows who joins us.

1435-1445. Sensitive address burglar alarm. . . . Dave was late on the scene and remained in the car chatting to the community constable. Dave was arranging a blind date for him but assured him "she isn't a dog, I promise you. And her Dad owns a business." "But what I want to know, is she a nympho?" . . . While they continued in this vein the area car driver approached, sucking the blood off a bad cut on his thumb. "I'm injured," he joked, "but justice has been done," confirming the retribution received by the youth in the van.

At tea, it emerged that the relief had gone drinking the previous night, and Dave had three hours' sleep before an early court. He remarked that he'd not seen his wife and boy for six days, due to her shift system and his failing to coincide. His hands were shaking. As the shift went on, I noticed that most officers had a tremor. The sergeant, Amanda, asked how the research was going. She started to discuss the importance of "explaining" in verbal interaction with citizens. She quite clearly saw it as a key tactic:

> I hate violence, I'm a pacifist. There's no place for violence but if its offered you, well, you'd better be good at it. But explanation is the biggest part. In there [charge room] or outside. I find that if you take them through what you have to do and why, then 90% of them are as good as gold.

The sergeant's remarks contrasted sharply with her officers' actions in the van. Perhaps because I sensed that with the police there was more openness to debate than with the racist politicians I had researched in an earlier study (Fielding, 1981), or because I was working on a team and the fieldwork would not be lost if I alienated the officers, I decided to breach my usual practice and explicitly react to events such as the beating in the van. I found this less damaging than I anticipated; as I took individuals to task, I often found that my views had already been assumed. I also found officers keen to use my reaction as a springboard to make a rejoinder to a particular issue that also concerned them.

When the chance arose to discuss the application of "street justice" to the man in the officer-in-distress incident, I initially wanted to gauge whether the officers considered how casual onlookers might regard what was happening. The police, too, wanted to discuss how the public would evaluate the beating, perhaps using the "public" reaction to check mine; that is, the researcher became the person to be persuaded. The officers all knew such things looked bad but wanted outsiders to know their reasons and to accord the reasons legitimacy.

In such discussions, one implicitly confronts dilemmas, rethinking choices officers have had to make. The researcher who breaks into this by moving away from the self-effacing role not only learns that such decision making is another aspect of police discretion but that officers are keen to get another view (the researcher's personal attributes may make such a move easier for some than others; see Punch, 1985). Dilemmas come from the difficulty in assessing the gains and estimating the probability of obtaining them, where the right choice depends on "judging the likelihood of the unlikely fortune" (Billig, Condor, Edwards, Gane, Middleton, & Radley, 1988, p. 11). Second opinions are eagerly sought in confronting such choices. If they take a stance seldom encountered, so much the better, as this grounds decisions in a wider range of potential criteria.

The problem with many psychologically oriented studies of decision making is that they reduce choices to a stark form that conforms to design methods and that can be studied clinically. By discounting social context, the research design reduces the dilemma to payoffs of a single desired utility and the subject's thinking to profit maximization (Colman, 1982). Like any utilitarian logic, this factors out the very complexities that generated the dilemma and renders a version of choice that is awesome in its banality. The effect when applied to events such as the beating in the police van is to make the episode incomprehensible. Policing is not an activity that can be studied through force regulations. Such activities require cultural knowledge to appreciate.

The first refinement of a conceptual schema of police beatings is to appreciate that not all beatings are the same. For example, police distinguish between the officers who may issue a "shout"; some are irresolute or unreliable and may make such calls lightly. In this case, discussion centered on the relative inexperience of the woman police constable. She was not a regular detective but a uniform officer temporarily assigned to a plainclothes squad. Against this inexperience, her colleagues emphasized that she had an intuitive feeling that the suspect was becoming unpredictable, a familiar feeling officers are inclined to endorse.

As an observer, I found the aftermath of the event disturbing; the officer I was accompanying switched effortlessly from cynical cracks about street justice to parley over the blind date. While this was expressed in crudely ribald terms, it was the extreme banality that disturbed me. I had just witnessed an event that I would have reported as a bystander, while the officers were clearly comfortable enough with it to turn to social chitchat. This provoked reflection about their unconcern over the event and made me ponder whether, as many have concluded, all police become brutalized.

Of course, this was the central thought the officers expected I would have. They had several rejoinders: the type that maintained the need for street justice as the courts were weak; the type that spoke of a Levitical restoration of balance (between black community and white and/or between decent citizens, represented by police, and criminals); the type that spoke of the compassion police feel and the mask they must wear to discharge their expected role at, for example, road accidents; and so on. In this case, the banality of the aftermath was complicated by the sequence of adrenalin-stirring events, which made available the argument that beatings were the inevitable culmination of stressors that escalated the participants' sense of danger.

Those not directly involved with "the beating," at least 20 officers in at least six vehicles, had rushed from the park in a high-speed traffic jam, arriving en bloc at the "sensitive" address. For the second time in a few minutes, they had moved with all haste to a place where there was literally nothing for them to do. Instead of excitedly discussing what had happened, they kidded about a blind date. The line we quickly thrashed out was that, if you did not make light of such things, the job would drive you mad. The awareness of stress is manifest throughout the field notes of the shift. Dave and I explicitly discussed it when he spoke of continually missing his wife and son. Once I learned that most of the shift had hang overs, I noticed that most of them had tremors.

Reaction to the "shout," and the almost immediate stimulus of the sensitive address alarm, could now be read as indexing the working situation of officers, making available the argument that the pressures of the job "made" officers act like this, that the beating was not only explicable as street justice but as the reaction of exhausted, benign people stretched beyond the limit, and so on. (None of these rejoinders is, necessarily, one I would buy; in this case, after all, the officers were at the beginning of a shift.) This then provoked discussion about whether police brutality arose from bias, the dynamics of the situation, or the nature of the job. In my role as spokesperson for the outside, I pointed out that I found the sergeant's remarks about violence intensely ironic, having just watched the shift she was in charge of acting in a way that contradicted her statements about the need to control suspects by persuasion and "tactics."

From this discussion, I learned that, far from ironic, her remarks could be read as themselves occasioned by the very events most in the station knew I had witnessed. Armed with the avowed focus of our research (on competence in street tactics), she had constructed a version that neatly fed me what I was thought to want and probed what I made of the events.

The point in attuning to the equivocal meanings of discourse is not to undermine its veracity (either as field note or as sign of what is "genuinely" thought by subjects) but to take account of the complexity that rational choice theory must gauge if it is to move beyond *homo economicus*. As Billig et al. (1988) put it:

> The point behind this hermeneutic analysis is not to expose inconsistencies as signs of hypocrisy. . . . In fact the charge of hypocrisy is completely misplaced, because the counter-themes are implicit rather than explicit; as such, the person expressing the discourse may not be fully aware of these counter-meanings in the way that an out-and-out hypocrite would be. (pp. 23-24)

Indeed, one promise of this approach to research on sensitive issues is to provoke awareness in the subjects that there is ambivalence, obliging them to recognize that it would certainly be hypocritical if they resumed a monocular perspective on the action.

Discussion

> It makes things worse if it is assumed that the critical value of comparativism is to permit the formulation of a decisive solution to a singular enigma. (Needham, 1981, p. 108)

Needham's remark is consistent with an approach to belief systems that sees them as uncertain and open to contest over interpretation by believers. "Ideology is not seen as a complete, unified system of beliefs. . . . Instead ideology, and indeed commonsense, are seen to comprise contrary themes. Without contrary themes, individuals could neither puzzle over their social worlds nor experience dilemmas" (Billig et al., 1988, p. 2). The perspective challenges some of the supposed secure generalizations so rare and consequently valued in social and behavioral science. Billig et al. cite the example of the concept of prejudice. "We find the concept of prejudice being used in a way that simultaneously claims a rationality for the speaker, by criticizing the irrational prejudices of others, and that permits the expression of discriminatory views against other groups" (1988, pp. 5-6).

It has been the simplistic and arrogant presumption that these complexities only touch the professions (e.g., the preoccupation in discussions of "sociological ambivalence" or cognitive dissonance with the practice of medicine). Taking an intercalary role in fieldwork forces us to acknowledge that the "great certainties" do not invest most behavior. The belief systems that grow around an occupation, forming its culture, are as much marked by dialectical contradiction as their political ideology counterparts. People think within the constraints of ideology and with the elements of ideology. Ideology is not merely a template patterning the thought of its bearers or an internally consistent pattern forming a holistic mental structure. The view that the schema filters stimuli and allows bearers to experience the world from a shared perspective underestimates the importance of deliberative thinking. Indeed, the dilemmatic elements in ideology enhance deliberation.

The success of the intercalary role rests on the degree to which the external audience can be made real to subjects. It remains a device reliant on knowledge of the setting; to react as a complete outsider would be to invite a sloganistic response couched purely in public relations terms. It is a matter of the degree to which researchers can establish their own credibility and enable members to reflect on their experiences and actions.

The intercalary idea is challenging, not least in its assault on the reassuring idea that culture, in all its distinctiveness, lies "out there," ready for the swoop of the collector's net. In fact, what lies out there is partial and mediated (Van Maanen, 1988, p. 95). This is more readily perceived when there are problems in the field. Van Maanen's experience when left to drive a giant squad car he had frequently ridden in made him appreciate how little he had grasped of the basic practical competence of officers and to see that, even in the "confessional" writing style he occasionally adopted to leaven ethnographic authority, he had been cautious about seriously entertaining alternative interpretations.

A "coproduction" approach to fieldwork could meet some of the problems raised by research on sensitive topics. It is not simply a matter of what the researcher recognizes to be sensitive. Sensitivity being a social construction, methods texts are little help, yet members represent a strangely neglected source. This does not excuse the researcher from effort to evaluate members' accounts; this would be to revert to simple naturalism and to amplify the tendency for accounts produced by powerful actors such as police to be treated as authoritative. In designing research, field-workers need to give serious attention not only to what they see as controversial but to what subjects find sensitive.[2] It is not just another obstacle in the field but a compelling part of a well-founded analysis.

Notes

1. The support of the (U.K.) Economic and Social Research Council is gratefully acknowledged.
2. This cannot be divorced from the problems in eliciting information about sensitive topics in the first place. Access, and the kind of cooperation that guides the researcher into the setting's social organization, is more readily granted to some than to others.

References

Barker, E. (1986). *The making of a Moonie*. Oxford: Basil Blackwell.
Barnes, J. (1963). Some ethical problems in modern fieldwork. *British Journal of Sociology, 13,* 118-134.
Barnes, J. (1979). *Who should know what*. Harmondsworth, UK: Penguin.
Becker, H. (1964). Problems in the publication of field studies. In A. Vidich, J. Bensman, & M. R. Stein (Eds.), *Reflections on community studies*. New York: John Wiley.
Billig, M., Condor, S. Edwards, D., Gane, M., Middleton, D., & Radley, A. (1988). *Ideological dilemmas*. Newbury Park, CA: Sage.
Colman, A. (1982). *Game theory and experimental games*. Oxford: Pergamon.
Douglas, J. (1976). *Investigative social research*. Beverly Hills, CA: Sage.
Fielding, N. (1981). *The National Front*. London: Routledge & Kegan Paul.
Fielding, N. (1982). Observational research on the National Front. In M. Bulmer (Ed.), *Social research ethics*. London: Macmillan.
Fielding, N. (1988). Competence and culture in the police. *Sociology, 22,* 45-64.
Glaser, B., & Strauss, A. (1967). *The discovery of grounded theory*. Chicago: Aldine.
Glassner, B. (1980). *Essential interactionism*. London: Routledge & Kegan Paul.
Hughes, J. (1976). *Sociological analysis: Methods of discovery*. London: Longman.
Lofland, J. (1971). *Analyzing social settings*. Belmont, CA: Wadsworth.
Needham, R. (1981). *Circumstantial deliveries*. Los Angeles: University of California Press.
Phillipson, M. (1971). *Sociological aspects of crime and delinquency*. London: Routledge & Kegan Paul.
Punch, M. (1985). *Conduct unbecoming*. London: Tavistock.
Rock, P. (1979). *The making of symbolic interactionism*. London: Macmillan.
Sharrock, W., & Anderson, R. (1980). *On the demise of the native: Some observations on and a proposal for ethnography* (Occasional Paper 5). Manchester: Manchester University, Department of Sociology.
Van Maanen, J. (1982). *Varieties of qualitative research*. Beverly Hills, CA: Sage.
Van Maanen, J. (1988). *Tales of the field*. Chicago: University of Chicago Press.

10

AIDS Prevention Research

Old Problems and New Solutions

BENJAMIN P. BOWSER
JOAN E. SIEBER

In prior centuries, all of the epidemics that became plagues in Europe had two qualities (Bullet, 1987). First, the manner in which townspeople organized and lived their lives lent to the spread of yellow fever and bubonic plague. Second, there was no cure for those infected. The AIDS epidemic has the potential to be the plague of the modern era. HIV disease not only exploits the structure of the human immune system, it exploits our cultural and social weaknesses as well. First, HIV disease defies the Western sense of physical reality. Persons carrying the disease cannot be physically distinguished from persons not infected. Second, HIV disease's multiyear latency before the disease is apparent exploits our desire to believe that we and our peers are invulnerable. Third, HIV disease is passed through the most personal, most sensitive, and most secretive of behaviors—sexual relations. Finally, HIV disease eventually kills those who are infected. With other diseases in this modern era, one could hope either to live with the disease or to be cured. HIV inevitably leads to death in a world where everything else seems relative and conditional.

There is no other incurable disease like HIV infection. While cancer and heart disease currently kill more people than AIDS, neither disease has the explosive epidemic characteristics of AIDS, especially for the young and for minorities (Selik, 1990; U.S. Department of Health and Human Services, 1985). AIDS could easily kill far more than all other diseases combined and still not run its course. The AIDS epidemic has already reached this level of infection in Central Africa (Koch-Weser & Vanderschmidt, 1988). Also, persons with cancer and heart disease can be treated and a high percentage can continue to live long and productive lives. In contrast, entire social networks can be exposed to the AIDS virus and be fatally infected before there are signs of danger. Under the best of circumstances, those infected might live five to ten years before the infection becomes evident (Hessol et al., 1989).

Until a vaccine is developed—if indeed one can be developed—successful prevention efforts are all that stand between us and a potential plague (Institute of Medicine, 1988). Successful prevention efforts are of utmost importance. What are they? After a decade of AIDS, there appear to be three limited successes. The first limited success has been media efforts to inform the public about AIDS and what can be done to keep from being infected. Surveys have shown that the general public is well informed about AIDS and how to minimize infection (Office of Technology Assessment, 1988). But, for most people who are sexually active, having knowledge about AIDS has not resulted in "safe sex" behaviors (Tucker, 1989). The second success is more limited. There have been efforts to reach injection drug users through community-health outreach workers. As the AIDS epidemic moved into the social networks of injection drug users, self-reported needle sharing has declined and the use of bleach to clean needles has increased dramatically (DesJarlais et al., 1985). Finally, the greatest successful prevention effort has been the "safe sex" general social movement among gay and bisexual men in the AIDS epicenters (Ekstrand & Coates, 1990). Through local mobilization and literal person-to-person persuasion, the gay and bisexual communities were not only able to successfully inform their members about AIDS, they achieved long-term behavior change as well.

A problem with these successes is that lasting behavior change across an entire group rather than among a few individuals occurred only after it was clear that the epidemic had struck that group. Group members began to question the social norms and behaviors that put their group at high risk of being infected. Similarly, when injection drug users began to die from AIDS, needle sharing behavior changed. Apparently, it is necessary for the disease to strike a given group before its members translate their knowledge about AIDS into behavior change on a large enough scale to prevent further spread of AIDS. But to wait until the disease begins to spread rapidly is clearly too late. What is needed is some way to induce behavior change before the disease strikes. This is certainly one of the major public health challenges of the twenty-first century. This is the major challenge to the social sciences as well.

The Challenge

To prevent HIV infections before the epidemic becomes evident within a social group is an extraordinary goal. It means changing behavior (toward abstinence, safe sex, and needle cleaning) prior to there being any immediate and apparent reason to do so. The challenge of developing early and successful prevention efforts now falls to AIDS activists, health service providers, public health specialists, and social scientists.

Do social scientists bring any special talents to the AIDS prevention challenge? Are they doing more than simply using their university and government affiliations to get research funding or to participate in the AIDS prevention general social movement? The major contribution of social scientists in the first decade of the epidemic has been to identify and describe groups at highest risk of becoming HIV infected (Miller et al., 1990). A lot has been learned about gay and bisexual men, out-of-treatment injection drug users, crack cocaine-associated HIV high-risk behavior, and adolescent AIDS risks (Fullilove et al., 1990). These studies have given us glimpses of each HIV high-risk group. The descriptive and accounting functions of social scientists, which have been their traditional strength, are certainly appropriate at the beginning of a research challenge. But, in this second decade of the AIDS epidemic, something more is needed.

Social scientists will now have to devise interventions, evaluate them, and keep refining them until the anticipated group behavior changes have occurred. This is the new challenge and the second potential contribution of social scientists to AIDS prevention efforts. Scientifically derived social change demands something very different than the trial and error persuasive efforts of AIDS activists. The scientists will have to understand why any particular intervention succeeds or fails. Ultimately, scientists will have to derive principles of successful intervention that are applicable across a wide range of social classes, racial groups, and subcultures. This is a formidable challenge. Changing the behavior of groups of people on such a scale, as a scientific goal, has never been done before (Turner & Turner, 1990). If AIDS prevention scientists are to be successful, they first must face and overcome a series of long-standing philosophical and methodological barriers.

The Research Enterprise

Social phenomena lack the underlying regularities and orderliness of physical and biological phenomena (Popper, 1968). It is virtually impossible to specify the necessary and sufficient conditions for any human behavior using our current theories and methods; and, even if it were possible to fully control and shape human behavior, as in a physics experiment, it may be unethical to do so.

What social scientists have to offer at this time is an orderly process of inquiry, a way to rigorously make decisions about possible conditions and associated factors, and a procedure to document the outcomes of AIDS prevention interventions. This may not be pure and exacting science, but it is better than no science or simple speculation. What is needed, in addition, is valid and relevant theory.

Even in physics, chemistry, and a nonexperimental science such as astronomy, sound theory has been initially derived deductively from experience, hunches, guesses, and even dreams. It is this use of deduction that most troubles social scientists, especially those who believe that science involves only the use of quantitative or probability methods. Deduction is a legitimate source of ideation and can be used, rather than avoided, in the name of objectivity. In fact, it is the main source of ideas and theories that we wish eventually to test objectively.

Critical to the success of any attempt to change behavior from high risk for AIDS to low risk is the development of sound theory about the causes of the relevant behavior. As yet, we have no such theory. The inductive method of the physical sciences is self-limiting and inadequate when applied to a problem such as AIDS prevention (Popper, 1968).

The proposed integration of inductive and deductive approaches might make some difference. The following sections of this chapter do two things: (a) illustrate how social scientists might reconceptualize their work and (b) outline a way to integrate a deductive stage into the research process to improve both methods and theoretical outcomes.

Grounding the Research Process

Given that the science behind AIDS prevention research is still in development, objectivity is more of a goal than a fact based on current methodologies. AIDS prevention research can be improved by using both inductive and deductive processes. Research does not occur in a social vacuum, nor is it some activity done from outside of the social worlds under investigation. AIDS researchers are, in fact, part of a community that comes to their research with an empirical literature, peer groups and peer pressures, a bureaucracy, managers and management, attitudes, beliefs, and biases not unlike any other self-defined group. Social scientists doing AIDS research have become specialists and a community unto themselves. A specialized language is developing, and an AIDS research political lobby is forming as well as systems of reward, sanctions, hierarchy, and status. This brings both a threat and an opportunity to the research.

The threat is that social scientists in the AIDS prevention research community could very well end up doing research for their own well-being and group interests. The new grants and new publications may become self-perpetuating and self-rewarding. In the first decade of AIDS research, investigators were close to and influenced by the AIDS prevention social movement. As any social movement matures, it either demobilizes and fragments or becomes established and self-perpetuating. With AIDS research becoming established, researchers' participation and effectiveness as part of the AIDS social movement will predictably decline. Not everything researchers do will necessarily lead, in the short or long run, to making the AIDS research community unnecessary or to preventing the further spread of AIDS.

If the emerging AIDS research enterprise is to be an opportunity rather than a burden for society, the issue of integrating deduction and subjectivity into social science research again arises, but in a different way. Not only is it necessary for AIDS researchers to acknowledge and use their own subjectivity in their formulation of theories and hypotheses, they must do the same for their subjects. Research subjects cannot simply be subjects. They must, in some way, be partners in AIDS prevention research. The meanings they give to their behaviors and to their motives for engaging in high- or low-risk behaviors are subjective. Researchers have to learn the subjective side of their subjects before they can conduct valid surveys or experimentation. The very best methods and good theory will not substitute or compensate for lack of knowledge and insight into subjects' subjectivity.

Community-Based AIDS Research

How does an AIDS researcher balance and strengthen inductive research methods? How do researchers use their own and their subjects' subjectivity and at the same time conduct research with some objectivity? Some answers to these questions have become apparent in conducting AIDS prevention research through a multiservice community-based organization with working ties to a university-based research group. It is necessary to do two difficult things well and simultaneously—to meet the methodological standards for peer review in the AIDS research community and to assist local service providers in slowing the spread of AIDS in their communities. To do one or the other would fall short of the mark. One could direct research and write papers, which might advance the literature for other researchers but would do little for communities at risk. Alternatively, one could work solely in the community and work with service providers and HIV high-risk groups. One might learn a lot and gain many insights, but ultimately very little would be done for lack of resources and inability to conduct and document interventions.

There are additional challenges that reinforce the need to revise conventional methods. Few high-risk subpopulations are accessible to random sampling. The universe of injection drug users cannot be enumerated for random selection. Very little is known in the literature about out-of-treatment injection drug users. Gay and bisexual men are not identifiable for random selection. Even less is known about African American, Hispanic, and Asian men who are gay and bisexual and who continue to be the highest HIV risk-takers. High-risk-taking adolescents are also a hidden population. In community settings, it is possible to get access to any of these and to other HIV high-risk subgroups. But it is impossible then to strictly and exactly fulfill methodological imperatives (e.g., random sampling) for groups that cannot be enumerated. But the challenge and the need to do AIDS prevention research and to develop interventions remain. Something can be done to address the limits of the science, the community burden of the research, and the needs of subjects and their communities. The innovative use of focus groups and the participation of people closest to the research population can make the activities of researchers beneficial to science, to communities at risk, and to the research participants themselves.

Use of Focus Groups

A way to integrate a deductive step into the research process is to use focus groups at various stages of the research. This simple and straightforward step can provide a "grounding" of one's theories and hypotheses in the reality of the subjects and can help craft the methodology to the social context of prospective subjects. The research will then measure something valid for subjects and will be an experience they can relate to, producing a higher participation rate than is the case with "nongrounded" research.

Focus groups were first reported in the social science literature by Robert Merton and Patricia Kendell in the 1930s (Morgan, 1988). More recently, focus groups were used as community review boards and as research communes, with mixed results, by urban anthropologists (Blauner & Wellman, 1982; Hessler & New, 1972). Apparently, when focus groups are used as the sole research technique to validate observations, the researchers' attention is limited and too much reliance is placed on community informants. Since World War II, focus groups have generally not been used in social and behavioral research. Focus groups were viewed as unscientific. Only in marketing research have focus groups been used as an integral part of the methodology.

In one of the few books that outlines how focus groups can be used to good effect in qualitative and quantitative research, David Morgan (1988) points out the following uses of focus groups:

(a) to orient oneself to a new field,
(b) to generate hypotheses based on informants' insights,
(c) to evaluate different research sites or study populations,
(d) to develop interview schedules and questionnaires, and
(e) to get participants' interpretations of results.

Given the difficulty of accessing and then gaining valid information about HIV high-risk sexual behavior in hidden and culturally distinct populations, all of these uses are needed to ground AIDS prevention research. Focus groups provide an orientation not only to a new field but to subpopulations for which there is very little useful prior information. Hypotheses based on informants' insights are essential. Even if these insights are biased or somewhat off the mark, they are closer to reality and more valid and representative than what someone outside of the experience and community of HIV risk-takers might initially bring to the research.

HIV risk-takers, like all other subpopulations, are not unidimensional. They are diverse and have their own social structure and social networks. Researchers have to get some knowledge of these structures and diversity to devise a method to ultimately reach the right sample population. The research instrument has to be sensitive to the communication style and language of prospective respondents. If the instruments are not sensitive, respondents may not only misunderstand the questions, they may be offended by them and not give valid responses. The researcher cannot user-refine instruments without having someone familiar with the target group to review the wording. Finally, once the researcher has results, participants add an important dimension by participating in the interpretation of the findings. We turn now to an example of the use of focus groups.

An Innovation

The Bayview Hunter's Point District of San Francisco, California, is a series of predominantly African American, low- to working-class communities. Bayview has many positive points, but it also has all of the social problems common to an economically marginal African American community that is in decline. In particular, its injection drug users, crack cocaine addicts, and sexually active adolescents constitute pockets of the highest HIV risk-taking behavior in the city. A social and health service organization, the Bayview Hunter's Point Foundation, has taken on the critical task of developing AIDS prevention interventions in the community. In past research at the Bayview Hunter's Point Foundation, focus groups were used as part of each project's conceptualization and to refine the research procedure.

No more than seven individuals are asked to come together at a time. The purpose is for them to discuss their experiences and to share with one another and with a researcher their knowledge and perspectives about drug use or HIV high-risk behaviors. Focus group participants are selected by social service staff based on their firsthand knowledge of in-house and street clients. On the surface, our focus groups might appear to be like any other focus group. But there is a subtle and very important difference with crucial implications for the quality of the research and for the extent to which foundation researchers could get valid information from respondents. The difference is that we did not simply use focus group respondents to gain information. Rather, they were empowered, as peers, to conceptualize strategies for accessing the research population. Our focus groups were more accurately described as "consultant focus groups." The focus group formally begins only after the participants fully understand the need for the research, feel that they are very important to the success of the project, and understand that they can make a real contribution. In our focus groups, participants were encouraged to become personally invested in the research. In ordinary focus groups, participants are primarily motivated by the social aspects of group discussion.

To empower participants and to get them to identify with the goals of the research are essential prerequisites for doing research on populations that are stigmatized, alienated from the mainstream, economically marginal, underclass, and distrustful of any mainstream interest or attention toward them and that also engage in illegal and deviant behaviors. Our earlier efforts have shown that persons who are drawn from this population, or who have been a part of it, would find a regular focus group just another mainstream exploitation of their circumstance. They would have nothing to do with a typical survey. In contrast, if the researcher accepts them as peers for their experience and knowledge, and provides them with a genuine opportunity to make a positive contribution, they will identify with the project and be highly motivated participants. The way in which consultant focus groups are organized and conducted is as follows:

(a) Focus group participants are recruited through individuals who are known and trusted within the subject population. This is important because trust for the researcher and the project is built out of existing trust. If the recruiter trusts the researcher, then the participant has reason to trust the researcher. It is also important for focus group participants to know that the researcher is obligated not to violate their trust of the recruiter.

(b) The focus group should be conducted in the subject's community and should be sponsored by someone trusted by the subject population. Location is important. Symbolically, to work in the subjects' community shows a willingness to accept them on their own terms and to learn from them.

(c) Once the group has gathered, the researcher must be introduced and vouched for by the recruiter and local sponsor.

(d) Before the group formally begins, the researcher talks casually with the participants in general as peers and people with whom the researcher has common interests. The researcher serves food and eats with the participants before the group begins. (The sponsor can suggest what food is appropriate.) The researcher does not talk in detail about the proposed project until both he or she and the group are comfortable.

(e) With the sponsor present, the researcher assures participants of confidentiality and sets the guidelines for the discussion. Everyone should have a chance to contribute. Real names are not to be used. The researcher asks for honesty, points out that participation is strictly voluntary, reviews the manner in which participants will be paid and how much of their time will be taken, and makes certain that there are no unanswered questions.

(f) The researcher briefs subjects on the proposed project (avoiding jargon) and discusses the project's potential benefits to the community. The researcher is open to questions and answers them in a straightforward fashion. The researcher uses respondents' suggestions to expand upon and to correct the initial list of benefits.

(g) Despite what the researcher has learned from prior projects and might know from the literature, the researcher tells respondents that he or she knows nothing of their world (and, indeed, despite prior projects and the literature, that may be so). In addition, what one may know as a researcher does not make one an expert in the eyes of such respondents. The researcher asks respondents to be project consultants and is honest about his or her dependence on them and readiness to listen.

(h) The researcher candidly discusses the intention and the necessity to publish the results of the ensuing research and points out that participants are gathered to help accurately frame the research and will be acknowledged in the publication. The researcher is specific as to where participants will be acknowledged, such as in a footnote, preface, or foreword, and gives them the option of a group acknowledgment or a listing of individual names. It is important for participants to be assured that they will not be exploited for the researcher's own personal and professional gain. Participants would indeed feel exploited if their insights, knowledge, and experience were taken from them without acknowledgment and then used for purposes of which they might not approve.

(i) Once all concerns and questions about procedures, purposes, and intent are addressed, the researcher presents the first discussion question and moderates in a nonjudgmental fashion. The researcher uses those who speak up to get a discussion going and to help bring out the more quiet or seemingly reserved participants. Those who seem reserved may only be holding back to see what is going to happen and how the moderator is going to conduct him- or herself.

(j) The moderator's questions should be short and clear. The directing of comments should also be short and to the point. The researcher should not make long statements but should observe, facilitate, and not attempt to control the discussion except to keep it on track.

(k) The researcher should use a micro-cassette recorder to record comments and should put it in plain view. Note taking during the discussion is very distracting both to participants and to the discussion leader.

Once the group is under way, it is the moderator's goal to get a lively discussion going in which each participant knows he or she can disclose information, feelings, and perspectives without judgment from the group or the moderator. The discussion leader sets the tone and maintains the openness. Once a lively and open discussion gets going, the researcher has an open window into the world of prospective subjects— a world in which the researcher hopes to do research.

Benefits to the Researcher

A successful consultant focus group may meet many times throughout the project. The group can be called together at any stage in the research, such as when formulating the research problem, design, and procedures; when problems arise; when information is obtained that is not understood; and when the researcher seeks to interpret the results. The focus group serves as the project's subject consultants. For methodological reasons, the investigator may wish to convene new focus groups at later stages in the project. There are several benefits to the researcher of conducting consultant focus groups in the manner described above.

(a) The most important benefit is that the researcher's initial theories and hypotheses that explain behaviors under investigation can be refined deductively, based on the insights and experiences of prospective subjects. This important enrichment of the research integrates the strengths of qualitative and quantitative approaches.

(b) Additional hypotheses invariably come out of the focus group discussion. These hypotheses are often quite different than the researcher's literature-driven list and may make a critical difference in the general success of the research project. These hypotheses are particularly important if behavioral intervention is the goal.

(c) The focus group discussion can enable the researcher to see his or her own motivation, biases, and subjective interest in doing the research. In moderating the discussion, the researcher remains a participant and has an opportunity to reflect on his or her own contribution to the research. By understanding one's own subjectivity with reference to the proposed research, the investigator is better able to step outside of his or her own biases both in conducting the research and in interpreting the results.

(d) Valuable information and tips can be obtained on how best to access and approach prospective subjects to maximize the likelihood that they will participate in the study. The focus group members are indirectly training the researcher to work with their peers.

(e) It is important that the investigator's work be useful and acceptable to the subject population. Focus groups motivate and encourage the researcher to work with subjects and to do so in a responsible way.

There are additional benefits to be gained from using consultant focus groups that are above and beyond those derived from a regular focus group. Consultant focus groups can benefit any research project seeking primary data from human subjects. But they are especially useful in engaging difficult-to-access, potentially mistrustful, and alienated subjects. Fortunately, there are benefits for the consultant focus groups as well.

Benefits to Focus Group Participants

In regular focus groups, participants might enjoy the discussion and be paid for their time and assistance. In consultant focus groups, there are additional and more important benefits to participants.

(a) The focus group becomes a unique opportunity for participants to make a positive contribution to their community. For substance abusers and others who live outside of the mainstream, much of what they have had to do to support their habit and to survive has been destructive of family and community. The focus group experience is often the first time participants have had an opportunity to give back to their family and community in a positive fashion.

(b) For underclass participants, to be accepted and treated as consultants by a person who represents higher education and a valuable mainstream activity is important self-esteem enhancement. This is particularly important to persons in substance abuse recovery who are making the transition from the "life" (the world of drug users) to the mainstream.

(c) In the consultant focus group, participants can have positive interaction with peers. Many of the interactions between people in "the life" reinforce negative self-concepts and narrow limits on participants' lives. A purpose of support groups for people in recovery is to experience, and practice, being rewarding to one another. Consultant focus groups can provide such an experience. But the potential benefit is larger than that. Ultimately, the community may benefit. In addition, participants often learn from one another. Typically, they had never thought before of some of the things that are discussed in the focus group, and it is not uncommon for participants to express a desire to meet again.

(d) In consultant focus groups, participants learn about themselves. When they hear what their peers did and think, this causes them to reflect back on their own experiences and thoughts.

(e) Participants indirectly learn something about research and have their first positive experience with research. They are surprised that researchers care about them, their peers, and their experiences. They are even more surprised to find that there might be books and articles written about their experiences.

Unpleasant But Important
Information for Researchers

There is an additional aspect of consultant focus groups. Not all of the benefits will necessarily be pleasant. Researchers may learn things they are unwilling or unable to accept. Points of view may be expressed that are abhorrent to them. Participants may deduce the researchers' central thesis and effectively challenge it. They may ask questions for which the researcher does not have good answers. They may express a high degree of pessimism about whether the research is worthwhile. They may want to know why the researcher personally wants to do this work and may not accept anything less than an honest and personal response. Participants may challenge the researcher's body language and comment on his or her general fitness to deal with their peers. The researcher may find out that he or she really cannot or does not want to deal directly with subjects on this topic.

These unpleasant problems and surprises are important opportunities to improve the proposed research as well as to improve one's skill as a researcher. What consultant focus group participants perceive about the researcher and the project should be viewed as indicators of important underlying problems in one's research—problems to be faced and corrected. Participants may indeed uncover the researcher's subjective biases in the proposed research. These biases no doubt affect the conceptualization, conduct, and interpretation of the research findings. The researcher's biases may very well mask what the researcher needs to know to devise an effective intervention or to understand the behavior of the research population.

As an alternative, one might be conceptually on the mark but may have personal habits or attitudes that will give subjects the wrong message and get in the way of obtaining valid data from them. In any case, it is useful to have information about one's biases and one's person, no matter how unpleasant, before the project begins. The difficult and unpleasant things one learns in focus groups can then be used to improve and extend both one's theory and one's methods. It may be important to ask questions in one's research interviews about issues or opinions one abhors and would not initially think to include. One may have to completely rethink, or add to, one's thesis. One may need to add a set of counterhypotheses. After the focus group, one may need to recruit others to conduct the interviews and interface with clients. The following is an illustration of how a consultant focus group improved a research project.

An Illustrative Example

In San Francisco, African American adolescents have dramatically increasing rates of the sexually transmitted disease (STD) syphilis. This is particularly alarming for two reasons. First, for any group, increasing rates of any STD indicate that the group is engaging in unprotected sex with multiple partners—a primary HIV risk behavior. Second, HIV high-risk behaviors and increasing rates of STDs precede an epidemic of AIDS infections. The Bayview Hunters Point Foundation began conducting research to determine levels of HIV risk taking and to develop ways to encourage adolescents in the community to reduce their HIV risk-taking behaviors. This research began with consultative focus groups.

The research literature provides extensive documentation that African American adolescents begin to have sexual intercourse earlier than others. This literature is primarily descriptive and provides few tested explanations. The most frequent assumptions are that poverty, peer pressure, low self-esteem, and belief that one cannot influence people and events in one's life are the primary explanations for early sexuality and subsequent STDs (Udry & Billy, 1987). It is clear from the literature that adolescents' knowledge of STDs and how to prevent them are insufficiently compelling to reduce STD risk behaviors. If we had conducted research without consultative focus groups, we would have proceeded with these assumptions as the basis of a series of hypotheses.

Through consultative focus groups with African American adolescent males, some of our assumptions were challenged. When young men were asked why they thought drugs were so pervasive in their community, several answered, "That's the way the White House wants it." Others acknowledged that they agreed, and a discussion began about the government's involvement in shipping, distributing, and marketing drugs through organized crime. Even more shocking was their view that AIDS had the same source—from the government, in its attempt to get rid of African Americans and other "undesirables." This is not what we had expected to hear, nor did we expect to get such a matter-of-fact tone and consensus on this point. The discussion leader then asked why, if they and others believed this, did they sell and use drugs? The answer was equally revealing. "People do it for the money regardless of where they think it's coming from." In addition, there was a consensus that there is rarely a distinction between drug users and dealers. "You cannot sell what you won't use." When we asked them about condom use, we got comments such as "only [gay men] wear them" or "wearing them means you've got a disease."

Many things were said in several focus groups and hours of taped discussion, but participants' comments on the origin of drugs and AIDS and attitudes toward condoms were the most revealing and had major implications for our research. Whether we agreed with them or not, this was their perception. It challenged our view and alerted us to three perspectives on AIDS and condoms that might be shared by their peers.

First, it was clear that we had to find out to what extent these attitudes existed and were representative of those of their peers. If these views were indeed common, then an AIDS education and intervention associated with the federal government might be perceived in just the opposite way to what was expected, such as that those associated with such a program are "in it for the money." Clearly, the only place an AIDS prevention program could come from and be received as legitimate would be from within the group.

Second, it was clear from many additional comments that the major barrier to AIDS prevention was participants' sense of manhood. This issue became very clear when they were asked what they would do if avoiding AIDS meant avoiding sex with multiple partners and using condoms. One participant responded that he would then "take his chances." It was clear that their sense of manhood was intricately tied to active sexuality. Their comments alerted us to the fact that this might be a more precise explanation than poverty, powerlessness, or peer pressure. In any case, we would investigate whether these additional explanations of high-risk behavior could be generalized to others in this research population. A further implication of our focus group participants' comments was that they would be extremely resistant to using condoms. If these views were shared by their peers, then an AIDS prevention intervention would have to be preceded by a change in their concept of "manhood."

Finally, the success of AIDS prevention among gay and bisexual men had resulted in our focus group participants' associating condoms and AIDS with gay men. Their own purpose for using condoms was to avoid getting their sex partners pregnant. Again, they had a revealing point for us. When asked when they would use condoms, they expressed two different views toward steady and casual sexual partners. They would use a condom with their steady partner—to avoid getting her pregnant. On the other hand, they might not use condoms with their steady partner if they were really close. In the same way, they might use a condom with a casual partner to avoid getting a sexually transmitted disease. On the other hand, these young men also reported that they might not wear condoms with a casual partner "who did not matter" to them. Despite general anticondom attitudes, there were conditions under which they would use condoms. To advocate and attain regular condom use in this population would, at a minimum, mean finding out more about their condom use and nonuse conditions. None of this would have been apparent had we not conducted consultative focus groups.

References

Blauner, R., & Wellman, D. (1982). The researcher and the researched: Decolonizing social research. In R. Smith & P. Manning (Eds.), *A handbook of social science methods.* Cambridge, MA: Ballinger.

Bullet, A. (1987). *Plagues and poxes: The rise and fall of epidemic disease.* New York: Demos.

DesJarlais, D., et al. (1985). Risk reduction for the acquired immunodeficiency syndrome among intravenous drug users. *Annals of Internal Medicine, 103,* 755-759.

Ekstrand, M., & Coates, T. (1990). Maintenance of safer sexual behaviors and predictors of risky sex: The San Francisco Men's Health Study. *American Journal of Public Health, 80,* 873-876.

Fullilove, R., et. al. (1990). Risk of sexually transmitted disease among black adolescent crack users in Oakland and San Francisco, California. *Journal of the American Medical Association, 263,* 851-855.

Hessler, R., & New, P. (1972). Toward a research commune? *Human Organization, 31,* 452-454.

Hessol, N., et al. (1989, July). *The natural history of HIV infection in a cohort of homosexual and bisexual men: Cofactors for disease progression, 1978-89.* Paper presented at the Fifth International Conference on AIDS, Montreal, Canada.

Institute of Medicine. (1988). *Confronting AIDS: Update 1988.* Washington, DC: National Academy Press.

Koch-Weser, D., & Vanderschmidt, H. (1988). *The heterosexual transmission of AIDS in Africa.* Cambridge, MA: ABT.

Miller, H., et al. (1990). *AIDS: The second decade.* Washington, DC: National Academy Press.

Morgan, D. (1988). *Focus groups as qualitative research.* Newbury Park, CA: Sage.

Office of Technology Assessment. (1988). *Does AIDS education work?* Washington, DC: U.S. Congress, Office of Technical Assessment.

Popper, K. (1968). *The logic of scientific discovery.* New York: Harper & Row.

Selik, R. (1990). Epistemologic trends of AIDS cases in the context of the 1987 revision of the case definition. In P. Volberding & M. Jacobson (Eds.), *AIDS clinical review 1990.* New York: Mercel Dekker.

Tucker, S. (1989). Adolescent patterns of communication about sexually related topics. *Adolescence, 24,* 269-278.

Turner, S., & Turner, J. (1990). *The impossible science.* Newbury Park, CA: Sage.

Udry, J., & Billy, J. (1987). The initiation of coitus in early adolescence. *American Sociological Review, 52,* 841-855.

U.S. Department of Health and Human Services, Task Force on Black and Minority Health. (1985). *Report of the Secretary's Task Force on Black and Minority Health.* Washington, DC: Government Printing Office.

PART IV

The Use of Feminist Methodologies in Researching Sensitive Topics

Because feminist researchers often study issues that are controversial or laden with emotion—such as reproductive freedom, divorce, physical and sexual abuse—they have made important contributions to the methodology of researching sensitive topics. While there is no single, unified feminist method—no feminist "how-to-recipes" as Duelli Klein (1983, p. 90) puts it—there are several principles underlying feminist research that are especially relevant to the study of sensitive topics. The chapters in this part apply and illustrate many of these.[1]

One of the most valuable contributions of feminist methodology has been its critique of traditional research practice. Central to this critique is the debunking of the myth of value-free scientific inquiry (Cook & Fonow, 1984; Reinharz, 1992; Roberts, 1981). The feminist reformulation of the research process calls for (a) open acknowledgment by the researcher of her or his assumptions, beliefs, sympathies, and biases, especially those emanating from her or his sex, race, social class, and/or sexual orientation; (b) rejection of the traditional separation of the researcher from the researched; and (c) adoption of the goals of research as consciousness-raising and empowerment.

As Rosalind Edwards points out in her chapter in this part, feminists recognize that the research process involves "double subjectivity" due to the characteristics and biases of the researcher as well as the research participants' perceptions of the research and the researcher. Both researcher and researched "place" themselves and each other and this, in turn, affects their interaction. These subjectivities are further influenced by the nature of the information the research participants are asked to reveal, which, in her study, was private and therefore sensitive. Depending on their placement of the researcher and the research, the research participants may be inhibited from or unwilling to share their ideas and experiences with the researcher.

Feminists have argued that, when both researcher and researched are women, the commonalities of experience that result from their sex helps to overcome this problem (Finch, 1984; Oakley, 1981). In addition, feminists advocate the use of self-disclosure or reciprocity on the part of the researcher not only to overcome participants' inhibitions but also to place the interaction between the researcher and researched on a "more equal footing" (Cook & Fonow, 1984; see also Melamed, 1983). Bristow and Esper (1988), for example, maintain that self-disclosure promotes "true dialogue" rather than "interrogation" in an interview situation. Edwards's research, however, indicates that race, in particular, may be a more powerful placement factor than sex and that self-disclosure may not be sufficient to remedy the distrust that minority respondents may feel toward a white researcher (see also Reinharz, 1992). Nevertheless, Edwards does find that self-disclosure can be significant in generating solidarity among women, regardless of race or social class differences among them.

Raquel Kennedy Bergen's chapter in this part also illustrates the value of self-disclosure and reciprocity when researching sensitive topics. Kennedy Bergen allowed the participants in her study on marital rape to guide the interviews. She offered information about herself and her personal life, and she freely answered participants' questions about herself and her opinions. She encouraged the participants in her study to "talk back" to her regarding the research (see also Cook & Fonow, 1984). Rather than biasing her data in a negative sense, Kennedy Bergen argues that self-disclosure and reciprocity were essential to the success of her project.

Kennedy Bergen's chapter also speaks to a fundamental ethical concern of feminist researchers that is also prominent in research on sensitive topics: specifically, how to handle research participants' requests for or obvious need of help or assistance. Whereas, traditionally, methodology texts view requests for help as impediments to research and advise against complying with them, feminist researchers "have questioned the moral implications of *withholding* needed information" (Cook

& Fonow, 1984, p. 2; see also Oakley, 1981; Reinharz, 1992). Kennedy Bergen, like other feminist researchers (e.g., Webb, 1984), recognizes the potential harm to participants in a study on a sensitive topic and advocates adherence to a feminist ethic by offering them direct assistance, which in her case was emotional support, counseling, and referral. Thus she also blurs "the distinction between the [participant's] role as subject and as human being" (Reinharz, 1992, p. 264).

Feminist researchers also have been credited with developing a variety of innovative methodologies, including the use of visual imagery, group diaries, drama, conversation and textual analysis, associative writing, and genealogy and network tracing (Cook & Fonow, 1984; Reinharz, 1992). These methodological techniques often are particularly appropriate for research on sensitive topics. Gillian Bendelow's chapter in this part illustrates this well.

In studying gendered notions of pain, Bendelow used a methodological strategy popular among feminist researchers—triangulation (see Cook & Fonow, 1984; Reinharz, 1992). By using three different data collection techniques—questionnaires, in-depth interviews, and visual imagery depicting various types of pain experiences—Bendelow enlarged her data base and also discovered that the use of an unconventional method can be especially helpful in eliciting information about a private, sensitive topic, such as pain. Bendelow reports that the use of visual imagery gave her respondents "an acceptable way of talking about the private in public" and was often therapeutic not only for them but for her as well. At the same time, the visual materials became "equalizers" in the research process; regardless of the reading or writing skills of individual participants, all except one (who had a visual impairment) were able to articulate opinions about the pictures they viewed—opinions, Bendelow notes, that were "very rich and philosophically profound."

The use of visual imagery as a research tool is relatively new and, as Bendelow indicates, requires some refinement. Nevertheless, this technique, along with the other innovative methods pioneered by feminist researchers, hold considerable promise for the study of sensitive topics.

Note

1. This part introduction is too brief to fully discuss all the central features of feminist methodology and clearly does not do justice to the rich debate that has characterized the

development of feminist methodologies. For a more thorough treatment of both of these topics, see Bowles and Duelli Klein (1983) and Reinharz (1992).

References

Bowles, G., & Duelli Klein, R. (Eds.). (1983). *Theories of women's studies.* London: Routledge & Kegan Paul.

Bristow, A. R., & Esper, J. A. (1988). A feminist research ethos. In the Nebraska Sociological Feminist Collective (Eds.), *A feminist ethic for social science research.* New York: Edwin Mellen.

Cook, J., & Fonow, M. (1984). Knowledge and women's interests: Issues of epistemology and methodology in feminist sociological research. *Sociological Inquiry, 56,* 2-29.

Duelli Klein, R. (1983). How to do what we want to do: Thoughts about feminist methodology. In G. Bowles & R. Duelli Klein (Eds.), *Theories of women's studies.* London: Routledge & Kegan Paul.

Finch, J. (1984). "It's great to have someone to talk to": The ethics and politics of interviewing women. In C. Bell & H. Roberts (Eds.), *Social researching: Politics, problems, practice.* London: Routledge & Kegan Paul.

Melamed, E. (1983). *Mirror, mirror: The terror of not being young.* New York: Simon & Schuster.

Oakley, A. (1981). Interviewing women: A contradiction in terms. In H. Roberts (Ed.), *Doing feminist research.* London: Routledge & Kegan Paul.

Reinharz, S. (1992). *Feminist methods in social research.* New York: Oxford University Press.

Roberts, H. (Ed.). (1981). *Doing feminist research.* London: Routledge & Kegan Paul.

Webb, C. (1984). Feminist methodology in nursing research. *Journal of Advanced Nursing, 9,* 249-256.

11

An Education in Interviewing

Placing the Researcher and the Research

ROSALIND EDWARDS

The privacy of family life and couple relationships is something that retains an especially strong currency. In particular, there is a general acceptance that domestic problems, conflicts, and tensions should be kept within "the family." Researchers often remark upon the strength of the norms of privacy as an obstacle in investigating family life and relationships (for example, Allan & Crow, 1990; Clark & Haldane, 1990). The idea of the domestic sphere as a fundamentally private place means that information about what goes on in it is regarded as a sensitive area of disclosure (Brannen, 1988).

Yet, the notion of a bounded family world that is *private* may not always have the same meaning for all sections of society because of the status and experiences of those groups. For instance, those espousing "traditional family values" may feel privacy and a lack of outside intervention from the apparatus of the state are necessary for the family to exist as the stable unit that they regard as the basis of society (Anderson & Dawson, 1986). For those who are working class, privacy may be bound up with notions of respectability (Allan, 1990). Black people, regarding their families as a haven from racism, may wish to keep their family lives especially private where white people and those in authority are concerned (Edwards, 1990a, 1990b).

This chapter considers the effects of these social, and political, contexts upon a research study. I explore the ways that interviews about a private, and therefore sensitive, subject can be made more, or less, sensitive by the sex, race, class, and educational experiences of both the researcher and the researched. In particular, I show how the process of the "placing" of the research and the researcher on the part of those interviewed can point up issues of wider significance.

The Research Study

The research on which this chapter is based involved repeated in-depth interviews with 31 women from different races and classes. The women were all at various stages of a full-time social science degree and were drawn from two universities and three polytechnics in the southeast of England. Each woman had at least one child who was either below school age or in full-time education. In addition, at least upon starting their degree courses, they had a long-term male partner. Most of the women were married or in cohabiting relationships akin to marriage upon commencing their studies, but several were in long-term relationships where their partners did not live with them permanently. The women defined their own status in terms of whether they considered themselves working class, middle class, black, or white. Of the white women, 10 referred to themselves as middle class and 12 as working class. Six women described themselves as black and one as black working class. Two others were of "mixed" race parentage and did not feel "black" or of a social class.

My research involved asking these mature mother-students about their experiences of gaining a higher education. (See Edwards, 1991, for the full study.) I wanted to explore their subjective experiences: how they interpreted, understood, and defined family and education in their lives. As part of this, I asked the women about the effects of their education on their relationships with their partners. In interviewing the women, and in fact in all stages of the study, I was guided by my understanding of a particular feminist methodology—a theory and analysis of how research should proceed—that has certain characteristics. These characteristics are primarily concerned with differing facets of the involvement of the researcher in the research as well the subjects of the research. This methodology seemed especially appropriate for this particular piece of research conducted by this particular researcher—I had been a mature undergraduate with family responsibilities myself. This chapter therefore examines my attempts to use a particular type of feminist methodology and method: "reciprocal" in-depth interviewing.

Feminist Methods and Methodology

Most writers on feminist research issues agree that there is no one method that can be termed *the* feminist methodology. Nevertheless, qualitative methods, and in-depth interviews as a method of gathering data in particular, have tended to be associated with feminist research. They seem to represent what Hilary Graham refers to as "a female style of knowing" (Graham, 1983, p. 136) and what Dorothy Smith calls "the standpoint of women" (Smith, 1987, p. 105). Moreover, particular topics of interest in my study—the women's family lives and patterns of power in their partner relationships—have been argued to be less accessible using the more "public" methods of surveys or statistical presentations (Graham, 1983).

At the root of the methodology I employed for my research is a critique of objectivity—of the supposed rational, detached, value-free research as traditionally espoused. Many feminists have argued that the unconscious bias of the male-defined intellectual position, which holds that the judgment of the researcher and the perspective of the subject are necessarily separate processes, is a political myth that creates invisible distortions (Bowles & Duelli Klein, 1983; Ferree & Hess, 1987; Harding, 1987; Smith, 1987; Stanley & Wise, 1983). In its place, some have called for an explicit investment of the researcher in the research and a conception of both researcher and researched as parts of a larger social "whole." From this critique, I have elsewhere distilled (Edwards, 1990a) three linked principles that are of importance at all stages of research, from conceptualization through to production.

First, women's experiences (varying according to ethnicity, social status, and so on) are important and, to understand them, women's lives need to be addressed in their own terms. There is a relationship between what goes on in the variety of women's lives at an individual level and the way society is structured at a more general level. Second, the aim of a feminist inquiry must be to provide explanations of women's lives that are useful to them as an instrument to improve their situations. An aim of such research is therefore to ensure that women's experiences are not objectified and treated merely as research fodder. Third, the

researcher is a central part of the research process and her own feelings
and experience should be analyzed as an integral part of it. This location
of self by the researcher may occur in two related ways. On an intellectual level, the researcher should make explicit the reasoning procedures
she used in carrying out her research. In addition, on what is often called
a "reflexive" level, the class, race, sex, assumptions, and beliefs of
the researcher must be available for scrutiny and must be explicated in
terms of their effects upon the research and upon analysis. I will also
be arguing that these understandings, when placed alongside the respondents' social characteristics and assumptions, can be especially
illuminating.

An implicit assumption in the feminist literature on methodology, and
an explicit one in much of the feminist literature on interviewing, is that
women researchers (and feminist women researchers in particular) have
some special sort of nonhierarchical woman-to-woman link with their
female interview subjects—a two-way rather than the traditional one-
way relationship. Anne Oakley (1981) and Janet Finch (1984) both posit
a cultural affinity between women interviewers and the women they are
interviewing because they "share a subordinate structural position by
virtue of their gender" (Finch, 1984, p. 76). Finch argues that her interviewees wanted to "place" her as a woman, "expecting me to understand what they mean simply because I am another woman" (p. 76).
They, and others, write of the readiness with which women have talked
to them about private matters (e.g., Graham, 1984). Feminist researchers have made important points with regard to woman-to-woman situations and have brought to light considerations that enhance our understanding of the effects of the shared characteristic of sex on the research
process. If, however, we accept that there are structurally based divisions between women on the basis of race and/or class that may lead
them to have some different interests and priorities, then what has been
said about woman-to-woman interviewing may not apply in all situations. It certainly did not in my research, as will be elaborated below.
In addition, I have explored these experiences and some of the issues
arising from them elsewhere (Edwards, 1990a).

Moreover, while still retaining the nonhierarchical woman-to-woman
link, some feminists (e.g., Griffin, 1987; Thorogood, 1987) have attributed to the open-ended interview an ability to help counter any implicit
racism on the part of white researchers. It is argued that, because this
method of gathering data allows women to speak for themselves, it can
avoid producing data that "pathologize" black women. For Thorogood,

for example, making black women's perceptions and experiences central to the data gathering and interpretation was a way in which the imposition of her assumptions and values could be countered. The same could be argued with regard to assumptions held by researchers relating to class or, in fact, any type of prior conceptions of respondents' lives held by researchers. Nevertheless, the caveat must be added that this is not such a simple process as it may appear. Collecting loosely structured accounts of women's lives is not just a matter of collecting data that already exist external to the researcher.

"Double Subjectivity"

Although my interviews were designed to allow the women's own perspectives to emerge, researchers are not just "recording instruments" through which subjects are able to make visible their personal experiences. While I tried my best not to prejudge the research process by defining its boundaries too closely and by allowing the women's definitions to emerge on their own terms, it must be recognized that the researcher is not simply a straightforward receptacle for the views of others. The researcher is a "variable" in the interview process in several ways. Researchers bring their own life experiences to their research, and they structure what the research is about. Therefore the topics are legitimately up for discussion and analysis—however unstructured the interviews are themselves. More important for the discussion here, interviewing itself is an interactive process. The women's accounts were the result of their interactions with me. The particular occasion for the telling of their stories was my intervention as a researcher. Moreover, their stories were also slanted by their perceptions of myself and the research.

Where people are the subjects of research, their views of the researcher and of the research itself will affect their responses and behavior. The whole research process is, as Jane Lewis and Barbara Meredith put it, subject to "double subjectivity" (Lewis & Meredith, 1988, p. 16): that of the respondent and that of the researcher. This, crosscut with the women's feelings about the private nature of their family lives, had several important effects upon this research, as outlined below. Rather than ignoring or minimizing them, the presence of such double subjectivities can be used and understood as part of the research process. To bring this to the fore, and to aid consideration of its effects upon the research, my final interviews with the women were concluded with some questions exploring how they had felt about taking part. In addition, to see what effects self-disclosure would have, I used my own mature student experiences. While interviewing the women, I did not enter into a great deal of discussion or exchange information about myself unless asked to do so, over and above the "placing" process described below. The latter involved the woman interviewed knowing I had been a mature undergraduate student with a family. Once the main part of the interview process was over, however, I initiated a much more explicit self-disclosure. Each of the women was given the same written account of my "family-education" experiences to read. These included the effects of my studies upon my relationship with my husband as well as other experiences.

The sharing of yourself—reciprocity—with the women who are the subjects of your research has also been a feature of much feminist writing on methodology and interviewing. This sharing is recommended to reduce the exploitative power balance between researcher and subject (Graham, 1984), to show solidarity between women (Oakley, 1981), and also, more instrumentally, because self-disclosure on the part of the researcher helps elicit more information from the subject. Oakley appears to take both "solidarity" and "instrumentality" positions. She argues that feminist researchers should seek to equalize the relationship with the women they interview as part of their commitment to sisterhood. She also says, despite her objection to an instrumental attitude to the interview, that a nonhierarchical relationship and personal involvement on the part of the researcher is required to reach the goal of being admitted to interviewees' lives. My own experiences, however, do not confirm this instrumental aspect but do throw some light upon the solidarity factor. In particular, it is relevant to the women's feelings about their disclosure of "private" information during the interviews.

A Sensitive Subject

Asking the women about their family lives, especially their relationships with their partners, meant that I was, in most cases, asking them about a private and sensitive area of their lives. This was indicated to me in both general and specific ways.

Many of the women seemed to recognize an invisible wall around their family lives. *Outside* was a word often used in the accounts of people and places in relation to family and home. The family as a separate unit, into which intrusions from those outside of it were not wanted, was referred to, and some also talked of "my private life." It was most often their relationships with men that, as David Clark and Douglas Haldane (Clark & Haldane, 1990) have suggested, were regarded as the ultimate privacy. For example, speaking of using her own life experiences as illustration in seminar discussion, Anne said:

> I mean, you know, your married life with your husband, things like that, I don't bring that up in the class. That's my business. On the other hand, things like unemployment or being on sickness benefit for a long time, the fact that I was divorced before I married Ivor and I spent some time as a single parent, you're talking in very general terms. You're just skimming off the top I suppose.

What went on inside the family was, however, felt to be less a matter for privacy by some women. Sandra, for instance, had frequently asked priests, her husband's employer, and friends to intervene in her marriage and to back her up in her efforts to get her husband to stay at home and be more involved in family life—unsuccessfully, both in terms of getting some of them to do it and in this having any effect upon his behavior.

Nevertheless, inviting a researcher into your home to talk about these matters specifically is not necessarily the same as other sorts of social interactions. (But see Jane Ribbens, 1989, for a discussion of the complexities of this.) Referring to the interview process, several women assured me, when asked how they felt about being interviewed, that I had not been "intrusive," including a few who had referred to themselves as "open" people. When it came to being interviewed about their "private lives," the women's willingness to talk about this subject could be made more, or less, sensitive by their "placing" of myself as the researcher and their perceptions of the research.

"Placing" the Researcher and the Research: Race and Class

Among other factors, racial, class, and sex differences and similarities enter into the consciousness of individuals and groups and determine their conceptions of themselves and others as well as their status in the community. This has implications for the process of research. Such social characteristics assist both the researcher and the subject to "place" each other within the social structure and therefore have a bearing on the relationship between them (Burgess, 1986). Differences of race, in particular, were infused in the process of this research in much the same way that others have argued that shared sex is.

In the first instance, I had difficulty in actually getting black mature mother-students to take part in the research. Indeed, some of them were angry about being asked to take part in the research and complained about it to their course director. For the black women I contacted, education institutions were regarded as white middle-class places (Edwards, 1990a, 1990b), and the people associated with them were white and middle class. When I contacted black women through the education institution, I became that institution—placed as white, middle class, and oppressive just by the use of an instutitional letterhead—no matter what my sex. This was despite my hoping to signal in my initial contacting letter to the women the basis for a nonhierarchical relationship and placing myself through writing as interested in doing the research because I had been a mature student myself.

The way the black women felt can be illustrated by Irene's remarks when she told me how she had reacted to being asked to take part in the research:

> I think about it before, as I say, a lot before I agreed to take part. And also wonder what does she want, you know. . . . And then I thought I don't want to go into it. [The polytechnic] didn't do anything for me, so why should I do anything—maybe making a connection between you and [the polytechnic]. Why should I bother, you know?

A relationship of woman-to-woman affinity was not something easily established on the basis of our shared sex alone. My status as a white person attached to a public institution was what placed me—and it placed me in a negative way. Unlike the experiences reported by other feminist researchers, I had to take very direct initiatives to place myself as a woman because the black women who agreed to take part in the research were not initially willing to do the placing for me in any way other than race. Black women's attitudes to the research and to myself alerted me to the way race structured their perceptions of certain aspects of their lives, especially with regard to their place as students in the education institution. The length and multiple nature of the interviews helped overcome their wariness and enabled us to establish rapport, as did my overt acknowledgment during the interviews of the difference between us on the basis of race and its ramifications in terms of my ability to understand what was said to me (something I did because I noted it helped establish rapport, not hinder it). Even so, the black women I interviewed were not always at ease discussing their family relationships with me.

I did not have quite the same experiences with the other women I interviewed, including the women of "mixed" race. Both of the latter, in fact, had one white parent and relationships with white men. As Marcia put it, "I'm in the middle. But I'm more in a white world now." I found that white middle-class women were willing to discuss "private" family matters with me without me having to place myself. Indeed, Julia Brannen (1988) has also noted the way that middle-class women are quick to realize shared status and assumptions with middle-class women researchers. For example, Madeline said: "I mean I don't know very much about you but I feel that you sort of—I mean obviously because you're interested in it, you've had a family, you've got children. . . ."

White working-class women sometimes showed a slight wariness until placing had occurred (i.e., they had asked for, or I had volunteered, information about my partner and child-rearing status) and then also talked freely. What is interesting here is that, after an initial hesitation, the white women seemed to want to share a social similarity with me rather than to look for difference, as did the women of "mixed" race to a certain extent. A typical response from white working-class women to my questions on how they felt about taking part in the research was the one made by Michelle:

> I mean in the best, in the best traditions of Anne Oakley, had I not felt that you were the kind of person that I could talk to anyway, then I probably wouldn't have agreed to the second interview. . . . I think if it had been someone that was, I don't know, perhaps different from me, say, then I probably wouldn't have done.

Indeed, being the same as, or set apart from, other people was an important theme in various forms in most of the women's accounts of being a mature mother-student, and it recurred throughout the interviews. Among other things, it structured the women's experiences as students.

Academic Understandings

The women could feel themselves as different, or even deviant, as students within the higher education system in various ways (see

Edwards, 1990b). They did not fit the image of the "proper," traditional student. These feelings may well have affected their attitudes toward taking part in the research and telling me about the effects of their education on their partner relationships. In particular, the black women's sense of difference tended to be as black rather than as women with families, as was the case with the white women. Their race and issues surrounding racism often became even more central to them because they were learning about them as part of their degrees. This enhanced awareness, however, could leave them with the feeling that the subjects that were central to their lives and perceptions were not tackled deeply enough.

Some also expressed a feeling that they were under surveillance as blacks:

> The first thing I looked to see how many colored students failed to the proportion of white students. . . . 'Cos I always think they would tend to think well, we did try with the colored students and we had a five percent failure, you know. . . . Because I always believe that we are under constant scrutiny. Probably we are not. I don't know if we are. But constantly I have that feeling, you know. I don't know why I feel like that. I think the onus on you is to do even better to be accepted at their standard, you know what I mean? (Val)

These perceptions, when placed alongside their reactions to being asked to take part in my research, help indicate why the black women should feel especially sensitive about trusting me, a white academic, with private and personal details.

While issues concerning social class were also part of their degree study, this did not appear to become the overwhelming issue for the white working-class women in the same way. Indeed, they could end up feeling that they were not "doing things properly" if they saw issues concerning class differently than the lecturers. In the main, the white working-class and middle-class women tended to give me their opinions on "women's issues" as part of what they were learning and to see motherhood as their "deviancy" from "proper" studentship.

Consideration of the effect of education also illustrates another set of understandings the women interviewed brought to the research. As students in higher education, they were all familiar with academic research texts. Some white women (although, interestingly, none of the black women) mentioned Oakley's work in connection with explaining to me how they felt about taking part in the research or in discussing what the finished product might be like. This could explain why they looked for similarities between us—much of white feminist writing having stressed women's shared position.

Several research texts mention that those being interviewed by researchers are entering a situation that is new and unfamiliar to them. Ken Plummer (1983), for example, says that it is often difficult for subjects to grasp what is entailed, particularly in the case of the more open and fluid types of interviews where they are often expected to lead rather than merely respond to a series of cues from a questionnaire. The women interviewed for this study, however, were familiar with academic research studies and texts. They knew what our respective roles should be:

> I've often thought how do your feel about, you know—I've wanted to ask you "well, how do you feel about it?" Obviously, I haven't because I think, you know, I think had I . . . I think you were quite right to sit there and not—your views would have influenced perhaps what I'd said, what I could say. (Jenny)

Reciprocity and Self-Disclosure

Those women who had wanted to know about my own experiences but felt it "illegitimate" to ask me about them had their curiosity satisfied at the end of my last interview with them, when I handed them the account of my own experiences. To some extent, it was, at this point, a "controlled" self-disclosure, in that only what was written down was revealed and each women had access to the same "revelations." The majority of the women tended to make comments on my experiences as they read. There were many smiles, and nods, and exclamations such as, "God, it's amazing!" The account also often sparked questions about my experience: "And what about your husband now? I mean how does he view it all now?" "Did you get very moody then?" It led to discussions about how their and my experiences compared, ranging in type from "I didn't have this" to "I thought it was only me. I didn't know if it affected other people like that as well"—sometimes both from the same person. There were also reiterations of things they had already told me in previous interviews. A few women, however, just made a brief comment and we passed on to discuss things such as protecting their anonymity within the study.

This self-disclosure, coming at the end of the interviews, did not in fact elicit any extra data, in terms of sensitive private information from the women. It did, however, have three important effects. First, the self-disclosure gave permission for the research "rules," of which the women were so aware, to be broken: "I must admit sort of, you know, when I was talking to you I wondered, you know, whether you was sort of the same" (Wendy). The women's varying degrees of curiosity about me were allowed to be given vent. While some asked very few questions about me, others asked a great deal and so came to know a lot more. In other words, in the end, the amount of my own self-disclosure varied from woman to woman.

Second, it often increased or confirmed the sense of identification the white women looked for with me but in this case also included the black women. All the women indicated at least some feelings or experiences that we shared. This leads to the third—and, to some feminists, probably the most important—aspect of using self-disclosure. Many women made the link between our two shared experiences and a wider sense of solidarity with those in the same situation:

> That was really interesting. 'Cos it made me realize that probably the things that I felt maybe the majority of people—well, not all the things, but there seems to be a very common thread, doesn't it, between all these things? (Victoria)

These "common threads" in the women's accounts are an integral and inevitable result of the situation whereby they are women who are trying to combine family and education. Their position within, and the values of, each institution create these common themes, even as the women's race and class produce differences within their situations (Edwards, 1991).

Some of those writing about in-depth interviewing on sensitive subjects express concern about the way this type of interaction can upset and cause emotional harm to those interviewed, and a few consider the emotional load this can place on the researcher as well. Judith Stacey has challenged other feminists' ideas of reciprocity, empathy, and mutuality within the woman-to-woman in-depth interviewing situation and has reminded researchers that it "represents an intrusion and intervention into a system of relationships, a system of relationships that the researcher is far freer than the researched to leave" (Stacey, 1988, p. 23). At its most extreme, after an interview, the subject may be left with her emotional life in pieces and no one to help put them back together—a situation that Clark and Haldane have graphically termed the "scientific equivalent of slash and burn agriculture" (Clark & Haldane, 1990, p. 143). From the other side, both Clark and Haldane (1990), and Brannen (1988), note not only the vulnerability of the interviewee but also that of the interviewer. Brannen feels that in one-to-one situations it is easy for the researcher to be drawn into the interviewee's problems without the same sorts of supportive systems that would be available to a counselor. This can lead to emotional exhaustion on the part of the interviewer. Certainly some of the women I talked to were either in, or close to, tears during parts of their interviews, and certainly I found this disturbing and wondered what on earth I was doing to them and to me. Janice, for example, indicated that my questions about certain areas of her life had left her feeling disturbed for days:

> The first interview was the most uncomfortable one I have ever experienced. I felt I needed to say it but I was saying, I felt, such horrible things that I felt about other people and my family that I felt awful. And I was quite worried for about two or three days afterwards, thinking shall I come out 'cos can I cope with this? But at the end of the day I thought no, because it's something I've experienced and it's something I have the right to say. I mean the second one I didn't feel terribly uncomfortable about at all. Certain aspects of this one have made me feel uncomfortable. [RE: Is that, do you think, related to particular areas?] It's because it's related to my husband and my children.

To overcome this disturbance of equilibrium, some writers advocate a final "debriefing" for interviewees. For instance, Paul Thompson recommends remaining a while after the interview is over to "give a little of yourself" (Thompson, 1988, p. 211). I would suggest that in situations where this is possible—situations where the researcher's own experiences may have some bearing—it is not "topics of general interest" that help restore equilibrium but topics of *particular* interest. The "giving of yourself" may be especially important.

Furthermore (taking an instrumental attitude myself), these are not interactions that take place after the collection of data but are themselves important contributions to understanding. In instances such as this, my attempts at self-disclosure, because of their "solidarity" potential, may well have proved beneficial. After she had read through my autobiographical piece, Janice remarked:

> Well that, that in a sense, because they're so similar, has actually helped, because I realized that my feelings are not me. So in a sense I don't feel isolated. I can relate what you've experienced to what I've experienced. And the

similarities that are there actually make it easier for what I've said. So that actually helped. It puts it on a more human footing.

Janice's earlier comments on feeling uncomfortable during some aspects of the interviews again reveal the strength of the norms of privacy and loyalty with regard to one's family life and relationships. As Katherine Gieve writes of her edited collection of women's accounts of combining paid work and motherhood: "Telling the story of one's life as a mother means telling the story of the lives of children and perhaps a partner. Each of the authors has had to find a balance between privacy and revelation" (Gieve, 1989, p. xii). This was so for the women in my own study. If they felt uncomfortable because the balance had tipped too far toward revelation, my own self-disclosures may have helped legitimate theirs. My revelations may have restored these women's equilibrium by shifting its axis and may have ended the interviews in a positive way.

Ribbens (1989) argues that researchers using open-ended interview methods need to be sensitive and able to take cues from the person being interviewed: suiting the interviewing style to the individual concerned. In cases where the subjects of research and the researcher herself share some aspects of their experiences, especially where these are sensitive and marginal (in this case, the marginality of being a mature mother-student), this style can include self-disclosure. Researchers may need to recognize that, under some circumstances, self-disclosure can help lessen any disturbing effects of a respondent's own disclosures on a sensitive research topic.

Conclusion

The reactions to my own self-disclosure, combined with the different way I had to go about interviewing black women (i.e., directly placing myself and overtly acknowledging racial difference) lead me to argue that researchers conducting in-depth interviews should not be so concerned with making sure that what goes into every interview is the same to ensure "reliability" and "validity." They should, instead, work toward ensuring that what comes out is the same in quality. That is, not in terms of content but in terms of gaining a validly re/constructed re/presentation of "what is" for each subject's situation and her understanding of it.

The collection of these understandings in the form of interviews is, as I have shown, subject to the subjectivities of both the researcher and the researched. Researchers need to recognize that their own sex, race and class, and other social characteristics, in interaction with the interviewees' own social characteristics and experiences, can increase or lessen the sensitivity of their research topics. This may happen in unexpected ways, with respondents assigning social characteristics to the researcher, or giving a particular weighting to certain of them, that are not necessarily congruent with researchers' own perceptions of those characteristics. They are influenced by interviewees' own experiences and understandings as are their assumptions about the research. Such "placings" and assumptions may be particularistic, but they can also give researchers pointers to the ways in which groups of people construct and make sense of their lives in circumstances other than the interview itself.

References

Allan, G. (1990). Insiders and outsiders: Boundaries around the home. In G. Allan & G. Crow (Eds.), *Home and family: Creating the domestic sphere*. Basingstoke, UK: Macmillan.

Allan, G., & Crow, G. (Eds.). (1990). *Home and family: Creating the domestic sphere*. Basingstoke, UK: Macmillan.

Anderson, D., & Dawson, G. (Eds.). (1986). *Family portraits*. London: Social Affairs Unit.

Bell, C., & Roberts, H. (Eds.). (1984). *Social researching: Politics, problems, and practice*. London: Routledge & Kegan Paul.

Bowles, G., & Duelli Klein, R. (Eds.). (1983). *Theories of women's studies*. London: Routledge & Kegan Paul.

Brannen, J. (1988). The study of sensitive subjects. *Sociological Review, 36*, 552-563.

Burgess, R. G. (Ed.). (1986). *Key variables in social investigation*. London: Routledge & Kegan Paul.

Clark, D., & Haldane, D. (1990). *Wedlocked?* Cambridge, UK: Polity.

Edwards, R. (1990a). Connecting method and epistemology: A white woman interviewing black women. *Women's Studies International Forum, 13*, 477-490.

Edwards, R. (1990b). Access and assets: The experiences of mature mother-students in higher education. *Journal of Access Studies, 5*, 188-202.

Edwards, R. (1991). *Degrees of difference: Family and education in the lives of mature mother-students*. Unpublished doctoral thesis, South Bank Polytechnic/CNAA.

Ferree, M. M., & Hess, B. B. (1987). Introduction. In B. B. Hess & M. M. Ferree (Eds.), *Analyzing gender: A handbook of social science research*. London: Sage.

Finch, J. (1984). "It's great to have someone to talk to": The ethnics and politics of interviewing women. In C. Bell & H. Roberts (Eds.), *Social researching*. London: Routledge & Kegan Paul.

Gieve, K. (1989). Introduction. In K. Gieve (Ed.), *Balancing acts: On being a mother.* London: Virago.

Graham, H. (1983). Do her answers fit his questions? Women and the survey method. In E. Gamarnikow, D. Morgan, J. Purvis, & D. Taylorson (Eds.), *The public and the private.* London: Heinemann.

Graham, H. (1984). Surveying through stories. In C. Bell & H. Roberts (Eds.), *Social researching.* London: Routledge & Kegan Paul.

Griffin, C. (1987). Young women and the transition from school to un/employment: A cultural analysis. In G. Weiner & M. Arnot (Eds.), *Gender under scrutiny: New inquiries in education.* London: Hutchinson.

Harding, S. (1987). Introduction: Is there a feminist method? In S. Harding (Ed.), *Feminism and methodology.* Milton Keynes, UK: Open University Press.

Lewis, J., & Meredith, B. (1988). *Daughters who care: Daughters caring for mothers at home.* London: Routledge & Kegan Paul.

Oakley, A. (1981). Interviewing women: A contradiction in terms. In H. Roberts (Ed.), *Doing feminist research.* London: Routledge & Kegan Paul.

Plummer, K. (1983). *Documents of life: An introduction to the problems and literature of a humanistic method.* London: Allen & Unwin.

Ribbens, J. (1989). Interviewing women—an unnatural situation? *Women's Studies International Forum, 12,* 529-597.

Smith, D. E. (1987). *The everyday world as problematic: A feminist sociology.* Boston: Northeastern University Press.

Stacey, J. (1988). Can there be a feminist ethnography? *Women's Studies International Forum, 11,* 21-27.

Stanley, L., & Wise, S. (1983). *Breaking out: Feminist consciousness and feminist research.* London: Routledge & Kegan Paul.

Thompson, P. (1988). *The voice of the past: Oral history.* Oxford: Oxford University Press.

Thorogood, N. (1987). Race, class and gender: The politics of housework. In J. Brannen & G. Wilson (Eds.), *Give and take in families: Studies in resource distribution.* London: Allen & Unwin.

12

Interviewing Survivors of Marital Rape

Doing Feminist Research on Sensitive Topics

RAQUEL KENNEDY BERGEN

Marital rape is a horrifying ordeal that approximately 2 million women experience each year in the United States (Bidwell & White, 1986). Due to the sensitive nature of this problem, however, relatively little is known about the victims of marital rape or their assailants. Marital rape is a sensitive topic primarily because of the threat, both emotional and potentially physical, that speaking about their sexual abuse poses to survivors of marital rape. This chapter will explore how my research with survivors of marital rape was influenced by the sensitivity of the topic and my own feminist agenda.

In the course of this chapter, I will briefly discuss the sensitive nature of marital rape, central themes in feminist research, and some problems I have encountered while interviewing women about marital rape. I will argue that the application of feminist principles to the interview method is an excellent way to conduct research on sensitive issues. Primarily because feminist principles require us to scrutinize our methods more carefully, we can avoid many ethical dilemmas, such as exploitation and deception, that historically have plagued social scientists (Duelli

Klein, 1983). Rather than revealing definitive answers to the methodological questions that sensitive topics pose to researchers, this chapter
will attempt to contribute to the growing dialogue by discussing some
of the difficulties I faced and how I addressed them.

The Sensitive Nature of Marital Rape

Recently, increasing attention has been focused on the nature of conducting socially sensitive research (Lee & Renzetti, this volume; Sieber
& Stanley, 1988; Stanley, Sieber, & Melton, 1987). Lee and Renzetti define
sensitive topics as those that have potential costs (or threats) to the participant and the researcher. They also identify several areas of research
that are likely to be sensitive, including research of a sexual nature and
that which examines the private sphere, deals with the sacred, and "impinges on the vested interest of powerful people." Marital rape is sensitive both in meeting the criteria set forth by Lee and Renzetti and
because, commonsensically, it is a difficult issue for both survivors of
marital rape and the general public to address.

Marital rape is a sensitive topic primarily because of the potential
threat it poses to the women who agree to share their experiences with
a researcher. Speaking about their experiences of rape is emotionally
traumatic for women who, to a greater or lesser extent, must relive these
experiences and uncover unpleasant memories. Those survivors who
have come to terms with their experiences and have moved forward in
their lives are asked to reopen old wounds. Those who are still suffering
severe emotional trauma may experience heightened anxiety and mis-
ery by speaking in detail about the rapes (Russell, 1990). In my study,
several women reported experiencing flashbacks, loss of sleep, and increased tension as a result of the interview, which raises important ethical
questions for researching sensitive areas.[1]

Speaking of their experiences of marital rape is also potentially
life-threatening for the women involved in the research process. In her
study of marital rape, Diana Russell (1990) found that many women
were hesitant to disclose information about their experiences for fear
that their husbands would read the information and try to harm them.
Studies indicate that approximately 15% to 20% of victims are raped
after they separate from their husbands and, for many, the threat of separation is the factor that triggers the first incident (Finkelhor & Yllo,
1985; Frieze, 1983; Russell, 1990). Similarly, several of the women in

my study had been physically and/or sexually assaulted after they divorced their husbands and wanted their anonymity maintained to prevent their ex-husbands from acting vengefully.

While the threats to the women themselves were much greater, this study also posed a potential threat to me as a researcher. The threat existed primarily because the interviews most frequently took place in the homes of the participants, which could have been visited by the (ex-) husbands themselves. For the most part, I felt safe conducting the interviews; however, the possible threat of angry men finding me interviewing their (ex-)wives about their experiences was sometimes daunting.

While the potential emotional and physical threats marital rape survivors face are the primary reason for the sensitivity of the topic, the study of marital rape is threatening in other ways as well. First, the study of marital rape is sensitive because it poses a threat to one of this society's most sacred institutions—the private sexual relationship of a husband and wife. By its very definition, the term *marital rape* confirms that a husband (or wife) does not have unlimited sexual access to his or her spouse's body as historically has been assumed within the marriage contract (Finkelhor & Yllo, 1985). That a spouse can be prosecuted for such a violation threatens ideals about the marriage contract and is potentially threatening to those individuals with a vested interest in it. Of course, those most threatened by a law prohibiting forced sex in marriage are husbands who use their marital contract as a "license to rape" (Finkelhor & Yllo, 1985).

Research on marital rape is also threatening because it delves into the private sphere, which is often perceived as sacred. The family has historically represented a haven of love and affection, a private sphere absent of the violence that characterizes larger society and free from outside interference (Lasch, 1977). In particular, the sexual relationship of a married couple has been traditionally constructed as a private one not to be discussed with outsiders (Kinsey, Pomeroy, & Martin, 1948). Thus research that reveals marital rape as a horrifying and brutal act is certainly sensitive because it poses a threat to the ideology of the family and implies that public interference in the form of legislation is necessary.

Some writers (e.g., MacIntyre, 1982) would presumably argue that a topic such as marital rape is too threatening to explore. MacIntyre (p. 188) writes that it is necessary that "certain areas of personal and social life should be especially protected. Intimacy cannot exist where everything is disclosed." Other researchers, presumably most feminists and other social scientists who study sensitive issues, would argue that topics should be fully explored regardless of their sensitivity because the goal of research is "that of discerning and uncovering the actual facts of [people's] lives and experience, facts that have been hidden, inaccessible, suppressed, distorted, misunderstood, ignored" (DuBois, 1983).

Indeed, uncovering the hidden and exploitive aspects of women's lives has been the focus of much feminist research, thus feminists have a history of involvement with sensitive topics. Feminists and others who research sensitive issues often face common research dilemmas, such as preserving the anonymity of hidden populations, collecting information that is potentially threatening, and applying findings to the "real world" that are potentially detrimental. In this chapter, I will argue that the feminist research model is a particularly useful one for resolving many of the research dilemmas that arise with sensitive topics.

Feminist Research

During the past decade, feminist social scientists have focused a critical eye on the methodological and epistemological questions of doing research (Acker, Barry, & Esseveld, 1983; DuBois, 1983; Duelli Klein, 1983; Finch, 1984; Harding, 1987; Mies, 1983; Oakley, 1981; Stacey, 1988). This chapter will not attempt to debate whether or not a distinctively feminist methodology should exist.[2] Nor do I wish to imply that a single coherent body of "feminist principles" governs feminist scholarship. Instead, I will address some general goals of feminism and several trends that currently dominate feminist research in the social sciences.

Feminist research is, above all else, woman centered. Succinctly stated, "Feminist scholarship . . . puts women at the center of research that is nonalienating, nonexploitive, and potentially emancipating" (Sculley, 1990, pp. 2-3). Rather than just "adding women" to the traditional, androcentric perspective of reality, "one distinctive feature of feminist research is that it generates its problematics from the perspective of women's experiences" (Harding, 1987, p. 7). By starting with the private experiences of women, feminists explore how "personal" problems are the result of structured gender inequality. Most significant, feminist researchers are not only involved in gathering knowledge about women's experiences but implement this knowledge by actively working with other women to transform the economic and social conditions that oppress all women (Cook & Fonow, 1984).

Duelli Klein persuasively argues that feminists want their research to "differ from patriarchal scholarship and to that end we have to think about how we are going to do what we want to do" (1983, p. 88). Certainly feminists use the same basic methods for collecting data that androcentric sociologists have used—observation, content analysis, experimentation, historical analysis, comparative analysis, and surveys. The ways in which feminists use these methods, however, must be very different, for as, Maria Mies notes:

> the methodological principle of a value-free, neutral, uninvolved approach, of a hierarchical, non-reciprocal relationship between research subject and object—certainly the decisive methodological postulate of positivist social science research—drives women scholars into a schizophrenic situation. (1983, p. 121)

Thus feminists have created new ways to do research that fully reflect feminist values (Maguire, 1987; Mies, 1983; Stacey, 1988; Stanley & Wise, 1983). In particular, feminists have transformed the traditional interview method by advocating conscious partiality, a nonhierarchical relationship, and an interactive research process. It is my contention that these practices are useful for studying sensitive topics.

Feminists have made important contributions to the field of sociology in their serious critique of the interview method.[3] Historically, social scientists have been taught to interact with research participants in a value-neutral way, always keeping in mind that the interviewee is the *object* of study. In her article detailing problems with the classic interview recipe, Oakley (1981) quotes from a textbook that instructs: "the interviewer's manner should be friendly, courteous, conversational and unbiased" (Selltiz, Jahoda, Deutsch, & Cook, 1965, p. 576). Another researcher cautions that the interviewer "while friendly and interested [should] not get too emotionally involved with the respondent and his problem" (Moser, 1958, pp. 186-187). To do so indicates a "form of personal degeneracy" (Oakley, 1981, p. 41).

In contrast to these archaic recipes for interviewing, feminists, such as Maria Mies (1983), instead advocate "conscious partiality," which stresses partial identification with the participants based on personal interaction and the treatment of participants as subjects with real emotions and feelings. In short, interviewing with conscious partiality demands that the researcher assume the role of empathic listener and neither exploit nor manipulate the researched. This method challenges the assumption that scientists should approach their research with complete objectivity to become experts about a "true" (emotionless) reality (Stanley & Wise, 1983). Instead, Mies's method places great value on personal interaction and identification with the subject's experiences as another woman to produce more insightful research in a more ethical manner.

The most valuable aspect of interviewing with conscious partiality is that researchers are forced to deobjectify the participants and critically examine how their research might affect them as real people. Considering the consequences (on both a personal level and in terms of policy implications) of the research for the participants is essential to the work of feminists as their goal is the liberation of all women. Thus feminists such as Acker et al. (1983) caution against exploiting women and manipulating their experiences to fit the researcher's own agenda and instead advocate an interactive process based on honesty and trust.

Feminists are particularly critical of the hierarchical relationship between interviewer/interviewee that has historically been the norm in sociological research. Oakley (1981, p. 35) criticizes the unequal relationship dictated by textbooks that claim that "the person who is interviewed has a passive role in adapting to the definition of the situation offered by the person doing the interview." Feminists strive to overcome this hierarchical relationship through methods such as coauthorship and collective consciousness-raising, which are grounded in a relationship of intersubjectivity. This is a dialectical relationship that will permit the researcher constantly to compare her work with her own experiences as a woman and a scientist and to share it with the researched, who then will add their opinions to the research, which in turn might change it (Duelli Klein, 1983, p. 94).

This interactive process is empowering for both the researcher and the researched. Researchers are empowered because they are able to recognize how the research process affects them as both researchers and women (Cook & Fonow, 1984). Research participants are empowered because they understand that their personal experiences are no longer raw material for the data mill but that they are actively involved in sharing their stories with others and evoking change. In establishing intersubjectivity, feminists hope to create research "for" women—that is, research that considers women's experiences and tries to improve their lives—rather than research merely "on" women (Duelli Klein, 1983).

One final way in which feminists have contributed to research methodology is by challenging the traditional goals of conducting research.

Maria Mies (1983, p. 123) argues that feminists "cannot be satisfied with giving the social sciences better, more authentic and more relevant data," which has been the hallmark of androcentric research, but must actively participate in the struggle for women's emancipation. This involves "passionate scholarship" in which researchers are allied with those being studied and work with great devotion to eliminate oppressive social structures and relationships (DuBois, 1983). To do this, Mies (1983) argues that feminist researchers must not do research from their ivory towers but must become involved with the people they study and the concerns of the women's movement. It is this personal commitment and great dedication that enables feminists to conduct high quality research on even the most sensitive of issues.

Researching Marital Rape

My research (which is still in progress) involves intensive interviewing of marital rape survivors to learn how they define their experiences and cope with the violence. The problems I faced at various stages in my research were the result primarily of the sensitivity of marital rape; however, my commitment to feminist principles was essential in resolving many of these dilemmas.

Creating Interview Questions

The choice of research method was shaped by the sensitivity of marital rape and my desire to have the survivors express their experiences as completely as possible. I felt that surveys would neither allow women to fully describe their personal experiences nor allow for an interactive process. Participatory research in the form of ongoing group discussions with survivors would be the most ideal method; however, difficulties in gaining access to women through formal organizations impeded my use of this method. To date, the best research on marital rape has been conducted by feminists using the interview method (Finkelhor & Yllo, 1985; Russell, 1990), and I felt that through in-depth interviews women would best be able to tell their stories.

Constructing the interview questions was extremely difficult due to the nature of this topic. The phrasing of questions is particularly important in the case of marital rape because, as Diana Russell (1990) found in her study, women are hesitant to answer affirmatively the question:

"Have you ever been raped by your husband?" Of the 14% of women in her study whose experiences met her definition of marital rape (forced oral, anal, vaginal, or digital intercourse), only 6% defined their own experiences as rape. Past research (such as Finkelhor & Yllo, 1985; Frieze, 1983; Walker, 1989) also indicates that women are more likely to respond to questions about "forced or unwanted sexual intercourse" than to discuss "rape." In my study, I wanted to avoid misinterpretations and forcing women to fit into my definitions; thus my goal was to compose several open-ended questions to begin the discussion but for the interview to be guided mainly by each woman and her self-expression.

Gaining Access to Participants

The sensitivity of marital rape led to problems of selection in this study. As with all hidden populations—such as incest victims, AIDS patients, undetected criminals—it is difficult to determine who to interview. A random sample of all women in my area was not feasible for financial reasons, so I relied on a self-selected sample. The social construction of rape as a private problem combined with the personal difficulty many women feel in publicly speaking of intimate sexual relationships (both violent and nonviolent) decreases the likelihood of women coming forward as survivors of marital rape. Thus the women I spoke to were only those who had privately recognized themselves as victims of marital rape and publicly asked for assistance from a women's organization.

Gaining access to marital rape survivors proved to be one of the most challenging problems of this research project. Dealing with "gatekeepers," the directors of these women's organizations, was a very significant constraint that many who research sensitive topics must confront. Often, and certainly in my case, an entire research project is contingent upon a gatekeeper's granting permission to do the project. To gain access, the research proposal must be presented in a form that will be acceptable to the gatekeeper, and this can compromise the research if the gatekeeper's interests are not those of the researcher (Brewer, this volume).

During the course of my research, I have contacted approximately 40 institutions that might have some interaction with marital rape victims. With most organizations, I have explained my specific research aims and my experience as a rape crisis counselor. Both my sex and my work as a counselor have been invaluable in making connections with women's centers. The vast majority of institutions thus far, however, have either rejected my proposal to interview their clients or maintained that they have no interaction with victims of marital rape.

The proposals have been flatly rejected for a number of reasons. Several of the organizations have been inundated with research requests and directors have felt that their clients were exhausted from talking about their experiences with researchers. A second problem is that many organizations are threatened by outside scrutiny, particularly if their facilities and services are not up to par. Thus these organizations dismiss any research proposals from nonmembers. Third, some organizations are hostile to outside researchers because of past experiences in which the women have been exploited and depicted negatively in research findings. To solve these problems, some organizations have established their own ethical review boards to evaluate all incoming proposals and the possible consequences of research for the women involved.

The most common reason for not granting me access to the organization is on the grounds that the center does not have any contact with victims of marital rape. This response is particularly distressing when it comes from battered women's shelters and rape crisis centers who have more contact with marital rape survivors than any other type of organization. It is estimated that approximately 40% to 50% of all battered women are also victims of rape (Finkelhor & Yllo, 1985; Frieze, 1983; Russell, 1990), thus shelters should have a significant number of marital rape survivors. My experience as a counselor also indicates that women who have been raped by their husbands make up a significant percentage of the clientele of rape crisis centers. The problem seems to be a lack of information about marital rape, which leads to ignorance within women's organizations surrounding this type of sexual assault. In her study, Thompson-Haas (in Russell, 1990) found that almost 30% of rape crisis centers, and a majority of battered women's shelters, do not educate their staff about the specifics of marital rape or do not require that the staff ask questions about spousal sexual assault. Thus many organizations believe they have little or no contact with marital rape survivors because they are not asking questions specifically about marital rape.

Regardless of the reasons my proposals were rejected, the fact that they frequently were made gaining access to survivors of marital rape an extremely trying process. In the end, I actively worked with only a handful of organizations who agreed to provide me with access to possible participants. In each case, I shared my interview questions with the gatekeeper and made changes when they offered good advice.

The next step was for a member of the organization to contact women who matched the criteria of a marital rape survivor.[4] The women were told by the phone contact that their consent was totally voluntary and that we would be discussing some difficult questions. The contact briefly described the study (or gave a letter of introduction prepared by me, when applicable), my credentials, and my phone number. Approaching potential participants in this way was useful because the women felt more comfortable speaking with me when they knew that my research had been approved by a women's center they had worked with in the past. More significant, each woman's privacy remained intact until she decided to contact me and make her identity as a marital rape survivor known.

The Interviews

When the survivors contacted me about the research, I tried to convey that the material might be difficult to discuss and that we would need a private location where we could talk. Privacy and safety (both the participant's and my own) were of the utmost importance, and one woman even agreed to meet me in a private room of a local library for lack of any alternative. In the vast majority of cases, I interviewed the women either in their homes or at the women's organization with which they were affiliated.

The location of the interviews was an important factor for the obvious reason of maintaining anonymity, but it also proved significant for other reasons as well. First of all, it would be extremely difficult to have an in-depth conversation about such a sensitive and often emotional topic without the benefit of privacy. More important, as Finch (1984) indicates in her research on women, a certain type of interaction is established when interviews are conducted in the privacy of the participant's home, as half of my interviews were.

When I entered a woman's home, a special relationship was established primarily because she felt comfortable in her home and in control of the situation. Rather than my setting the agenda, each woman determined the general rules of the interaction, such as where we would talk, when we would eat, and so on. This was an important element of establishing an interactive relationship because, rather than taking a passive role and following my lead, each woman played an active role as hostess. The role of hostess was important because it was a familiar one to the women (who were in an unfamiliar position of interviewee) and one in which they were successful. In fact, the women went to great lengths to be hospitable by offering me beverages and snacks. On occasion, I even joined the family for dinner, which I interpreted as a strong indication that we had surpassed the traditional interviewer/ interviewee model of interaction and established a level of personal interaction.

Being in their homes also gave me greater insight into the experiences of these women. For example, at home, women tended to speak freely about their families and either showed me pictures or introduced me to their children. From these conversations, details frequently emerged about the children's reaction to violence, which might otherwise have been missed. Some women also shared important details about the assaults by showing me rooms in which they were raped. In one case, I learned much about a woman's current coping strategies when she received several phone calls during the course of our interview. When the phone began ringing, she became visibly nervous and insisted on screening each call with an answering machine. After this happened several times, she explained to me that she had been receiving threatening phone calls (and visits) from her ex-husband and that she was terrified of speaking with him. This is a detail that probably would not have been mentioned if the interview had been conducted in a public place. Thus I feel that interviewing women in their homes was an important aspect of establishing a relationship and fully understanding the emotional and physical trauma that these women have suffered.

From the beginning of each interview, I tried to establish an interpersonal relationship rather than act in "an indifferent, disinterested, alienated [way] towards the 'research objects' " as positivism requires (Mies, 1983, p. 122). I immediately explained my counseling experience and my interest in marital rape. This seemed to place most of the women at ease because they realized that I was genuinely interested in helping marital rape survivors, not just using their experiences for exploitive purposes. To further identify with me, most of the women felt understandably inclined to ask me personal questions. I was commonly asked if I was married, whether I had been a victim of rape, and my personal reasons for doing the study. I tried to answer all of their questions and freely discussed my opinions about violence against women. Rather than biasing their responses, as many social scientists feel that sharing personal information does, I think this exchange of information was essential in establishing a relationship based on trust and mutual interaction.

Although marital rape is an extremely personal and sensitive issue, most survivors did not seem uncomfortable discussing their experiences once we began talking. In fact, many seemed anxious to speak in great detail about very intimate aspects of their experiences. Relatively early in the interviews, I asked the question, "What was sex with your husband like?" This question usually prompted women to tell their stories, including descriptions of actual incidents and how they coped. As other feminists have found (Acker et al., 1983; Devault, 1990), a central element of interviewing is being a good listener and trying to understand the perspectives of the women involved. As my goal was explanation and validation of these women's experiences rather than verification, I tried not to interrupt the storytelling with minor questions of clarification. When there was prolonged silence, however, I usually asked specific questions about their experiences of oral and/or anal rape, and any childhood abuse they had endured, because this was information that they did not usually volunteer in their dialogue. Once the discussion was under way, however, most of the survivors felt comfortable speaking about even these very difficult issues.

The women with whom I spoke experienced a wide range of emotional reactions during the interview. Some were relatively unemotional and described the events much as if they were an outsider who had observed someone else being assaulted. Others became visibly distressed when remembering their past experiences. During the most emotionally difficult interview, I spent a long time offering support to a woman who became extremely upset when she described her husband anally raping her in front of her child. This experience emphasized the need for researchers (especially those working on sensitive topics) to interview with conscious partiality. If I had been a detached and objective researcher merely collecting data, I might have either terminated the interview and discarded the data or possibly suggested that the woman receive outside counseling. As a feminist researcher, however, I was interacting with this woman on a personal level and her distress was deeply affecting. Thus it was not problematic for me to comfort this woman (both during and after the interview) as I had not compartmentalized my identity into counselor, researcher, and woman.

After each woman told her story, I spent time discussing my research with her. I asked each woman for suggestions on how to improve my research and whether there were topics that I was not addressing. Most of the advice I received was insightful and I implemented their comments immediately. Several women even called me after the interview to make more suggestions or to give me additional details about their experiences that they had forgotten to mention.[5]

I was particularly concerned with the survivor's emotional reaction after the interview because of the potential harm involved with discussing such a sensitive issue (Lee & Renzetti, this volume; Sieber & Stanley, 1988). On the whole, most women seemed happy to have spoken to me and were hopeful that their information would help other women. Several women had negative reactions, such as flashbacks and nightmares after the interview, and I either counseled them myself or advised them to seek help from their regular counselor. Even these women, however, claimed that speaking about their experiences was cathartic and said they were grateful to have a sympathetic listener. Indeed, one woman said, "I couldn't believe it when she [the contact] called and said someone wanted to talk about marital rape—I didn't think anyone was interested in it." If they gained nothing else, participating in the research validated each woman's interpretation of her experience because she understood that she was not alone in her suffering and that people are actively working to end this heinous form of violence.

Conclusion

By now, it has become quite obvious that studying any sensitive issue, particularly one as potentially threatening as marital rape, is challenging. The sensitive nature of a topic has implications for the entire research process but particularly for the interaction between researcher and subject. A special relationship develops between the researchers of sensitive topics and their subjects due to the threatening nature of the project. Thus these researchers must be particularly careful to anticipate the consequences (both personal and political) of the research as well as to consider the ethical issues involved (Cook & Fonow, 1984). Feminist methods, such as interviewing with conscious subjectivity and intersubjectivity, are particularly valuable because they help researchers avoid some of the pitfalls of traditional research methods—primarily because of the focus on women as subjects (rather than objects of study) and the great emphasis feminist researchers place on forming nonexploitive relationships.

Certainly this chapter does not solve the problems that plague much sensitive research, such as gaining access to hidden populations, obtaining responses to potentially threatening questions, or coping with emotional subjects. In discussing my research and the problems I faced, however, I hope others will be encouraged to study issues such as marital rape and to at least consider the benefits of implementing feminist research methods to study sensitive topics.

Notes

1. I have tried to deal with this problem by notifying women before the interview about potential after-effects they might suffer and through counseling during the interview. Those women who did experience problems after the interview were either counseled by me or received other supportive help.

2. For a discussion of this debate see Acker et al. (1983), Dubois (1983), Duelli Klein (1983), Harding (1985), and Mies (1983).

3. Positivistic methods have been subjected to a sustained critique by both feminists and nonfeminists in recent years.

4. This included both those women who contacted the agencies for help with their husbands as well as those who were raped (or battered) by another individual, but also responded that they had been raped by their husbands at least once.

5. Another way to further the goal of accurate representation of their experiences is to send each woman the transcript form the interview. This allows women to make any changes or additions to our original discussion and promotes a more interactive process.

References

Acker, J., Barry, K., & Esseveld, J. (1983). Objectivity and truth: Problems in doing feminist research. *Women's Studies International Forum, 6,* 423-435.

Bidwell, L., & White, P. (1986). The family context of marital rape. *Journal of Family Violence, 1,* 286-287.

Cook, J., & Fonow, M. (1984). Knowledge and women's interests: Issues of epistemology and methodology in feminist sociological research. *Sociological Inquiry, 56,* 2-29.

Devault, M. (1990). Standpoint feminist strategies for interviewing and analysis. *Social Problems, 37,* 96-116.

DuBois, B. (1983). Passionate scholarship: Notes on values, knowing and method in feminist social science. In G. Bowles & R. Duelli Klein (Eds.), *Theories of women's studies.* London: Routledge & Kegan Paul.

Duelli Klein, R. (1983). How to do what we want to do: Thoughts about feminist methodology. In G. Bowles & R. Duelli Klein (Eds.), *Theories of women's studies.* London: Routledge & Kegan Paul.

Finch, J. (1984). "It's great to have someone to talk to": The ethics and politics of interviewing women. In C. Bell & H. Roberts (Eds.), *Social researching: Politics, problems and practice.* London: Routledge & Kegan Paul.

Finkelhor, D., & Yllo, K. (1985). *License to rape: Sexual abuse of wives.* New York: Holt, Rinehart & Winston.

Frieze, I. (1983). Investigating the causes and consequences of marital rape. *Signs, 8,* 532-553.

Harding, S. (1987). *Feminism and methodology.* Bloomington: Indiana University Press.

Kinsey, A., Pomeroy, W., & Martin, C. (1948). *Sexual behavior in the human male.* Philadelphia: W. B. Saunders.

Lasch, C. (1977). *Haven in a heartless world.* New York: Basic Books.

MacIntyre, A. (1982). Risk, harm and benefit assessments as instruments of moral evaluation. In T. L. Beauchamp, R. R. Faden, R. J. Wallace, Jr., & L. Waters (Eds.), *Ethical issues in social science research.* Baltimore, MD: John Hopkins University Press.

Maguire, P. (1987). *Doing participatory research: A feminist approach.* Amherst: University of Massachusetts, Center for International Education.

Mies, M. (1983). Toward a methodology for feminist research. In G. Bowles & R. Duelli Klein (Eds.), *Theories of women's studies.* London: Routledge & Kegan Paul.

Moser, C. A. (1958). *Survey methods in social investigation.* London: Heinemann.

Oakley, A. (1981). Interviewing women: A contradiction in terms. In H. Roberts (Ed.), *Doing feminist research.* London: Routledge & Kegan Paul.

Russell, D. (1990). *Rape in marriage.* New York: Macmillan.

Sculley, D. (1990). *Understanding sexual violence: A study of convicted rapists.* Boston: Unwin Hyman.

Selltiz, C., Jahoda, M., Deutsch, M., & Cook, S. W. (1965). *Research methods in social relations.* London: Methuen.

Sieber, J. E., & Stanley, B. (1988). Ethical and professional dimensions of socially sensitive research. *American Psychologist, 43,* 49-55.

Stacey, J. (1988). Can there be a feminist ethnography? *Women's Studies International Forum, 11,* 21-27.

Stanley, B., Sieber, J. E., & Melton, G. (1987). Empirical studies of ethical issues in research: A research agenda. *American Psychologist, 42,* 735-741.

Stanley, L., & Wise, S. (1983). "Back into the personal" or: Our attempt to construct "feminist research." In G. Bowles & R. Duelli Klein (Eds.), *Theories of women's studies.* London: Routledge & Kegan Paul.

Walker, L. (1989). *Terrifying love: Why battered women kill and how society responds.* New York: Harper & Row.

13

Using Visual Imagery to
Explore Gendered Notions of Pain

GILLIAN BENDELOW

The following chapter describes the development and use of an innovative research technique used in conjunction with a survey and in-depth interviews to provide a blending of quantitative and qualitative approaches. The central aim of the research was to explore how men and women perceive, evaluate, and act upon their own symptoms of pain and whether social characteristics, particularly gender, are seen to be important in affecting this process. A central hypothesis of this research is that the mind/body dualism and the dominance of a somatic ideology inherent in medicine tends to define emotional expression in experiences of pain as socially undesirable, whereas attributes such as stoicism tend to be valued. It is further hypothesized that this moral evaluation may be gendered.

The best known studies in this tradition are those of Zola (1966) and Zbrowski (1952), which looked at different cultural groups and the expression of pain. Zbrowski found marked differences between Italian Americans, Jewish Americans, and largely Protestant so-called "Old Americans."

For instance, the Italians placed great emphasis on the immediacy of experiencing painful sensations but quickly forgot their suffering once it had gone, whereas members of the Jewish group were mainly concerned with the meaning and significance of the pain in relation to their health and welfare, their anxieties focusing on the future. The latter group was much less emotional and more detached in reporting pain, often having an idealized notion of how to react and to avoid being a nuisance. Zola reported similar reactions by Italian Americans, whereas the Irish Americans in his sample appeared to value stoicism, the response being to ignore or play down the symptoms.

Other contemporary research suggests that the understanding and interpretation of personal beliefs about affliction and pain are a fundamental component of pain perception (Williams & Thorn, 1989). These beliefs include emotional, psychological, sociological, philosophical, and existential aspects as well as the sensory dimensions. Methodological issues are raised by the above considerations, as traditional clinical or experimental studies are generally unable to encompass the more abstract and subjective aspects of pain beliefs. In addition, reviewing the academic literature on pain perception indicates that, on the whole, gender is not viewed as a variable of any significance in the perception of pain (see Lander, Fowler-Kerry, & Hargreaves, 1989). The focus on thresholds appears to be the only issue concerning gender that has received much attention in relevant research. There may be variation in acute or chronic, physical or emotional, components, depending on the individual's experience, and a closer examination of the methodological aspects of these studies reveals a good deal about the social context of pain perception.

Pain perception involves emotions and feelings, which may be problematic to elicit and to measure. Although, by its very nature, pain may become a public concern, there can be little argument that it is a highly personal experience that may be difficult to discuss because it is so emotionally charged and subject to the exposure of vulnerabilities. To explore the complexity of beliefs and meanings around the conceptualization of pain, a phenomenological approach is needed and a principal aim of this study was to allow the subjects to define for themselves what they mean by *pain*. Although theoretical approaches to pain have broadened since the 1960s, becoming more eclectic and multidisciplinary, and encompassing both phenomenological and hermeneutic philosophies, these developments have yet to be fully reflected in the methodological design of studies, although there is an expanding emphasis on the subjective nature of pain. For example, the widespread use in pain clinics and hospices of the McGill Pain Questionnaire (Melzack, 1975), which requires respondents to choose descriptions of the nature of their pain from lists of adjectives, emphasizes the importance of language and expression. Attempts from within the social sciences to provide a taxonomy of pain reveal limitations of powers of expression:

> To demonstrate their distress, most people readily offer dramatic affective language, describing pain in terms of tension, fear and autonomic distress. Expressions such as *exhausting, frightful* and *sickening* are often accompanied by paralinguistic vocalizations of moaning and groaning and non-verbal signs of affective discomfort to signal the sufferer's distress to observers. (Craig, 1984, p. 153)

The inclusion of subjective approaches in the research design makes even more apposite the focus on gender, as theoretical and methodological work within the sociology of health and illness by feminist scholars over the last 15 years has highlighted the links between qualitative methodology and the representation of gendered experiences. Feminist critiques within medical sociology have identified a long-standing and unquestioning acceptance of the values and norms of the existing society that are reflected in medical practice and provision (see Clarke, 1983). (It is recognized, however, that gender does not operate in isolation, being crosscut by other social characteristics such as race and class.) In addition, much of this work is grounded in ethnographic and humanistic traditions, an essential feature of which is to emphasize the subjective and to reveal the "lay" voice rather than that of the expert or professional. As a discipline, sociology has the flexibility and methodological imagination required to allow insights into the complexity of pain beliefs, as located in the context of such issues.

The research design incorporated three different, but complementary, methods of data collection, namely, a questionnaire, an in-depth interview, and a sequence of visual imagery portraying various types of pain experience. This chapter attempts to evaluate the use of the latter method as a research tool. The qualitative fieldwork was designed to examine the themes of the questionnaire in greater depth and to provide deeper insights into the complexity of pain beliefs and perceptions by using a different, more subjective, approach that would enable definitions of pain to be broadened and more contextualized. The main themes followed from the two major "findings" of the questionnaire: First, that most people perceived women to have a superior capacity to men for coping with pain, or for there to be no gender differences; a minority said that men were better at coping with pain. The female reproductive role was consistently used to explain this notion. Second, analysis of the questionnaire data showed men were significantly less inclined to think the emotional component of pain perception had any importance.

Eleven men and eleven women took part in the interviews. This subsample was a self-selected group from a larger random questionnaire sample of 107 attendees of a general practice in North London. The interview began by recalling the questionnaire and asking for more details about the most painful experience the respondent could remember. In each case, this gave rise to a "pain story," the length of which varied considerably. In relating their experiences, every person without exception talked about their feelings while recalling the relevant episode and/or incident(s). The theme of physical versus emotional pain and the separation or interlinking of those two were universally explored, often without my prompting, although I did explicitly ask, if it had not already arisen, whether the interviewee thought that there was such a thing as "emotional pain." At this point in the interview, a sequence of visual images was introduced, aiming to further explore social perceptions and beliefs about pain. The final part of the interview centered on the questionnaire responses to gender differences and pain perceptions.

The use of imagery in the context of data collection appears to be somewhat unusual, and the development of the technique is described below in detail.

Rationale and Development of the Visual Imagery Technique

The striving of technical scientific language toward neutral objectivity appears to be discordant with the human ability to convey emotional and experiential qualities of pain. As a consequence, turning to the arts and literature is sometimes recommended as a strategy for better understanding the subjective nature of pain.

My personal interest in using visual images to probe more deeply into beliefs and attitudes about illness and pain emerged initially from a "lay" appreciation of the relationship between art and society following the work of Berger (1964) and others challenging the exclusivity of "high culture." Despite the impact of sociological theories on art history throughout the 1970s and 1980s (particularly Marxist and feminist critiques; see, for example, Fischer, 1964; Lippard, 1976; Nochlin, 1971; Pollock, 1982), there have been few reciprocal attempts to enhance social perspectives. Within the social sciences, the study of perception, in particular, and pain, in general, has traditionally been embedded in scientific models, with a consequent lack of acknowledgment of the ways in which the social order is represented and endorsed by art. Wolff (1975, p. 7), in her comprehensive account of a sociological perspective on art as a social product, speculates as to why phenomenologically orientated sociologists have not turned to the arts, a seemingly logical progression: "Like society, art is a creation of individual members who are in many ways formed by society."

There are methodological difficulties in developing a sociology of art, if the initial assumption is made that a work of art may express the ethos or ideology of a period or particular social group. Wolff contends that the underpinnings of both positivism and phenomenology lack structural and historical perspectives, which may not supply a context, and suggests a hermeneutic approach to the analysis of imagery. This, in turn, involves the combination of two disparate epistemological inquiries: "the micro-analysis of the individual, phenomenological linguistic experience and the macro- or social knowledge-constitutive determining interests" (Wolff, 1975, p. 36).

Generally, imagery as a research tool in social science appears to be underused and confined to certain areas, such as facilitating psychoanalytic diagnoses, for example, in the use of the Rorschach tests. An isolated study by Petrovich (1957) used a test consisting of 25 cards depicting a man in various painful situations—the Pain Aperception Test (PAT)—to test pain reactivity. The study was unusual in that the focus was on reaction rather than sensation, attempting to tap the emotional response to painful situations experienced by others. Petrovich claimed that high scores on the PAT correlated significantly with anxiety and neuroticism, using Taylor's Manifest Anxiety Scale (1953) and Eysenck's Personality Inventory (1956). Despite the interest in access to emotional responses that this test provided, the study proved difficult to replicate and was heavily criticized on these grounds. Identification with the sufferer in the test cards was thought to differ from subject to subject (the point that this may have been a gender issue as the subject was male is not raised). The criticism appears effectively to have curtailed any further development of the technique until Elton, Quarry, Burrows, and Stanley (1978) tried to replicate it in Melbourne 20 years later. They argued that the imagery material was considered too complex and ambiguous by the subjects and that the extraneous clues were too confusing. Subsequently, they developed a new measure, which they named the Melbourne Pain Aperception Film (MPAF), that depicted a bare hand and forearm in situations of increasing pain as follows:

1. hand slapped
2. hand pinched
3. finger pricked with a pin
4. hand hit with a wooden ruler
5. thumb hit by a hammer
6. hand caught in a door
7. fingers burnt by a match
8. hot water spilled on a hand
9. hand cut deeply on the ball of thumb by a knife
10. fingers chopped off by an ax

Elton and colleagues supported the view that the extraneous details in Petrovich's study were confusing. Their own presentation of pain as "disembodied," however, clearly implies a lack of respect for any broad cultural model of pain. The respondents in this study were men and women from three different groups: "pain-prone" patients, "organic" pain patients, and a control group. They were given 10 seconds between each segment of film to record their responses on seven-point scales. As with the Petrovich study, the analysis is limited, concentrating on significant correlations between variables but not taking factors such as gender into account. There were no significant differences found between any of the groups, and the authors concluded that, although these types of tests do not have much use as a *clinical* measure of pain reactivity, "they may be useful in determining intercultural differences in responsiveness to pain, and individual differences. When used in conjunction with other methods, they may tap some of the more elusive dimensions of pain" (Elton et al., 1978, p. 30). It was precisely this quality that I was seeking for the kinds of questions I wanted to ask.

Use of visual images in the context of a sociological interview has something in common with the vignette technique as used by Finch (1987) and others. She advocates the use of a hypothetical situation permitting the interviewee to define the meaning for her- or himself and

allowing for features of the content to be specified, so that the respondent is being invited to make normative statements about a set of social circumstances, rather than to express his or her "beliefs" or "values" in a vacuum. It acknowledges

> that meanings are social and that morality may well be socially specific. (Finch, 1987, p. 106)

The method was developed in the United States in the late 1960s by using *factorial* vignettes to mimic experiments. A basic story was presented that remained constant but the outcomes were varied, and responses were recorded and analyzed in survey fashion. The most common practice has been to follow the vignette with fixed responses. For instance, Lomas Cook (1979) used eight vignettes per interview to explore public support for welfare claimants, following these with a fixed set of five questions seeking the opinions of the respondents with yes/no responses.

In another study of the distribution of household income, Alves and Rossi (1986) included 50 vignettes per interview and followed each with a nine-point rating scale indicating approval/disapproval. Finch herself used a more complex form of vignette in her study of the public morality of obligations to assist kin. This involved the construction of characters in a story with up to three possible different outcomes. She stresses the flexibility of the technique:

> Asking concrete questions about third parties has the effect of distancing the issues. This seems to make the questions less personally threatening, which may be very important when the sensitive features of relationships are being explored. It also has the effect of breaking away from the limitations imposed by the personal experience and circumstances, (Finch, 1987, p. 111)

Generally, there seems to be a consensus that the use of vignettes is extremely valuable in tapping general imagery but does not foretell actions.

In this study, a series of paired images were used instead of vignettes. As the major focus of the study was gender, I was hoping to portray salient gendered images of pain (for example, childbirth for women and battle for men). I was unable, however, to find either a photographic or artistic image of a woman in pain in childbirth (the images I found depicted serenity, joy, or even ecstasy). Nonetheless, the gendered pairs that emerged seemed to provide complementary contexts. Some of the images also raised other issues, such as age and race, that I wanted to include. Acknowledgment must be made of the subjectivity of the final choices, which are influenced by my own definitions and beliefs about pain and by features of my own background, including my professional training in psychiatry.

Another complicating factor is that artistic material, particularly fine art, is highly culturally embedded. The collection of images I used is no doubt Eurocentric and also covers varied time spans, which may serve to distract from or influence responses. In the interview situation, respondents were presented with the six pairs of images, one at a time, without any information about the artist or the background (if desired, the information was offered at the end of the sequence) and asked:

1. What is happening to the people in the picture?
2. Is anyone in the pictures in pain?
3. Is there more pain in one picture than the other?

Respondents were then shown all the images together and asked:

4. Who is in the most pain out of all the images?
5. With whom do you identify most?

Although there was no time limit, respondents were asked to give as immediate a response as possible and were reassured that there was no right or wrong answer and that I was not making any judgments about their responses, which were both noted and tape-recorded. Due to the size of the subsample, it was possible to assimilate all the material in an immediately accessible manner. The word-processed transcripts were manually "cut and pasted" and the relevant quotes were pasted around each pair of images, forming a "poster" that could be hung on the wall and studied at length. This process facilitated the effective extrapolation of various themes, although no doubt it could be criticized for providing data that lack a dynamic and remain "static."

Overview of Reactions to the Images: Common Themes

One of the most immediately striking features of the responses is that, despite the diversity of backgrounds of respondents, and their different levels of articulation, there are common responses to each pair of images. An "overarching" view of each image is apparent from the analysis and is presented below.

Pair 1

(A) *The Sick Child* by Edvard Munch (1907 National Gallery, London) depicts two figures, one childlike, debilitated, and in bed; the other, presumably the mother, is bowed despairingly over the side of the bed.

(B) *The Hopeless Dawn* by Frank Bramley (1888 Tate Gallery, London): The setting is a spartan room, suggesting Victorian poverty. Through a window, waves lash as if there is a storm. An older woman is trying to provide comfort to a younger woman, who is lying prostrate in her lap.

On the whole, picture A is seen as the most distressing and more concerned with physical illness. Many of the interpretations of the pictures are concerned with defining the *type* of pain, for example: "They don't seem to be in *physical* pain there, seems more like *mental* pain."

Well [B] looks like *emotional* pain—she's crying to her mother because her boyfriend's left her or it could be that they are both in pain because somebody's died. [A] it looks like the person in the bed could be in *physical* pain and the person by the side of her could be in *emotional* pain but there is a *physical* pain there whereas that [B], I think is purely *emotional*.

The theme of emotional pain is expressed continuously, sometimes with ambivalence, as there are doubts as to whether it constitutes "real" pain, especially for the males in the sample. Whereas picture A is thought to convey different types of pain, picture B is seen as overtly emotional in quality and therefore less likely to be about pain. Both male and female respondents included deeply personal feelings in their interpretations, including their own experiences of illness and hospitalization. These experiences were related repeatedly to other themes suggested by the images such as mother/child relationships and bereavement. Only two respondents felt that neither of the images portrayed pain of any type.

Pair 2

(A) *Jamshedpur India* by Werner Bischof (1951 Magnum Photofile) is a black and white photograph depicting an emaciated elderly Indian woman, appearing to be in dire poverty and raising her hands in a manner that appears to be pleading.

(B) *Old Man Grieving* by Vincent van Gogh (1882 Van Gogh Museum, Amsterdam) is a black and white sketch depicting an elderly man in peasant-type clothing, sitting abjectly in a chair holding his head in his hands.

The reactions to these images again reveal a common theme. The choice of these particular pictures was influenced by the fact that, as well as portraying gender, they also raised issues of age, class, and race. The man's plight is seen as private and personalized, whereas the woman is seen as representative of a universal suffering, the public "pain" of the underdeveloped world. For example: "This one [B] conjures up the pain of the individual whereas this one [A] is the more harrowing picture-graph and it makes you aware of the plight of people."

Whether or not the content of the pictures is defined as pain, the "public" nature of the plight of the woman appears to act to *reduce* empathy for her; even though there is a consensus that *she* is probably suffering more, *his* personal grief seems to produce more immediate sympathy:

> I feel upset looking at him—that could be me when I get old, I don't want to end up like that. He's probably fought in the war, all sorts of things but just to end up in pain, old, alone—he's probably got cancer or something. I know she's probably even worse off, she could be starving even but I'm much more sorry for him.

> The man is in anguish, what he's going through is agony, but it's a personal anguish whereas the woman—it should be more shocking because it could be torture, death but somehow it's not personalized.

There are several responses that do not consider these images to be conveying pain as such and that use definitions such as *despair, hopelessness, anger, grief.* Again, these pictures convey emotional qualities, which for some respondents (more males than females) gives rise to a reluctance to define them as pain without the physical component.

Pair 3

(A) *The Lady of Shalott* by John William Waterhouse (1988 Tate Gallery, London) is a highly stylized oil painting depicting a woman in medieval clothing floating down a river in a boat, appearing to be in extreme anguish.

(B) *Melancolie* by Edvard Munch (1918 Munch-Museet Oslo) is a black and white impressionistic sketch depicting a man sitting staring into the sea in an attitude of despondency.

This pair of images elicited negative reactions; on first impression, the majority of the sample did not think the images portrayed pain at all, although there was a much more sympathetic response to image B, who was perceived to be in a state of extreme desolation and loneliness. The isolation of the male figure was seen as a more valid form of suffering and was true for both males and females. The males also repeatedly expressed personal identification with the man in image B after reflecting on the images. The responses to picture A were also fairly uniform between the sexes. Even if the woman is thought to be in pain, it is seen as the pain of "romantic love," which is portrayed as melodramatic, somewhat ridiculous, not to be taken seriously, and certainly not "real" pain. Some respondents even indicated a narcissistic, self-inflicted quality, verging on martyrdom. For example, in response to the question: Is she in pain?

> Yes, but possibly quite enjoying it. I know that sounds very cynical and I wouldn't have said that 20 years ago, I'm sure but yes, she probably feels she is but sort of pain and love and beauty are sort of all intermingled.

Only two of the respondents appeared to empathize or feel there was any genuine plight in picture A, one of whom was nursing her husband through a terminal illness and expressed the worry that the woman would kill herself because of the pain she was experiencing. Suicidal tendencies were also attributed to both images by another interviewee who had described himself as having suffered from paranoid schizophrenia for many years. He said:

> She is showing the pain of an inadequate world—a melancholic love of life as known by her, a more esoteric life. He is really black and white—lonely, empty—a black snake in a human body. There is no emotional comfort there whatsoever. I used to feel like that in the mental hospital. I'd rather be the woman.

Pair 4

(A) *San Sebastien* by Gerit von Honthoust (1590 National Gallery, London) is an oil painting depicting a martyrdom—a male body is bound and studded with arrows in the torso, arms, and legs. Blood is seeping from the wounds but the face is peaceful, as if in sleep.

(B) *The Broken Column* by Frida Kahlo (1944 Collection of Dolores Olmeda, Mexico City): This time, a female body is depicted bound and studded with nails, and the woman's spinal cord has been replaced by a broken column in a rather surreal fashion. Her face is detached and expressionless.

For the first time, the images actually depict physical pain being inflicted on the subjects. This invokes mixed reactions; many initial reactions are of fear and revulsion, and three of the female respondents found the images quite offensive and shocking. Sadomasochistic themes were interpreted by many of the respondents, which for both men and women were disturbing, and a few of the men revealed that their disturbance was made more complex by the fact that they found the images almost erotic. The ambiguity of responses is increased by the lack of expression in both the faces, which obscures the reactions of many of the respondents. This results in a distancing of feelings; sometimes the images are described as intellectualized appreciations of pain rather than "true" impressions, often attributed to the artistic style.

It feels like a theater stage set so in a way it gets you in the pit of the stomach but you don't necessarily think in terms of pain in terms of the picture, you're more thinking in terms of what the spirit is doing, in terms of what it's about—I think that is the purpose of the picture. My feeling is that it is trying to talk about a certain type of pain—more like an intellectual exercise.

The pain from [B] is about what you should be feeling and you will feel but you won't, well I think that it represents pain but I don't think you can feel it from that image but you are aware of what it means—the pain is made real. It's symbolism, when you're not actually feeling it in your gut but you feel it in your head.

Although most respondents of both sexes respond more immediately to picture A as the image depicting the most pain, after some reflection, B emerges overall as the more evocative but as a symbolic interpretation. Many of the females in the sample felt a strong personal identity with image B.

Pair 5

(A) *Scene from a London Playground* by Network Photographers (1987 Aladdin Books Ltd.) is a black and white photograph of a black child, presumably a boy by the clothing, weeping; his face is screwed up and grimacing. A (white) adult's arm is around him.

(B) *Hungary 1947* by Werner Bischof (Magnum Photofile) is a black and white photograph, again depicting a crying child of indeterminate sex but weeping more passively. Tearstains on her or his cheeks and spittle running from the mouth suggest the crying has been prolonged.

This pair of images gave rise to the most immediate emotional reactions, usually of sympathy or pity. Many of the female and some of the male interviewees claimed the images made them feel upset and evoked incidents from their own childhood experiences or those of their own children. There is little debate that the children are in pain, except for three responses out of the whole sample. These were from the two oldest people in the sample, one male and one female and the youngest man, and all expressed the view that children's tears were not to be taken seriously, in the following vein: "Yes, but children cry. Small children can be absolutely heartbreaking for the lack of another Smartie—you can't always take it so seriously, tremendous tears, upset—they don't look in pain."

Although the rest of the sample consensually acknowledge that the children *are* in pain, the child in A is thought possibly to be in more physical pain than the other, which in turn gives a tendency for him or her to be considered as being in more overall pain.

Pair 6

(A) *Two Followers of Cadamus Devoured by a Dragon* by Cornelius van Haarlem (1624 National Gallery, London): This oil painting depicts two naked intertwined bodies, the face of one of which is being attacked by a dragon. A severed, bitten off head lies at the forefront of the picture, whereas in the background there appears to be the mouth of a cave in which a knight in armor is lurking.

(B) *Judith Decapitating Holofernes* by Artemisia Gentileschi (c. 1618, Uffizi Gallery, Florence): This oil painting portrays a man being held down on a bed and having his throat cut with a sword by two well-dressed women, from a long-bygone age. The man's eyes are wide open and astonished, and the woman who is using the sword has an extremely self-satisfied appearance.

The final pair again depict gory, violent images and produce responses of horror and some refusals (all female) to look at the images. For example: "I don't know what to say about these—they're both so revolting I don't even want to have to look at them."

> Oh good God that's a sacrilegious thing isn't it, they're cutting his head off, good God and they're cutting his throat—this is terrible what they've done, this is the worst one, they're crucifying him, cutting his throat and it makes me shudder—that one does as well but that is worse—it upsets all your system as soon as I look at it.

For most of the sample, however, after an initially shocked reaction, there was a process of distancing. As in the responses to pair 4, the artistic style was often used to create this distance. Picture A, especially, is described as being unreal, a myth, a fantasy, something out of a horror movie, and humor may be employed to construct an analytical, more intellectualized response, which serves to reduce the possible distress. Although the distancing process was also applied to a lesser extent to picture B, it was felt to be more realistic, more likely, and subsequently depicting more pain. The males in the sample expressed more personal identification and worries as to why this should take place. For instance:

> Bloody hell, that's one way of getting rid of the husband isn't it? I can familiarize with that more because that is real, has gone on, did go on and still goes on now—it looks like he's been asleep and they've come in and caught him by surprise, by the time he's realized what's happened it's too late he can't do nothing to save himself so I feel more pity for him.

> I suppose I could say I'm surprised it takes two ladies to get a bloke while he's asleep. There is a certain amount of pain in that face but it's more pain of surprise than pain of pain. You can feel from this that the person is obviously rich but there's no real clues to why. I suppose it's revenge.

Links Between the Public and the Private: Advantages and Disadvantages of Using Visual Imagery in Data Collection

The chapter has described an exploratory use of visual imagery as a research tool to elicit beliefs about pain as an alternative to more traditional studies of pain perception that use experimental psychophysical approaches, often involving the infliction of noxious stimuli on subjects. In contrast, the research has been experienced as positively supportive, and on the whole the subjects responded well to the request to look at and discuss visual images. Nobody refused to take part, and most respondents claimed to enjoy the exercise. Some even claimed to find it therapeutic, particularly the subjects who had experienced traumatic hospital treatments or severe emotional disturbance (for example, long-term treatment for paranoid schizophrenia or constant debilitating anxiety attacks). These respondents expressed the view that contemplating the plight of the people in the images somehow helped to put their own dilemmas into perspective and gave them an opportunity to "cope" with the feelings that their own personal events had aroused in them. In the same way that Finch (1987) demonstrates how the vignette technique provides a form of "desensitization"—an acceptable way of talking about the private in public—many respondents claimed it was a relief to take part in the imagery exercise after having revealed in some depth their own "pain stories" and to contemplate something that was happening to someone else. This desensitization was mutually beneficial, from the point of view of the so-called burden of interviewing. Many of the "pain stories" were extremely harrowing to listen to, so that the change of discussion to a third party was also a personal relief.

An important methodological point is that using images enables the subject matter to be standardized—the images stay the same whereas questions may be altered in context or expression from interview to interview. In addition, the use of images elicits an *immediate* response and does not necessarily require a high level of articulation, although obviously how people talk affects what they say. Preliminary discussions about using this type of material had raised the issue that some people might relate to artistic representations better than others; in other words, there would be a social class advantage in that the higher social classes would be more familiar with the materials. In fact, given the responses from this sample, this would not seem to be the case. Obviously, there were differences in the styles of articulation, and people with an artistic background or knowledge discussed the images more analytically, to the extent that they sometimes became inappropriately diverted by discussing technical styles (for instance, the merits of photographs over paintings or vice versa). It appeared that the less the respondent knew about the picture, or art in general, the more spontaneous was the response. Some subjects used comparisons with television programs, popular novels, or media advertising, and the quality of responses was very rich and philosophically profound, as the quotes illustrate. Even the two subjects who felt that the exercise was pointless did not refuse to take part and made appropriate and relevant contributions. The only person who was unable to use the material at all suffered from visual disability and was unable to decipher many of the scenes but still attempted to do so with my assistance. Another respondent was unable to read or write and found the exercise much more appropriate than completing the questionnaire, which I had read aloud to her.

The inherent advantages of using imagery to elicit beliefs and personal experiences of pain would seem to offset the more practical difficulties in presenting material of this nature. It must be emphasized, however, that the study described was of an exploratory nature and, if used as a method, would need to be developed and standardized. A follow-up study has been devised and is currently being undertaken with a sample of 40 (20 male and 20 female) attendees of a pain clinic in a London hospital to test the potential efficacy of the use of imagery in this way.

References

Alves, W., & Rossi, P. (1986). Who should get what? Fairness in the judgments of distribution of earnings. *American Journal of Sociology, 84,* 541-564.

Berger, J. (1964). *Ways of seeing.* Harmondsworth, UK: Penguin.

Clarke, J. (1983). Sexism, feminism and medicalism: A decade review of the literature on gender and illness. *Sociology of Health and Illness, 5,* 62-82.

Craig, K. (1984). Emotional aspects of pain. In P. Wall & R. Melzack (Eds.), *A textbook of pain.* New York: Churchill Livingstone.

Elton, D., Quarry, P. R., Burrows, G. D., & Stanley, G. V. (1978). The Melbourne Pain Aperception Film. *Melbourne Psychology Reports, 45,* 1-12.

Eysenck, H. J. (1956). The questionnaire measurement of neuroticism and extraversion. *Revisita di Piscologia, 54,* 113-140.

Fischer, E. (1964). *The necessity of art.* Harmondsworth, UK: Penguin.

Finch, J. (1987). Research note: The vignette technique in survey research. *Sociology, 21,* 105-114.

Lander, J., Fowler-Kerry, S., & Hargreaves, A. (1989). Gender effects in pain perception. *Perceptual and Motor Skills, 68,* 1088-1090.

Lippard, L. (1976). *From the center: Feminist essays on women's art.* New York: Thames and Hudson.

Lomas Cook, F. (1979). *Who should be helped? Public support for social services.* Beverly Hills, CA: Sage.

Melzack, R. (1975). The McGill Pain Questionnaire: Major properties and scoring methods. *Pain, 1a,* 277-299.

Nochlin, L. (1971). Why have there been no great women artists? In T. Hess & E. Baker (Eds.), *Art and sexual politics.* Harmondsworth, UK: Penguin.

Petrovich, D. V. (1957). The Pain Aperception Test: A preliminary report. *Journal of Psychology, 44,* 339-346.

Pollock, G. (1982). Vision, voice and power: Feminist art history and Marxism. *Block, 6,* 6-9.

Taylor, J. A. (1953). A personality scale of manifest anxiety. *Journal of Abnormal and Social Psychology, 48,* 285-290.

Williams, D., & Thorn, B. (1989). An empirical assessment of pain beliefs. *Pain, 36,* 351-358.

Wolff, J. (1975). *Hermeneutic philosophy and the sociology of art.* London: Routledge & Kegan Paul.

Zborwski, M. (1952). Cultural components in response to pain. *Journal of Social Issues, 8,* 6-30.

Zola, I. (1966). Culture and symptoms: An analysis of patients' presenting complaints. *American Sociological Review, 31,* 615-630.

PART V

Disseminating Sensitive Research Findings: Structural and Personal Constraints

The first chapter in this part, by Pamela Brink, describes her research on women's secret societies in Nigeria. In it, she reprises some of the issues raised in this volume by Ayella and Brewer: the problems of gaining access and maintaining trust. The primary theme of the chapter, however, is the problem raised for the researcher by coming to know the secrets of those being studied. The rituals surrounding membership in women's secret societies among the Annang of southern Nigeria are a sensitive matter, not to be disclosed to outsiders. Brink describes the difficulties involved in eliciting information on secret matters and the further dilemmas involved in making those secrets available to a wider audience.

As Brink's chapter makes clear, what goes into published reports is often shaped by events occurring long before the actual writing takes place. Innocuous material may be published because the researcher has deliberately chosen a noncontroversial topic for study. Agreements made to gain access have sometimes allowed a gatekeeper the right to veto, inspect, or control what is to be written. Neither is it unknown for researchers to be hoodwinked by research participants or to have obtained only their grudging participation (Barnes, 1979; Becker, 1964)—both factors likely to lead to less than full reporting.

In addition, as the Adlers point out in their chapter, self-censorship is common in the reporting of social science findings, especially in research on socially sensitive situations. Self-censorship functions to protect both the researcher and the researched from possible harms induced by publication as well as helping to preserve good relations with those who are or have been studied. They also note that researchers have also sometimes remained silent about particular—sometimes discreditable —features of their own activities in the research setting. It is understandable that social scientists resort to self-censorship where publication might potentially jeopardize a carefully cultivated research relationship or bring down retribution on themselves or on those they study. This gives rise to an unwelcome paradox, however. The greater the sensitivity of a particular topic, the greater the likelihood that self-censorship will protect those in the research setting (Barnes, 1984; Jahoda, 1981). Unfortunately, situations of this kind are also more likely to be those where there exists a clear and urgent social interest in accurate reporting (Fichter & Kolb, 1953).

As the Adlers make clear, when we censor our own work, the wider social science community is "duped, deceived, or misled." This kind of deception can, in turn, have wider consequences. Whatever the particular merits of the many issues raised by the "Springdale" case (Whyte, 1958), this was, of course, the basic point that Vidich and Bensman (1964) made. Identifying with those studied can lead the researcher through self-censorship to present a sanitized view of their activities. For Vidich and Bensman, the result was a social science that concealed elite impropriety while leaving the powerless open to scrutiny. The powerful could encourage self-censorship because they were articulate enough and had the necessary resources to react in negative ways to portrayals of them that were unflattering.

To a certain extent, this argument has been turned on its head in recent years. A number of writers have claimed that pressures toward "political correctness" have encouraged the self-censorship of research findings that conflict with the politically liberal assumptions upon which social science disciplines such as sociology are based (Gordon, 1980; Lynch, 1989; see also Felson, 1991). If one considers, for example, institutional practices in social science, such as the peer review process (Bakanic, McPhail, & Simon, 1987, 1989), the alleged chilling effects of ideological pressures are much less evident than some critics have contended. Nevertheless, the basic point remains that self-censorship produces a biased universe of research findings, the dimensions and contours of which are unknown and will remain unknown without discussion and disclosure of the kind produced by the Adlers.

A number of writers have argued against an overly "sentimental" approach to withholding information from published research findings (Barnes, 1979; Becker, 1964; Fichter & Kolb, 1953). While one should be alive to the potential harms produced by publication, these harms need to be explicitly assessed rather than simply assumed, and they need to be weighed against the gains to the wider community of making the information available. Writers like Becker (1964) and Johnson (1982) stress that it is desirable, where feasible, to discuss the possible consequences of publication with those being studied. This helps them to recognize the dilemmas faced by the researcher and may prepare them for consequences potentially flowing from publication. A strategy of this kind might be especially appropriate in the kind of situation the Adlers describe, where self-censorship is prompted by loyalty toward someone in the setting. Here it might be argued that researcher and researched have conflicting expectations about publication rather than conflicting interests. In situations of conflict, violence, or repression, on the other hand, the researcher's interest in full scientific disclosure conflict with the safety and well-being of research participants. In this case, alternatives to censorship may be hard to find.

The pressures that lead to self-censorship in academic writing discourage some writers from making their work available to wider audiences. As the example of the Adlers again shows, researchers sometimes have preferred the obscurity of publication in scholarly journals to bringing their work, and the people they study, to the attention of the mass media. There are, of course, good reasons for making research results available via the media to a wider audience. The public contributes to social science research as taxpayers and participates in it as respondents, informants, and subjects. Members of the public presumably have some right to see what has been produced (Roberts, 1984). Dissemination can potentially enhance the credibility of social research in the eyes of the wider community and among potential users, policymakers, and political elites (Mazur, 1987; Stocking & Dunwoody, 1982). Making social science procedures more understandable also helps to demystify research procedures and encourages greater understanding of the ethical difficulties faced by researchers—both factors that might be useful in the study of sensitive topics (Stocking & Dunwoody, 1982). Against this can be set the danger of what Sieber, in an earlier chapter, described as "press-mediated sensitivities," where stories about social research are reported in a sensationalist manner.

As Channels (this volume) acknowledges, media coverage of social science research is, *in general,* accurate (see also Weiss & Singer, 1988). Nevertheless, the interpretations and meanings that reporters assign to research findings reflect their priorities with respect, for example, to newsworthiness rather than those of the researcher. Even otherwise innocuous studies are not immune to misleading interpretations. For instance, a rather staid research study on the social and religious correlates of attendance at Roman Catholic schools in England and Wales (Hornsby-Smith & Lee, 1979) was described by one British national newspaper as having been about the sexual fantasies of convent schoolgirls.

It is most probably the case, however, that sensationalization or trivialization most often affect researchers whose topics or methods are unusual or sensitive in some way. Peterson (1991), for example, notes that stories featuring cultural anthropologists occur more frequently in the U.S. tabloid press than in "quality" newspapers. The focus of these stories, however, is on the allegedly bizarre practices of "primitive" tribes, the intrepid or "wacky" character of the researcher, or the cost to the taxpayer of apparently "useless" or trivial research. Even where media stories are accurately reported, they still can be surrounded by eye-catching layouts or titles that give a misleading impression of the article's content (Frisch & Watts, 1980; Richardson, 1990). Against his advice, the publisher of Brewer's (1992) book on the police in Northern Ireland serialized it in a popular Sunday newspaper with some unfortunate results (see Brewer, this volume).

Channels argues that particular difficulties arise from the potential loss of control over information and interpretation that occurs when the results of research find their way into the media. Very often in research, one is not interested simply in the direct effect of a particular variable— in Channels's case, the race/ethnicity of those being processed by the criminal justice system. Instead, analysis is directed toward indirect and interaction effects. The media, however, are averse to technical detail and to academic caution about drawing simple conclusions from complicated data. One may face an unpalatable choice between, on the one hand, allowing inaccurate coverage and, on the other hand, being circumspect in ways that encourage the public to reject the research as insubstantial.

Echoing a point made by Channels, Richardson (1990), a sociologist who has attempted to write directly for a popular audience, argues that researchers are sometimes too reticent to present themselves as an authority on their topic. In so doing, she argues, they risk depriving themselves of control over the content of their writing and diminish their bargaining power with editors. Like Richardson, Channels and others (e.g., Stocking & Dunwoody, 1982) encourage researchers to be more proactive in their dealings with the media. Indeed, Channels recommends that researchers, particularly when sensitive topics are involved, explicitly design their research with an eye to the possible implications of media coverage. This, of course, is less easy for researchers involved in qualitative or exploratory studies. Some of those who study sensitive topics may still need to remain cautious in their dealings with journalists.

References

Bakanic, V., McPhail, C., & Simon, R. J. (1987). The manuscript review and decision making process. *American Sociological Review, 52,* 631-642.

Bakanic, V., McPhail, C., & Simon, R. J. (1989). Mixed messages: Referees' comments on the manuscripts they review. *Sociological Quarterly, 30,* 639-654.

Barnes, J. A. (1979). *Who should know what? Social science, privacy, and ethics.* Harmondsworth, UK: Penguin.

Barnes, J. A. (1984). Ethical and political compromises in social research. *The Wisconsin Sociologist, 21,* 100-110.

Becker, H. S. (1964). Problems in the publication of field studies. In A. J. Vidich, J. Bensman, & M. R. Stein (Eds.), *Reflections on community studies.* New York: John Wiley.

Brewer, J. D. (1992). *Inside the RUC.* Oxford: Oxford University Press.

Felson, R. B. (1991). Blame analysis: Accounting for the behavior of protected groups. *American Sociologist, 22,* 5-23.

Fichter, J., & Kolb, W. L. (1953). Ethical limitations on sociological reporting. *American Sociological Review, 18,* 544-550.

Frisch, M., & Watts, D. L. (1980). Oral history and the presentation of class consciousness: The *New York Times* versus the Buffalo unemployed. *International Journal of Oral History, 1,* 88-110.

Gordon, R. A. (1980). Research on IQ, race and delinquency: Taboo or taboo. In E. Sagarin (Ed.), *Taboos in criminology.* Beverly Hills, CA: Sage.

Hornsby-Smith, M., & Lee, R. M. (1979). *Roman Catholic opinion.* Guildford, UK: University of Surrey.

Jahoda, M. (1981). To publish or not to publish. *Journal of Social Issues, 37,* 208-220.

Johnson, C. G. (1982). Risks in the publication of fieldwork. In J. E. Sieber (Ed.), *The ethics of social research: Vol. 2. Fieldwork, regulation, and publication.* New York: Springer-Verlag.

Lynch, F. R. (1989). *Invisible victims: White males and the crisis of affirmative action.* New York: Greenwood.

Mazur, A. (1987). Scientific disputes over policy. In H. T. Englehardt, Jr., & A. L. Caplan (Eds.), *Scientific controversies: Case studies in the resolution and closure of disputes in science and technology.* Cambridge, UK: Cambridge University Press.

Peterson, M. A. (1991). Aliens, ape men and whacky savages: The anthropologist in the tabloids. *Anthropology Today, 7*(5), 4-7.

Richardson, L. (1990). *Writing strategies: Reaching diverse audiences.* Newbury Park, CA: Sage.

Roberts, H. (1984). Putting the show on the road: The dissemination of research findings. In C. Bell & H. Roberts (Eds.), *Social researchings: Politics, problems and practice.* London: Routledge & Kegan Paul.

Stocking, S. H., & Dunwoody, S. L. (1982). Social science in the mass media: Images and evidence. In J. Sieber (Ed.), *The ethics of social research: Vol. 2. Fieldwork, regulation and publication.* New York: Springer-Verlag.

Vidich, A. J., & Bensman, J. (1964). The Springdale case: Academic bureaucrats and sensitive townspeople. In A. J. Vidich, J. Bensman, & M. R. Stein (Eds.), *Reflections on community studies.* New York: John Wiley.

Weiss, C. H., & Singer, E. (1988). *Reporting of social science in the national media.* New York: Russell Sage.

Whyte, W. H. (1958). Freedom and responsibility in research: The "Springdale case" [Editorial]. *Human Organization, 17,* 1-2.

14

Studying African Women's Secret Societies

PAMELA J. BRINK

This chapter examines the sensitive nature of studying secret societies in a small, isolated African village. The anthropologist enters the field foreign to the language and customs of the people being studied, is clearly identifiable as a stranger by virtue of skin color, language, and clothing styles, and is ignorant of the correct or appropriate behaviors of the culture group being studied. The fieldwork context lends itself to several sensitive issues.

This chapter will discuss some reasons the field situation made studying women's secret societies "sensitive." The first springs from the nature of the population itself, which can pose an ethical dilemma for the anthropologist. The population cannot give fully informed consent given that many of them have no idea what research means and do not relate to the anthropologist as a researcher. They relate to the fieldworker as a person who is initially a stranger and then becomes either a friend or a fictive relative. Because research and researcher are not part of their worldview, they do not fully understand to what they are consenting. The anthropologist is ethically bound to protect this population from having their anonymity and/or confidentiality violated. How this is done, when fulfilling the mandates of the research, is part of the subject of this chapter.

At one time in anthropology and sociology, covert participant observation was a common practice. The goal of the researcher was to explore and describe an unknown population, with or without their permission; if they did not give permission, then it was permissible to do the research covertly.[1] In this case, the end justified the means. Today, covert observation is an untenable situation and is considered unethical. Researchers wishing to do covert observations must clearly outline the benefits that will accrue that will outweigh risks to subjects when they find out they have been misled and have been in a research project about which they were unaware. When a vulnerable population is at risk, simply because informed consent cannot be obtained, then the researcher has the double responsibility of making the research overt. The dilemma occurs because the population being studied is a vulnerable population. For this reason, the dilemma is a "sensitive" issue.

Second, studying "secret societies" is sensitive given that the subjects "trust" the researcher not to violate their trust and not to reveal their secrets. A dilemma for the anthropologist when she or he discovers "secrets" in the fieldwork situation, and in which the population being studied "trusts" the anthropologist with those secrets, is what can be published that does not violate that trust, while fulfilling the mandates of the research for which funding was obtained.

A third reason this research is sensitive is the degree to which the population protects these "secrets" from outsiders. Most secret societies have sanctions against persons who reveal their secrets. I was at personal risk of being "punished" several times. If I had been in the field in September, the time when the secret "police" society[2] functioned in controlling the bad behavior of clan members for infractions during the past year, I might have been punished severely for asking about secrets.

The Annang are suspicious of strangers who go about asking too many questions that may be construed as "personal." They are afraid that the questioner is working for the tax collector. They may not be sure just how the questions are associated with taxes but, to be on the safe side, they refuse to answer questions and chase the questioner away. Martin (1956) described a similar experience in her work among the Ibibio, a neighboring tribe similar to the Annang in customs and language.

Finally, the Annang protected their secrets by "not knowing" any girls who were in the "fattening room." Not a single informant would admit there was a fattening room girl in their village, yet we saw one walking home one night from where she had obviously been on display in the village market all day. A second fattening room girl was observed in the village of my major informant, who was obtaining all the senior women for me to interview. Although he was helping me in my research, he said he did not know there was a fattening room girl in his village. These methods of maintaining secrecy persisted throughout all my field visits.

To place these dilemmas in context, I will first describe traditional anthropological fieldwork methods in which the anthropologist sets out alone to live with a hitherto unknown people. Usually, the language, customs, social structure, physical environment, and political climate are completely unfamiliar because no one else has reported on their culture. To do this, I will overview some basic principles of anthropological field methods, share my field work experience among the Annang of southeastern Nigeria, share some of my problems in data collection, and address the dilemmas this field research posed for me. Finally, I present a discussion on studying secrets in the field.

Anthropological Field Methods

In the early years of anthropological research, there was a studied avoidance of teaching fieldwork methods on the assumption that these methods should not be taught. "The field worker was simply told to bring back as much material as possible documenting the way of life of the people he [sic] had lived among. To plan more rigorously would probably bias observation, it was thought; or even worse, it would prevent the collection of valuable—and often disappearing—data" (Cohen & Naroll, 1973, p. 7).

Anthropologists going into the field relied on *Notes and Queries on Anthropology,* the first edition of which was issued in 1874 by a Committee of the Royal Anthropological Association (CRAA). In a section titled "Secret Societies" was the simple statement: "Where secret societies are powerful it may not be possible to get information from members as to the ritual and function, but information from non-members, though possibly unreliable as regards ritual, will be valuable in showing the effect of the institution on social structure" (CRAA, 1967, p. 194).

The primary anthropological research design is called *ethnography*, which means "to map a culture" and requires multiple methods of data collection to accomplish that goal. The primary method is participant observation over a long and continuous time to learn to behave appropriately within a new cultural context and to understand the meanings implicit in appropriate behavior. The entire point of participant observation is to learn to think and behave appropriately to the culture—to become as much of a participant as possible while retaining as much objectivity as possible to later write up the data. The purpose of learning to think and behave appropriately is that this validates that the researcher has "got it right," that his or her observations are accurate and repeatable. It is not at all unusual to leave the field situation and suffer from reverse culture shock simply because the field-worker must now rethink and reorient to the home culture when she or he has been so immersed in the new.

Field stays range from six months to more than two years but the preferred minimum length is one year to observe the complete cycle of events during a calendar year. The researcher is expected to learn the language of the people and become facile enough to understand and use humor appropriately. In the early stages of fieldwork, contacts are random and informal, while, in later stages, contacts are formal and purposive. The researcher has learned who to interview about what and the proper protocol to observe while interviewing.

The primary and most important field instrument is the researcher. The trust and rapport that is established between the researcher and the people being studied is critical to the success of the research. And that trust is based upon a belief in the integrity of the field-worker—a belief that shared secrets will not be revealed to anyone else. Violation of that trust ruins the fieldwork situation and the researcher is barred from further fieldwork in that location. Not only is that particular field-worker barred from further contact, but so are all later field-workers.

The Fieldwork Experience

My first African field experience was not my first trip to Nigeria, nor was it my first anthropological field experience. Professor Donald Hartle of the University of Nigeria, Nsukka, had cleared the way for me to study in Nigeria. He had arranged housing for me in the village. Although I had been studying Efik under Professor William Welmers at the University of California, Los Angles, I did not have sufficient language skills to conduct interviews by myself in Annang. I was therefore dependent upon interpreters or English-speaking informants. For a variety of reasons, this first visit was limited to 6 months, which was insufficient for me to become proficient in Annang. Later visits were even shorter, limited to summer holidays.

There were several problems in doing field research that had an impact on the quantity and quality of data that could be collected. I was a white North American woman professor living in a black rural village culture that was male oriented and male dominated. Finding a place for me within the culture was problematic. Although women have lower status than men, "professor" was considered a very high status. As a white person, I was also assumed to be wealthy, which was also a very high status. As a stranger, I was immune to witchcraft, but I was also considered stupid given that I did not know the language as well as the small children. I could sit with the men and listen to men's talk and I could also be counted upon for monetary assistance. There was always the question, however: Should I be treated as an Annang or as a white? Should everything be explained to me as if I were a child, or should one assume that I knew the rudimentary facts of Annang life?

Field status is of critical importance in fieldwork. The field site was a closed and remote community that had little direct contact with the outside world. Villagers may meet the occasional missionary family or have members of their own families go off to the city and return, but mostly they are unaffected by the urbanization and industrialization of Western culture. Most social contact was through kinship and extended kinship ties. The researcher must be fit into that system somehow or always remain an "outsider."[3]

I was adopted as a junior sister (*eyen eka*—same mother, same father) by my chief informant's father. As a result, I was given protection and status in his village. I became auntie to all of my fictive brother's children (four by his first marriage, seven by his second) and junior sister to his two brothers and to his sister. This was fortunate, as his sister was head of all women's secret societies in the village. As a relative, I was privy to information about the Annang not available to nonrelatives. Also, as a relative, I was financially responsible for them. If there was anything wrong with any of them, I was there to help. I took them to hospital, paid their bills, bought medicines, and so on. I was treated as any other wealthy relative.

In the early days of fieldwork, I did not know where I belonged or what status I should take. Being adopted into a village family gave me kinship status and provided some protection from those who thought I had no business in Afaha Obong. Being white, with no obvious job, also made me a suspicious character. Why would a white woman, who was not a missionary, live in the village? And then there were those who wanted me to write about the Annang so they would be known to the world.

The first field visit was the most successful simply because I was there a longer time so people came to know me. Also, I was living inside a village, so I heard about events quicker. The last two visits were significantly shorter, living in a nearby town, requiring that I commute to the village. On the first two visits, I had a car at my disposal while on the third visit I had to hire taxis.

There were several logistical problems in the field. Due to my lack of facility with the language, I always needed an interpreter around to rescue me from my own failings. This posed a problem given that most of the English speakers were male (most of the educated Annang were men). Also, most of the individuals who were looking for jobs were men. If I wanted to talk to women about women's affairs, I really needed a woman interpreter and they were hard to find. I sometimes scheduled interviews during school holidays when one of my fictive sisters could go with me to interview one of their elderly relatives. I felt the most comfortable on these occasions.

During the last field visit, a young woman interpreter had been found to help me and she turned out to be very skilled. She was not, however, a relative of any of the women we interviewed and was not a fictive relative of mine. In addition, she was a Christian and had not been through any of the secret societies herself. Therefore informants did not have an established trust relationship with her. So, although she was a woman skilled in both languages, she was not a member of the right clan and was not a member of the secret societies. She was, herself, someone to be suspicious of, but better than a man.

These field problems (lack of time in the field, lack of facility with the language, lack of skilled women interpreters who were themselves members of the secret societies) prevented the richness of detailed data that could have been obtained. On the other hand, the data that were acquired are sufficiently detailed to present a dilemma of what to report.

Field Problems

Other field problems were a direct result of the logistics of short field stays, lack of facility with the language, and being interested in women's secrets. I could not "hang around" in someone's compound and broach the subject of secret societies spontaneously. I was treated as a "very special person" whenever I visited a compound and was given the status of having a "formal visit" arranged. Formal visits always resulted in a crowd of people (both men and women) watching a white woman in their village. This atmosphere was not conducive to sharing secrets. In contrast, during my last field visit, I took a young white woman as my research assistant. We established her as being junior to me. While I was having formal visits with the men and senior women, she was gossiping in the kitchens with the women and children.

Most of the interviews in 1989 were arranged for me by a man who was the senior male in his extended family and village. My research assistant and I would arrive in a taxi, driven by a man from another clan, pick up the young woman interpreter, pick up our sponsor who had arranged the interview, and then proceed to the home of the informant. The men would either stay and listen to the interview or be near enough for the women to be uncomfortable. Frequently, they would remove themselves from sight when we asked them to leave, but we could hear them chatting together.

There were several persons who wanted to help me in my research and could not see why others would not want to help as well. In their enthusiasm, they would say, "Oh, it's all right to ask questions." Or even, "Go ahead and take pictures, it's all right." And when I would take the photographs or ask my questions, someone would protest, loudly interrupting the proceedings until all had been explained. This happened three times, once in 1974 and twice in 1989.

In 1974, as I was interviewing a senior woman, having had the interview arranged by a neighbor, we were interrupted by angry shouts and a man burst in on us. He shouted and gesticulated, pulling the old woman out of her room and into the courtyard. Here he harangued us all. Many women crowded around and some men began to gather. Then the old woman's son appeared and shouted at the original man. He talked and talked and talked until at last all the bystanders began to disperse and eventually the original tormentor left as well, mumbling and gesticulating at all of us. My friend came over to find out what the concern was and I explained what I was doing and why I was doing it. He explained to me that the man was angry because the old woman was telling me "secrets," and if I wanted to learn these secrets I had to pay for them and I had not paid. I was also told that the man had expected me to interview his wife rather than the old woman I was visiting. He felt his wife knew more about "these things" than the old woman. Frustrated and shaken by this experience, I found it hard to settle down and get back to the interview.

This very uncomfortable situation brought home to me several lessons about fieldwork. The first one was obvious—how easily one could get into difficulty during the early days of fieldwork. The second was how ignorant I was about the customs of the people, trusting that my informant of the moment would not put me in a situation that would violate group norms or endanger me. The third was the Annang custom of paying for secrets, about which I was ignorant. And the final lesson was that I should have stuck to my original research questions and not gone off on wild-goose chases simply because someone thought I was interested in a different topic. These individuals, believing I was interested in secret societies, were eager to help me get the information I wanted.

The second situation occurred in 1989, again in the early days of fieldwork. This time, our principal informant came to get me and my research assistant and take us to one of the villages where a second burial[4] was in progress in the village square. "Bring your camera and let's go," he shouted, and off we went. He placed us in an advantageous spot and I began to take pictures. All of a sudden, the crowd turned on us and a man was heard shouting violently. He was a member of one of the secret societies and was angry that I was photographing secrets. In fact, we were all in the village square, a very public place. It was quite frightening for a while, but the incident was finally resolved by my taking a picture of the entire society, promising a copy to each man.

Both incidents were based upon the anger of a single man who felt I was violating Annang secrets. His anger would arouse others to question my right to be there. The men were always placated by being told that I was "paying" for these secrets as an Annang would pay.

A third incident, again in 1989, involved a fattening room girl (*mbobo*) and her mother. One of my fictive sisters found out there was a mbobo in a nearby village and wanted me to see her. We arrived at the mbobo's compound as she was returning from the blacksmith's on the back of his bicycle. He had been installing the *awok* (brass winding bracelets) on her legs. When the man went away, she went into the house and took off all her clothes except a pair of panties (mbobo must be undressed always). She went around the back of the house to the toilet and then returned to the house where she entered a bedroom (evidently hers) and opened the door and windows. She pulled a bowl of food out from under her bamboo bed and sat on the floor with her legs crossed out in front of her. She pulled out a small carved doll (*udeng*) from the waistband of her panties and first fed it from the bowl, and then herself. She called out to a small boy to fetch her some water, which she first gave to her udeng. As all these events were happening, my fictive sister kept saying, "Take your pictures, it's all right!" I was too uncomfortable to take the pictures without permission and the mbobo was studiously ignoring me, although she was laughing and chatting with our male taxi driver. When the mbobo's mother arrived and found us there, she was very angry. I asked permission to interview and take pictures, but she refused saying I had to pay a lot first. And the amount she quoted was indeed a lot! Because we didn't have that kind of money with us, we went away without our pictures and without some of our questions answered. We had seen a mbobo at home, however, and we had seen how the house had been arranged for her.

The Dilemmas

These incidents, and others, have created several dilemmas for me. I have taped the songs sung by the celebrant, I have photographed the contents inside the secret box where the ritual paraphernalia is kept, and I have a listing of the contents. I have a list of the foods used during the initiation rites, the songs that are sung, the money and other materials used. They are all very secret. I have paid for these items, but readers have not. Do I have the right to publish this material? In looking at the manuscripts on mbobo written by students for their bachelor's theses (Akpan, 1990; Bassey, n.d.; Ibanga, 1985; Idem, 1979), there is very little detailed information. One can only wonder if they were also avoiding secrets. In fact, most of the other literature on fattening is superficial (Elake, 1963; Kirk-Greene, 1957; Malcolm, 1925; Messenger, 1957, 1959; Nzekwu, 1959; Talbot, 1915; Udo Ema, 1940).

This dilemma, for me, is real and has not, as yet, been resolved. To what extent can I, or should I, report on what I know about Annang women's secret societies?

A second dilemma was in relation to the fieldwork itself. To participate fully in the secret societies, I needed to be inducted into the societies. There were two problems with becoming a member of these societies. In one society, *Ngwongwo,* clitoridectomy was part of the induction ceremonies (Brink, 1989). I was not willing to discover, personally, the extent of this surgery, and was therefore barred from participant observation in the society.

The second problem was the requirement that women seek the advice of a diviner (*Idiong*) who would prescribe one or the other of the societies as a cure for illness. *Ndam* is the society that is prescribed for the treatment of intractable headaches. I don't have headaches and I was not willing to test the diviner's ability to diagnose accurately. There are social sanctions against lying to diviners that are similar to the sanctions that call in the police society. The second society (*ngwongwo*) is prescribed for women with problems of infertility or persistent leanness. Not being lean and being too old to bother about fertility, I was not eligible for that society. Therefore I never became a member of either society. I was, and still am, limited to hearsay evidence. To what extent, therefore, are the data that I have collected valid? At best, I can triangulate my findings by comparing one person's statements with another's. I can validate one informant's accuracy by comparing their verbal accounts with verifiable observations of my own. I can describe peripheral or circumstantial hearsay evidence but cannot describe what it is like to be initiated or be a member of that society.

Although I was interested in studying the fattening room, that experience requires initiation into the other two societies as a prerequisite to entrance. Being barred from those societies, I was barred from any further observation of mbobo. I am left with the advice from the Committee of the Royal Anthropological Association: "Information from non-members, though possibly unreliable as regards ritual, will be valuable in showing the effect of the institution on social structure" (CRAA, 1967, p. 194).

A final difficulty in knowing what to report and what not to report stems from the same phenomena as that which occurred in the field. After writing my reports, I usually send them off to my field informants to validate what I have written. Mostly, I cannot get a critique of my work. Instead, my friends are so happy that I am writing about the Annang that they offer no criticism at all. I am left, therefore, with the possibility of flawed reporting. Although I have checked my materials in the field, the way I write my final reports and the conclusions I have reached may not be a true reflection of the Annang.

Resolving the Dilemmas

There are several solutions to studying secrets in an ethnographic field situation, some of which are discussed over coffee at conventions and others whispered about by graduate students about to go into the field. The least acceptable solution is to "go native," or to abandon the role of researcher and become a full participant in the culture. When the researcher stops collecting data and/or refuses to publish the collected information, the anthropological community believes it has lost valuable data. As a graduate student in anthropology, I heard about Frank Cushing and his dilemma in studying the Zuni Indians. He became so close to the Zuni that he became a Bo priest. Once he had achieved that status, however, he never published about the Zuni again. His book, *Zuni Breadstuffs,* I was told, was the last time he published anything closely resembling a Zuni secret.

A second method, widely discussed and accepted for a time, was to manufacture a different name for the culture under study. The question was this: "Does one reveal secrets and protect the culture by giving them a different name, or does one use the group's real name and not publish the secrets?" Two outcomes have resulted. One story is told of Margaret Mead, who had written up a study she had conducted but had provided anonymity by giving the group a new name and location. In a talk to some members of a graduate department of anthropology, however, she shared who the group really was. Later she was horrified when she learned that one of her listeners had revealed the name of the group in a published work.

Another result of manufacturing pseudonyms reported more recently in anthropological circles involves the researcher's relationship with the group. There have been times when the researcher has returned to the field proudly bearing the ethnography (either in book form or in dissertation form) as a gift to the village. Upon looking at the title, the elders exclaim, "Do you mean to tell us that after living with us for two years, you still do not know our name?" Here we see an example of what happens in a vulnerable population that does not understand what the researcher was about. They believed their name would be known to the world and on that basis had agreed to the research. The researcher believed she was "protecting them from themselves" when she introduced the pseudonym. This does not endear the researcher to the population and makes reentry into the field much more difficult. The use of the pseudonym is not as much in vogue for fieldwork outside of urban settings but remains a popular form of maintaining anonymity in North American cities (see Becker, 1969). When pseudonyms are not used, the dilemma remains of whether to reveal "secrets" and, if so, to what degree (see Ellen, 1984, p. 151).

For each field-worker, the dilemma of what to tell and how much to tell is a personal dilemma. Because we are trusted, we have an obligation to behave in a responsible manner. We have learned to think the way our informants think, and we have learned their explanatory models. They expect us to think and act within their frame of reference. If we think and act appropriate to our own frame of reference, as researchers, and that frame of reference is contrary to and/or in conflict with theirs, they trust us to respect their frame of reference *as our primary responsibility.* Clearly, there are no easy solutions.

Notes

1. In his famous article, Rosenhan (1973) describes what happened to eight individuals who presented themselves to psychiatric outpatient clinics with a single presenting complaint and were admitted to inpatient psychiatric wards. In all cases, the patients had "invented" their symptoms and presented them in context of their life histories. Once admitted, they never referred to their symptoms again. Instead, they became participant observers of the psychiatric units, eventually taking notes openly and interviewing the staff. Not once were these individuals "spotted" as researchers. When the article appeared in print, there was a loud hue and cry in the psychiatric community, accusing Rosenhan and his research assistants of manufacturing data. There were more "Letters to the Editor" in the next issue of *Science* than ever before.

2. This secret society (*Ekpo*) was greatly feared. During my last field visit in 1989, I was told of a woman who was killed driving through the clan territories on her way to work. Ekpo were near the road at the time and accused her of "looking at them," an accusation subject to immediate punishment. A young man on the grounds of the Catholic Junior Seminary was shot in the eye and later died. This society went about the village beating people for alleged infractions during the year.

3. Peggy Golde (1970, pp. 5-10) discusses many of these issues thoroughly in the introduction to her book *Women in the Field.* She also identified the special needs of young single women, in contrast to single older women or married women, in the fieldwork situation.

4. The "second burial" is similar to a memorial service but very elaborate. The senior son is responsible for all expenses and, because the proceedings are very costly, the second burial is sometimes delayed for years. The entire village is invited in addition to all the members of the deceased's secret societies and all important people in the village or clan. Bands are hired to play, new cloth is purchased for all women relatives to have new clothes, a cow or pig is purchased and slaughtered, a cement sculpture is commissioned to commemorate the deceased and placed in a prominent area where all can see it, and so on. The celebration may take place in one day or over several days depending upon the status of the deceased. Part of the celebrations take place in the village square, where there is dancing by the members of the secret societies.

References

Akpan, C. R. (1990). *Traditional institution: Mbobo culture in Ibibio Land.* Unpublished bachelor's thesis, University of Cross River State, Uyo.

Bassey, E. E. (n.d.). *Traditional marriage institution in East Itam in Itu Local Government Area.* Unpublished bachelor's thesis, University of Cross River State, Uyo.

Becker, H. S. (1969). Problems in the publication of field studies. In G. J. McCall & J. L. Simmons (Eds.), *Issues in participant observation.* Reading, MA: Addison-Wesley.

Brink, P. J. (1977). Decision making of the health care consumer: A Nigerian example. In Western Interstate Commission for Higher Education (Ed.), *Communicating nursing research: Nursing research in the bicentennial year.* Boulder, CO: Western Interstate Commission for Higher Education.

Brink, P. J. (1984). Value orientations as an assessment tool in cultural diversity: Theory, method and examples. *Nursing Research, 33,* 198-203.

Brink, P. J. (1989). The fattening room among the Annang of Nigeria. *Medical Anthropology: Anthropological Approaches to Nursing Research, 12,* 131-143.

Cohen, R., & Naroll, R. (1973). Methods in cultural anthropology. In R. Naroll & R. Cohen (Eds.), *A handbook of method in cultural anthropology* (pp. 3-24). New York: Columbia University Press.

Committee of the Royal Anthropological Association (CRAA). (1967). *Notes and queries on anthropology.* London: Routledge & Kegan Paul.

Elake, P. (1963). Ekue rites. *Nigeria Magazine, 76,* 45-46.

Ellen, R. F. (1984). *Ethnographic research: A guide to general conduct.* New York: Academic Press.

Golde, P. (1970). Introduction. In P. Golde (Ed.), *Women in the field: Anthropological experiences.* Chicago: Aldine.

Ibanga, M. J. (1985). *Fattening "Mobopo" in Ikot Etok Udoh (Abak).* Unpublished bachelor's thesis, University of Cross River State, Uyo.

Idem, S. B. (1979). *The changing role of women in the Old Calabar Province.* Unpublished bachelor of science paper, University of Nigeria, Nsukka.

Kirk-Greene, A. H. M. (1957). A Lala initiation ceremony. *Man, 5,* 9-10.

Malcolm, L. W. G. (1925). Note on the seclusion of girls among the Efik at Old Calabar. *Man, 25,* 113-114.

Martin, A. (1956). *The oil palm economy of the Ibibio farmer.* Ibadan, Nigeria: Ibadan University Press.

McCall, G. J., & Simmons, J. L. (1969). *Issues in participant observation.* Reading, MA: Addison-Wesley.

Messenger, J. (1957). *Anang acculturation: A study of shifting cultural focus.* Unpublished doctoral dissertation, University of Michigan.

Messenger, J. (1959). Religious acculturation among the Anang Ibibio. In W. Bascom & M. Herskovitz (Eds.), *Continuity and change in African cultures.* Chicago: University of Chicago Press.

Nzekwu, O. (1959). Iria ceremony. *Nigeria, 63,* 341-352.

Rosenhan, D. L. (1973, January 19). On being sane in insane places. *Science, 179,* 250-258.

Talbot, D. A. (1915). *Women's mysteries of a primitive people: The Ibibios of Southern Nigeria.* London: Cassell.

Udo, R. K. (1970). *Geographical regions of Nigeria.* Berkeley: University of California Press.

Udo Ema, A. J. (1940). Fattening girls in Oron, Calabar Province. *Nigeria, 21,* 386-389.

15

Ethical Issues in Self-Censorship

Ethnographic Research on Sensitive Topics

PATRICIA A. ADLER
PETER ADLER

Douglas (1971, 1976) has argued that human society is conflictful, rife with layers of fronts disguising various levels of private and less-than-public information that insiders would prefer to conceal from the prying eyes of outsiders. The mandate of the researcher is to penetrate these fronts and thereby discover the truth about science and society. While not everyone will agree with the polemical slant of this statement, it remains true that a surprising amount of the research undertaken by social scientists falls into the realm of sensitive topics, comprising private knowledge and thereby challenging researchers to obtain it and to think seriously before revealing it. This is especially true of ethnographic research, because the personal nature of the interactions and relationships between ethnographers and their subjects leads the latter to discover more depth insights into their subjects' attitudes and behavior than practitioners of many other methods. Whether the sensitivity of the setting and/or its people is recognized in advance or it emerges as a surprise, researchers often discover that they have unearthed information

AUTHORS' NOTE: We would like to thank Charles Gallmeier, Jim Henslin, Raymond Lee, and Carol Warren for helpful comments on earlier drafts of this chapter.

that could prove hazardous or embarrassing to some members of the research setting (including themselves).

Self-censorship, the practice of omitting selected facts and features of one's research findings, has been practiced by data gatherers for as long as the ethnographic tradition has existed. This usually involves deleting experiences that reveal personal, sensitive, or compromising features about researchers or their subjects. Goffman (cited in Lofland, 1971) has referred to researchers' discussions of their perils in the field as "reporting only the second worst thing that happened to them" (censoring the worst), while Warren (1980) has suggested that what we read is more likely to be the tenth or twelfth worst. The fact that field researchers censor their presentations, as well as the nature of those censorings, are not among the more openly discussed aspects of field research. When these tales are told, it is usually done in private, face-to-face exchanges (referred to as "corridor talk" by Van Maanen, 1988). In this chapter, we will peer behind the closed doors of self-censorship, examining the types of intentional omissions made in the reports of field researchers. Although we address many practical issues related to self-censorship, we must never forget that this utilitarianism must be always balanced with an ethical awareness that privileges what Lee and Renzetti (this volume) have referred to as "scrupulosity over callousness."

Background

Our interest in self-censorship was sparked by some difficult decisions we had to make in two of our research settings: those of drug traffickers (see Adler, 1985) and college athletes (see Adler & Adler, 1991). We conducted our study of drug traffickers over a 6-year period, from 1974 to 1980, which involved daily participant observation with members of a dealing and smuggling community. We stumbled onto the community by accident, befriending a neighbor who turned out to be a smuggler. Over the years, we became close friends with both him, his (ultimately divorced) wife, and his whole network of associates, spending frequent time together, testifying at his various trials, and taking him into our home to live with us for 7 months after he was released from jail. We also maintained close ties with his former wife and the new dealing network she entered after leaving him, working in her legitimate business front, caring for their children, and following her many escapades (e.g., extramarital affairs, airline scams, drug dealing). Although we did not deal ourselves, we participated in many of their activities, partying with them, attending social gatherings, traveling with them, and watching them plan and execute their business activities. We thus came to know members of this subculture and formed close friendships with several of them. In addition to observing and conversing casually with these dealers and smugglers, we conducted in-depth taped interviews and cross-checked our observations and their accounts against further sources of data whenever possible.

Although committees for the protection of human subjects were nascent at this time, we were first approached by a member of this body to secure clearance for the research in 1977, by which time we were well into the project. Consulting our subjects, they urged us not to go through the procedures, as it would have required them to sign consent forms with their real names. This, they believed, would not have given them the kind of protection they desired. Once sensitized to this concern, we began to think about other activities of ours that could potentially endanger them. For this reason, we turned down an offer by a friend to help us gain research entrée with agents of the Drug Enforcement Administration (DEA), data that would have given our work a multiperspectival vantage on dealing but that might have brought our research and our subjects to the attention of the authorities. We also feared being subpoenaed to testify in the trial of a former graduate student, whom we had heard through our informants had gone native after he had been arrested for dealing, and he was trying to claim research as his defense. This would also potentially disclose our research and endanger our subjects, we feared. Finally, when we felt adequately immersed in the setting to develop our ideas, write about them, and publish them, we encountered our fourth set of qualms. How could we publish articles about our subjects when most of them were still actively involved in illegal activities? In all conscience, we felt we could not. So, despite the fact that we regarded a sociological journal as a place where topical information might rarely reach the public notice, we censored ourselves. As graduate students, we were approaching entry to the job market and needed the publications, yet we made a conscious decision not to submit any articles while our subjects were engaged in activities through which they could be recognized. We also used disguise to alter facts about the identities of some of our subjects and cut out unflattering descriptions of their appearances (to avoid insulting them). Our first articles (Adler & Adler, 1980, 1982) did not appear until we had moved out of town and our subjects had significantly altered their activities. By the time more articles and a book were published, our subjects were all out of the trafficking business.

For our next research project, we spent five years (1980-1985) studying the socialization of college athletes on a university basketball team. The university was a medium-sized private school in the mid-south-central part of the United States. During these years, the team placed in the top 20 of nationally ranked Division I teams for several years, achieving an overall winning record of four times as many wins as losses. It thus held the distinction of being the most successful basketball team in the university's history. At the same time, it was the most successful and popular team in the city, because there were no professional sports teams located there. The focus of major attention, all of the players and coaches became well known to the team's many fans.

In conducting this research, we assumed differentiated roles in the setting. Peter became an active member (see Adler & Adler, 1991), taking an official role as an assistant coach on the team (while still teaching classes). In this position, he served as an adviser, counseling athletes on their academic schedules, their future career possibilities both inside and outside of athletics, the interpersonal dynamics of their relations with teammates and coaches, and how this influenced both their on- and off-court performance. At the same time, he advised the coaching staff on matters pertaining to players' academic course work, the interface between the coaching staff and the university's academic administration, and some of the dynamics concerning their interpersonal dealings with the players. As a member of the coaching staff, he sat on the bench during games, traveled with the team on road games, and made occasional appearances on the head coach's radio and television shows. Patti assumed the role of a peripheral member, working as a professor at the university, interacting with members of the scene as a coach's wife, and forming close friendships with several of the players, who became our key informants. Although we were both insiders in the scene, our roles and perspectives were different; this difference included both our degree of self-identification with the team and the degree to which others identified us as being a part of the team.

Peter's clearly delineated position as a coach and his frequent media appearances led to the players' and coaches' celebrity status being extended to him (see Adler, 1984). During the season, reporters combed feverishly for knowledgeable "experts" to interview, and Peter became a regular source, receiving considerable publicity. While we immediately realized the fact of his celebrity, it took us longer to recognize some of the consequences of that celebrity.

When we first began to feel that we were familiar enough with the setting to consider writing about it, we once again experienced feelings of constraint. Peter's celebrity and his publicly known association with the setting made us feel that any work we published on the topic might receive more media attention than we desired. While our subjects were not engaged in illegal activities, the publicity that publication of our research might bring might destroy the anonymity of the setting and its members. While some social scientists have decried the importance of confidentiality and anonymity in studying public figures (see Spector, 1980), we did not feel that way. We had visions of our presentations finding their way back to our subjects, such as had happened to Morgan (1972) in the infamous "British Association Scandal." We neither wanted to upset or alienate our subjects, as had happened in his case, nor to rankle any number of other relevant parties. This might invoke potential ethical or legal problems, we feared (although, ironically, it was not prohibited under the guidelines of the regulatory and review board in charge of protecting human subjects; see Olesen, 1979; Wax & Cassell, 1979).

After wrestling with this problem for some time, we decided it would be best to adopt the following two forms of self-censorship: (a) we would not write about certain topics and (b) we would not publish in certain forms or venues. Regarding the former, we excluded from our scope of interest any material concerning NCAA violations, booster organizations, or extensive discussion of drug use. The latter decision involved holding back from either doing extensive media interviews about our findings or publishing our research as a book (we felt that a book would be more visible to the media than articles published in relatively remote scholarly journals), for as long as either the coach, any team members, or we remained at the university.

Ironically, we had stronger feelings about the problem of self-censorship in the basketball as compared with the drug dealing setting, even though members of the latter setting were engaged in much more illegal behavior (and one of our respondents was dating a sociologist, which gave him a much greater likelihood of access to the data presentation; see Warren, 1980). This stemmed from several factors. First, the unorganized character of the drug traffickers and their turnover in the business led us to feel that these people would be harder for outsiders to locate two or three years into the future. In contrast, we believed that the danger of discovery through outsiders "busting the code" would be more pronounced for our basketball subjects due to their membership in a publicly visible and organized group that was difficult to veil. This problem was particularly enhanced by the celebrity of our subjects and the consequent media attention that both they and our work received. We feared, even, that members of the media might intermediate between us and them if their identities were discovered. As it turned out, we were embarrassed by two situations in which prominent newspaper reviews of our book identified both the school and the coach with whom we did the research, the second reporter going out of his way to solicit a comment from the coach on his thoughts about the book. With the exception of our primary key informant in the trafficking setting, Dave, we also felt a greater sense of loyalty to our subjects in the basketball research, due to their openness to us and their enormous help and loyalty. All of these factors allowed us to reveal more about the drug dealing setting and to censor ourselves less.

Analyzing our feelings and decisions, we realized they were prompted by various pulls toward self-censorship that are generic in character. In the remainder of this chapter, we discuss these factors.

Factors Prompting Self-Censorship

The Development of Loyalties

One of the strongest reasons people omit material from their presentations is rooted in the personal loyalties they develop toward their settings and to the individuals they study within them. In both cases, these were primarily to individuals. Our strongest ties were to Dave, who had lived with us and became our closest friend. Even after leaving the setting, we continued to maintain close ties with Dave and to exchange visits with him in our new location. In the basketball setting, our loyalty was to the head coach, who had served as the gatekeeper to the setting for us, authorizing our presence and sponsoring us to the rest of the team and setting members. Not only did we appreciate the degree of entrée and trust he had accorded us, but he had extended his personal loyalty as well, and we felt obligated to extend ours in return. Beyond this, we greatly admired the man as both a coach and a moral human being (eventually dedicating the book to him) and did not want to do anything to distress him either personally or professionally.

This is the classic Chicago School type of self-censorship, based on an unexpressed research bargain sensed by researchers and members to protect the latter (see Haas & Shaffir, 1980). After all, members usually allow researchers to become familiar with their lives only after they become convinced that the researchers are "nice guys" and will not harm them. Researchers must then answer the question, "Whose side are we on?" (Becker, 1967). Following Becker, they have usually chosen to align themselves with their subjects, who are often low status members of society. As Klockars (1979) has noted, this may involve the suppression of selective information. For example, in Klockars's (1974) case study of a fence, he omitted any mention of a critical way his subject both maintained relations with the police and enhanced his ability to operate his illicit business: "Vince" fed small-time thieves (not the professional operators with whom he regularly dealt and who had status and position within the criminal subculture) to the police (Klockars, personal communication, 1991). Fine (1987) found in his study of Little League baseball players that even the youngest athletes may require protection in the form of the researcher's self-censorship. He agonized at length over whether to include data on the more nasty and deviant aspects of the youths' subculture, then finally decided that their parents (whom he anticipated would read the book) would be too upset with his subjects if he included these in the final version (see Fine & Sandstrom, 1988). Letkemann (1980) also voiced concerns about whether and how to self-censor to protect his subjects, who had been critical of persons in power, in his book about incarcerated safe-crackers. Finally, Roadburg (1980, p. 283) noted numerous occasions in his research on professional soccer players when his subjects specifically asked him to censor his work ("I hope you don't write about this in your book," they asked him) because he was observing behavior that fell within the acceptable confines of societal norms but that violated the norms of their professional roles (playing cards, going to pubs or discos). These constraints thus fall within the ethical dimension.

Ironically, even when researchers feel they are being evenhanded and fair to their subjects, they often experience what Lofland (1971) has called "the agony of betrayal." Portrayals that appear to researchers to be neutrally cast may seem critical or even negative to participants (see Gallagher, 1964; Gurel, 1975; Vidich & Bensman, 1964; Warren, 1980; Whyte, 1964). This is especially true when researchers attempt to take an "objective" or "detached" perspective and to look at the setting in a different way than the members. Then, they are betraying the participants not only by portraying too much about them but also by analyzing them in a way that suggests that their own perceptions about themselves may not be correct. This was a special worry to us in the drug trafficking research because we had conceptualized Dave as the epitome of a "failure" and studied him closely to determine how someone could flop so miserably in this arena of "easy money." One of the reasons that we eventually concluded was responsible for his lack of business success was his self-deception: He routinely violated the simple rules of dealing (don't sell to people you don't know; don't store the product where you live; don't talk openly about drugs on the phone) even though he denied that he did. Yet our observations from knowing and living with him showed us that he regularly forged "creative" interpretations of his behavior that allowed him to act as he pleased, even when it went against his rational business policies. For us to contradict his perceptions of himself in writing would constitute an act of betrayal.

Self-censorship due to loyalty and commitment take their extreme form when researchers go native and either adopt the members' perspectives completely or fail to return from the field. One version of this is the ethnomethodological epistemology of "becoming the phenomenon," where going native and renouncing the professional social science audience is a requisite (Heritage, 1984; Mehan & Wood, 1975). Studying deviant or illegal activities also fosters this type of self-censorship, because these are particularly sensitive topics.

Ongoing Involvement in the Research Site

In the basketball research, we also chose to keep a low profile because we anticipated a continuing relationship to the setting. In contrast to the drug trafficking study, where we knew we were leaving town as soon as we got our degrees, in the athlete study we were employed by the school and thought we would have a long-term relationship with the basketball program. At the time we were doing the research, we did not anticipate ever fully leaving the setting, and we thought it might be disadvantageous for our future research to reveal anything negative or that might be perceived as negative (to the best of our ability to judge) about the setting or its members. Thus researchers who sense the need for maintaining positive relations with an organization or its members may feel compelled to censor their published presentations. This may account for the relative paucity of academics' direct studies of interactions with colleagues, as Douglas (1976) noted in discussing his interest in, yet complete self-censorship of ideas about, the social order and organization of academic faculty meetings. Letkemann (1980, p. 298) worried about this same problem in deciding how to prepare his work on incarcerated safe-crackers for publication: "There were questions of self-interest. Perhaps I would someday wish to do prison research again; should I therefore be less critical of prisons in this report, so that I might again have the cooperation of the prison administrators?"

Researchers who take an active or complete membership role (see Adler & Adler, 1987), who participate in the central, core activities of the group and/or who have a deeper, more personal form of self-identification with the group, are especially prone to have long-term involvement in their settings. This is particularly true for those who choose their research topics in an opportunistic (Riemer, 1977) manner, capitalizing on existing membership in a group by turning it into a research subject.

Sponsorship

A third factor influencing our self-censorship lay in the practical and legal realm. Outside the athletic program, the greater university framed both the participants' activities and our own. We did not want to "bite the hand that fed us" and be critical of the administration that signed our paychecks.

We felt that the university might react sensitively to the publication of our findings because of the revenue it relied on from supporters in the community. We also feared that negative legal outcomes might arise for the university if we published data about sensitive areas governed by NCAA regulations. While the coach ran a fairly straight program, the rules and regulations seemed subject to change and interpretation, and we suspected that it might be impossible for an "up and coming" team to run a competitive Division I program without occasionally overstepping the bounds.

Researchers may especially feel the pull to self-censorship if their research is sponsored by a funding agency. As Broadhead and Rist (1976, p. 325) have noted, "Sponsorship not only influences the formulation and execution of a variety of researchable issues, but directs the analysis and presentation of findings as well." When this occurs, researchers are often tempted to tell the funding agency one thing while they do what they want.

Snow (1980) has discussed this form of self-censorship in the context of disengagement, in referring to pressure from granting agencies and sponsors to quit the field. This pressure may be based on their fear that researchers will reveal something to reflect poorly on them or on the program they are supporting. Some form of this may have happened with us in the athletic research as well, because, at one point in the third year of the study, Peter began to hear rumblings among the faculty that his research was not "sitting well" with the administration. He should quit the research and abandon the setting, he was told by the chair of his department, or else it might have "serious repercussions for his tenure." In consulting other faculty members around the university, he found that they all advised the same course of action. As a result, he began to disengage from his active membership role, first stepping down as an assistant coach but remaining unofficially associated with the team and then, subsequently, withdrawing altogether. This cessation was frustrating and painful to us and felt like the university was acting to censor not only our potential publications but our data gathering as well.

A final impetus to self-censorship in this category comes when the individual, group, or agency sponsoring the research has a political or policy agenda. Researchers may be given grants, sponsored to attend conferences, or provided access to research settings with the implicit understanding that their work will reflect favorably on the sponsor and/or follow the preferred political agenda. Many sensitive topics are mined with specific agendas that researchers must tread carefully to avoid becoming ejected. This is certainly true in the area of drug policy, which is laden with moral overtones, and in many other political and policy areas as well.

Institutional Setting

In addition to the three factors prompting our self-censorship, there are several that have influenced other sociologists. One of these may arise in the negotiations researchers have to do to gain entrée in studying more formal organizations. In contrast to the informal, unspoken research exchange that often constrains ethnographers in unstructured research settings, field-workers studying bureaucratic organizations may have to make explicit promises or agreements with organizational gatekeepers to gain entrée. This can sometimes lead to their censoring their findings, either partially or totally, at a later point in their research. In Whyte's negotiations to study the Phillips Petroleum Company, he promised management that he would submit his manuscript for clearance before publishing it. Upon receiving the completed book, Phillips refused Whyte permission to print it, and so his study died in manuscript form (Whyte, 1984).

Other sociologists, faced with such research bargains or obligated to give copies of their reports to gatekeepers, have forged other solutions. After studying a battered women's shelter, Ferraro (1981) decided that she could not give the shelter director a copy of her report. As a result, she ended up having to write two versions, one for the director, the other for publication (see also Warren, 1980).

One researcher's muckraking may also evaporate the institutional support and future entrée of another, which we found when we tried to study the San Diego Chargers. We had negotiated for weeks with management to gain access to players for casual conversation and interviews and were successfully obtaining clearance as we worked our way up the institutional ladder. Suddenly, another researcher who had been working with the team for a year published his book, a muckraking exposé of drug abuse in this professional football club (see Mandell, 1976), and the doors shut in our faces.

Political Climate

The political climate surrounding researchers can make their data gathering and its publication highly sensitive. Ethnographers, with their capacity to unearth deep and hidden data, are the most likely of all researchers to discover taboo information that might pose a political danger. They may feel a desire to censor the data they gather for the purpose of protecting either their respondents or the organizations that surround those respondents.

Researchers gathering data in Third World countries are likely to encounter the types of situations that would provide them this impetus to self-censorship. For example, much to his dismay, Asad's (1973) research was used by colonial powers. In Peneff's (1985) study of entrepreneurial activities under a newly socialist government in Algeria, he felt compelled not only to censor his findings but to replace an overt with a covert approach (thereby hiding his research).

Personal or Family Factors

At times, ethnographic researchers censor their reports because they want to protect themselves or family members. Researchers studying politically sensitive or deviant groups may fear reprisals from the people they are studying if they reveal too much. This happened in Mitchell's (n.d., 1991) research on survivalists in Oregon, where he feared for his own safety if he published something unfavorable and his subjects learned of it (Mitchell, personal communication, 1991). Parsa (1989) also encountered this problem in his study of the Iranian revolution and the fall of the shah, originally written as a doctoral dissertation. As a student, Parsa encountered frequent protests of pro-Khomeini demonstrators whenever he gave talks from his research, which made him fear reprisals against his family still living in Iran if he did not censor his presentations. His father, a member of a religious minority group that was particularly vulnerable, went underground in 1984 when he was placed on Khomeini's death list. In 1989, when Khomeini issued a price upon the head of another author, Salman Rushdie, Parsa's book was already in press. This caused Parsa considerable concern, and he pulled the work out of press to further purge facts, modify attributions, change words, and delete sentences. His aim was to make his work appear as academic as possible and thereby less threatening, hoping to lessen the danger to other members of his family. Although he considered himself the foremost authority on the Iranian revolution and believed he had a moral imperative to be forthcoming, he decided to specifically censor information about the nature of the oppression occurring under the Khomeini regime. He was able to skirt total censorship, in part, by attributing some of his own thoughts to other people who had said similar things (Parsa, personal communication, 1991). This tactic of attribution was also noted by Warren (1980) in her discussion of the sensitive nature of data presentation and was used by us (Adler, 1985) in our comments on some of the "dope chicks" in the dealing crowd.

In other cases, researchers censor their reports to hide not only the behavior of their subjects but their own as well. This may be caused by their desire to shield themselves from family members and close friends. They may not want their spouses, children, or parents to know how involved they were in the field setting, especially if they did things that they sense might bring disapproval.[1] In Becker's (1963) research on becoming a marijuana smoker, for example, he never mentioned his own drug use, and Rasmussen and Kuhn's (1976) research on massage parlors never indicated Rasmussen's romantic involvement with the masseuses. Perhaps most infamously, Humphreys's (1970) research on tearooms never discussed his homosexuality; he even offered a cover story that he took the role of the "watch queen." This account became especially dubious when he later left the ministry, divorced his wife and children, and came out of the closet to become a gay rights activist, a situation he described as typical of tearoom participants. Researchers studying sensitive topics may similarly want to downplay their involvement in some of the deviant activities common to various sensitive subcultures such as drug use, adultery, homosexuality or lesbianism, or law/rule violations.

The Contagion of Stigma

Finally, as Kirby and Corzine (1981) have noted, researchers may censor their reports to avoid incurring the stigma of their subjects on themselves. This is especially likely to occur when ethnographers engage in what Warren (1980) has called "discreditable research" into topics that carry deviant overtones such as sex (see Weinberg & Williams, 1972) or drugs (see Henslin, 1972). This happened to one of us, Patti, when we moved out of the drug research setting and into a morally conservative state. When queried by neighbors about her dissertation topic, she found that ethnographic research among drug dealers met with disapproval (she was shown the door). She modified this to a study of drug use and was similarly stigmatized. Only when she self-censored and morally distanced herself from her subjects by describing her research as a study of drug and alcohol *abusers* was she able to avoid the contagion effect. Peter also encountered the contagion of stigma during the course of our basketball research, when he was rumored to be giving away undeserved grades to athletes in his classes or when his long hours spent in the dorms hanging out with athletes, helping them to study for their exams (among other things), were perceived by outsiders as constituting special treatment. The image of athletes as dumb jocks who would want someone to help them cheat in their classes fostered this suspicion. To avoid the contagion of such stigma, ethnographers may have to minimize their discussions of the extent of their personal participation and involvement in the activities of the setting and its members.

Discussion

The unspoken practice of self-censorship has many causes and dimensions; it is more prevalent than most people admit, especially to those outside the community of qualitative researchers. Self-censorship can be directed toward veiling either researchers' own activities or the activities of their respondents. These intentional omissions are usually directed toward the anticipated reactions from respondents, the media, the professional audience, the government or the police, employers, the community, or family members.

The practice of self-censorship is subject to the whims of fad and fashion in ethnographic writing. In a sense, we are moving into an era where self-censorship is not as fashionable as previously. In the 1940s and 1950s, closer to the codification of participant observation as a methodology, ethnographers tried to project a "scientific" and therefore "objective" front on their methodology (Adler & Adler, 1987). This favored detachment as a mode of self-presentation and facilitated self-censorship. More recently, however, we have seen the rise in popularity of the "confessional tale" (Van Maanen, 1988), where researchers engage in methodological introspection for the purpose of gaining further insight into field research epistemology. This mode fosters more self-revelation about researchers' involvements, leading to less self-censorship.

Yet self-censorship occurs because there are immediate and tangible reasons or persons who deserve privacy or who demand to be protected from the potentially threatening disclosures researchers can make (Sagarin, 1973). This includes people whose reputations or livelihood may be threatened by potentially damaging or embarrassing disclosure of their secrets. Our obligation as scientific researchers and moral human beings includes the protection of our subjects against such outcomes.

But there is a potential cost associated with self-censorship that cannot be ignored. This cost is incurred in two arenas: the loss to scientific knowledge and the loss to society. First, the community of scholars loses when we are duped, deceived, or misled by the transformation or omission of relevant data. We suffer a loss whenever scientific knowledge is compromised. How can we know the nature of behaviors, the extent of behaviors, and the connections between social factors when they are not reported? Second, potential social problems may go unreported by researchers who protect their subjects, leading to harm against others. Thus, for example, if we fail to report violence or sexual abuse against children when we witness it in connection with interviewing spousal abusers, or if we fail to report police brutality that we witness while conducting a participant observation study of the police (Van Maanen, 1983), we neglect to alert society about information that is potentially pressing. And, while our subjects, family, and institutions are all very present, representing a visible lobbying force arguing for the protection of their own interests, society and the scientific community are distant and disembodied. Who, then, is to stand up and advocate for science and society, to argue against this seemingly minor or benign form of omission?

Self-censorship constitutes an ethical dilemma that must be resolved by each individual involved in the research endeavor. It involves a cost-balance accounting between competing claims, determined by the moral, personal, and professional dictates of social scientists. Offering his view of the moral guidelines to follow in evaluating our self-censorship, Gans (1982) has suggested that, while researchers must try to prevent harm from coming to their subjects, if they observe a miscarriage of justice, they have the obligation to report it.

At the same time, alternatives to self-censorship do exist. When seeking to avoid the costs of both withholding knowledge and harming individuals, researchers have recourse to several possible options. First, a distinction can be noted between disguise and self-censorship. By significantly altering descriptions of people's appearance, location, relations, and activities, valuable information may be included rather than omitted altogether. Second, as noted in our discussion of Parsa's work, the manipulation of attribution may enable researchers to avoid complete self-censorship. This could involve constructing fictitious pseudonymical characters to which real people's thoughts or behaviors could be attributed, so that the actual actors are not identified. Another option would include failing to mention the primary or original authors of various thoughts or behaviors, attributing them instead to secondary and less vulnerable sources. A final option would involve researchers discussing with their research subjects the ethical issues the former face and enlisting the latter's aid in making the decision. This adheres to the principle of involving one's subjects in all aspects of the research process (Reiman, 1979) and offers them a knowledge base of the various potential consequences from which they can assist researchers in making ethically informed decisions.

Note

1. In a striking example of one of the consequences of lack of self-censorship, we wrote openly of our drug use as an invaluable methodological tool in doing the drug

trafficking research. While we sent the book to both sets of parents, interviewed at academic jobs on the basis of this work, and presented methodological papers on this research to the federal government without any negative repercussions, media people reporting on the work found this issue the most salient. After a prominent review of *Wheeling and Dealing* had recently appeared in the local newspaper, our 10-year-old daughter came home one night ashamed and embarrassed because her classroom teacher had read it and teased her about her parents' drug use at school that day.

References

Adler, P. (1984). The sociologist as celebrity: The role of the media in field research. *Qualitative Sociology, 7,* 310-326.

Adler, P. A. (1985). *Wheeling and dealing.* New York: Columbia University Press.

Adler, P. A., & Adler, P. (1980). The irony of secrecy in the drug world. *Urban Life, 8,* 447-465.

Adler, P. A., & Adler, P. (1982). Criminal commitment among drug dealers. *Deviant Behavior, 3,* 117-135.

Adler, P. A., & Adler, P. (1987). *Membership roles in field research.* Newbury Park, CA: Sage.

Adler, P. A., & Adler, P. (1991). *Backboards and blackboards: College athletes and role engulfment.* New York: Columbia University Press.

Asad, T. (1973). *Anthropology and the colonial encounter.* London: Ithaca Press.

Becker, H. (1963). *Outsiders.* New York: Free Press.

Becker, H. (1967). "Whose side are we on?" *Social Problems, 14,* 239-247.

Broadhead, R. S., & Rist, R. C. (1976). Gatekeepers and the social control of social research. *Social Problems, 23,* 325-336.

Douglas, J. D. (1971). *American social order.* New York: Free Press.

Douglas, J. D. (1976). *Investigative social research.* Beverly Hills, CA: Sage.

Ferraro, K. J. (1981). *Battered women and the shelter movement.* Unpublished doctoral dissertation, Arizona State University.

Fine, G. A. (1987). *With the boys.* Chicago: University of Chicago Press.

Fine, G. A., & Sandstrom, K. L. (1988). *Knowing children: Issues of participant observation with minors.* Newbury Park, CA: Sage.

Gallagher, A., Jr. (1964). Plainville: Twice-studied town. In A. M. Vidich, J. Bensman, & M. Stein (Eds.), *Reflections on community studies.* New York: John Wiley.

Gans, H. (1982). *The urban villagers* (2nd ed.). New York: Free Press.

Gurel, L. (1975). The human side of evaluating human services programs: Problems and prospects. In *Handbook of evaluation research* (Vol. 2). Beverly Hills, CA: Sage.

Haas, J., & Shaffir, W. (1980). Fieldworkers' mistakes at work: Problems in maintaining research and researcher bargains. In W. Shaffir, R. Stebbins, & A. Turowetz (Eds.), *Fieldwork experience.* New York: St. Martin's.

Henslin, J. M. (1972). Studying deviants in four settings: Research experience with cabbies, suicides, drug users, and abortionees. In J. D. Douglas (Ed.), *Research on deviance.* New York: Random House.

Heritage, J. (1984). *Garfinkel and ethnomethodology.* Cambridge, UK: Polity.

Humphreys, L. (1970). *Tearoom trade.* Chicago: Aldine.

Kirby, R., & Corzine, J. (1981). The contagion of stigma. *Qualitative Sociology, 4,* 3-20.

Klockars, C. B. (1974). *The professional fence.* New York: Free Press.

Klockars, C. B. (1979). Dirty hands and deviant subjects. In C. B. Klockars & F. W. O'Connor (Eds.), *Deviance and decency.* New York: St. Martin's

Letkemann, P. (1980). Crime as work: Leaving the field. In W. B. Shaffir, R. Stebbins, & A. Turowetz (Eds.), *Fieldwork experience.* Beverly Hills, CA: Sage.

Lofland, J. (1971). *Analyzing social settings.* Belmont, CA: Wadsworth.

Mandell, A. J. (1976). *The nightmare season.* New York: Random House.

Mehan, H., & Wood, H. (1975). *The reality of ethnomethodology.* New York: John Wiley.

Mitchell, R. (1991). Secrecy and disclosure in fieldwork. In W. Shaffir & R. Stebbins (Eds.), *Experiencing fieldwork.* Newbury Park, CA: Sage.

Mitchell, R. (n.d.). *Dancing at Armageddon: Doomsday and survivalists in America.* Unpublished paper, Oregon State University.

Morgan, D. H. J. (1972). The British Association Scandal: The effect of publicity on a sociological investigation. *Sociological Review, 20,* 185-206.

Olesen, V. (1979). Federal regulations, qualitative social science and institutional review boards: Comments on a problematic era. In M. Wax & J. Cassell (Eds.), *Federal regulations: Ethical issues and social research.* Boulder, CO: Westview.

Parsa, M. (1989). *Social origins of the Iranian Revolution.* New Brunswick, NJ: Rutgers University Press.

Peneff, J. (1985). Reflections: Fieldwork in Algeria. *Qualitative Sociology, 8,* 65-78.

Rasmussen, P., & Kuhn, L. (1976). The new masseuses: Play for pay. *Urban Life, 5,* 271-292.

Reiman, J. (1979). Research subjects, political subjects, and human subjects. In C. B. Klockars & F. W. O'Connor (Eds.), *Deviance and decency: The ethics of research with human subjects.* Beverly Hills, CA: Sage.

Riemer, J. W. (1977). Varieties of opportunistic research. *Urban Life, 5,* 467-477.

Roadburg, A. (1980). Breaking relationships with research subjects: Some problems and suggestions. In W. B. Shaffir, R. A. Stebbins, & A. Turowetz (Eds.), *Fieldwork experience.* New York: St. Martin's.

Sagarin, E. (1973). The research setting and the right not to be researched. *Social Problems, 21,* 52-64.

Snow, D. A. (1980). The disengagement process: A neglected problem in participant observation research. *Qualitative Sociology, 3,* 100-122.

Spector, M. (1980). Learning to study public figures. In W. Shaffir, R. Stebbins, & A. Turowetz (Eds.), *Fieldwork experience.* New York: St. Martin's.

Van Maanen, J. (1983). The moral fix: On the ethics of fieldwork. In R. Emerson (Ed.), *Contemporary field research.* Boston: Little, Brown.

Van Maanen, J. (1988). *Tales of the field.* Chicago: University of Chicago Press.

Vidich, A. J., & Bensman, J. (1964). Academic bureaucrats and sensitive townspeople. In A. J. Vidich, J. Bensman, & M. Stein (Eds.), *Reflections on community studies.* New York: John Wiley.

Warren, C. A. B. (1980). Data presentation and audience: Responses, ethics, and effects. *Urban Life, 9,* 282-308.

Wax, M. L., & Cassell, J. (1979). Fieldwork ethics and politics: The wider context. In M. Wax & J. Cassell (Eds.), *Federal regulations: Ethical issues and social research.* Boulder, CO: Westview.

Weinberg, M. S., & Williams, C. J. (1972). Fieldwork among deviants: Social relations with subjects and others. In J. D. Douglas (Ed.), *Research on deviance*. New York: Random House.

Whyte, W. F. (1964). On *Street Corner Society*. In E. W. Burgess & D. Bogue (Eds.), *Contributions to urban sociology*. Chicago: University of Chicago Press.

Whyte, W. F. (1984). *Learning from the field*. Beverly Hills, CA: Sage.

16

Anticipating Media Coverage

Methodological Decisions in Criminal Justice Research

NOREEN L. CHANNELS

Social scientists who conduct research intended to inform lay people or influence public policy must recognize that their research findings are unlikely to have a direct impact on either public opinion or policy agendas. Rather, we must rely upon other interested parties and organizations to put our research findings into the public eye. The media are of particular importance in this role, as they select among research topics and transform "scientific results" into "news" (Krumholz & Cogger, 1978; Pettigrew, 1985).

This dependency upon the media is often troublesome to social scientists because with the dependency comes a loss of control of the information and its interpretation as it is disseminated. And this loss of control is especially critical to social scientists whose research deals with sensitive topics because we are especially concerned with the accuracy and thoroughness of the media reports themselves and also with the impact of media choices upon the recipients of the information.

There are, in the social science literature, many discussions of the relationship between social science and the media; these often include advice to the scientist about how to talk with reporters who would cover our research. I will review some common problems cited by social scientists on this matter and then turn to examples of methodological strategies and choices to be considered in anticipation of media coverage. In these examples, I will draw upon the work of Sharon Herzberger and myself on the progress of African Americans, whites, and Hispanics through the criminal justice system. In this research, the findings about racial/ethnic differences in the criminal justice system are both socially and politically sensitive, and images of specific segments of the population and of government systems may be affected. The sensitive nature of this research makes it particularly important for us to anticipate media coverage and recognize the role of the media in introducing interpretations and assigning meaning to the findings.

Social Science
Coverage in the Media

Journalists and social scientists, in important ways, work on tasks that are seen as substantially overlapping. As Weaver and McCombs (1980) summarize the similarities, both are interested in understanding reality through empirical observations of the external world. And, in seeking to do so, both professions are likely to gain their information not through direct personal experience but through the reports of others. Also, there is general recognition now that journalists are not merely "reporting" but are attempting to find meaning in and interpret the material they cover (Weaver & McCombs, 1980). In these efforts, journalists are increasingly likely to use social science perspectives and methodology, including the analysis of large-scale data bases (Crespi, 1980; Weaver & McCombs, 1980).[1]

In spite of these broad similarities between the work of journalists and social scientists, there are often problems with the coverage of social science in the media. Weiss and Singer (1988), to learn the variety of views about media coverage of social science research, gathered data from journalists and scientists and conducted a content analysis of reports of social science research. They learned that criticisms from social scientists center primarily on the practical level, in the criteria for the selection of stories and the specific content of the coverage given to research, rather than on the more global level of the goals of the two professions. Further, they note that these problems are due to the structure and values of the news-making enterprise and are not best explained as characteristics of the journalists themselves.

Weiss and Singer's survey of social scientists whose own research was reported in the media showed that 54% said the story was accurate, 60% said the emphasis was appropriate, and 42% said nothing essential had been omitted. Social scientists who were simply quoted on an area of expertise had higher levels of satisfaction, probably due at least in part to the fact that the information they provided was less extensive and complex.

The social scientists in the sample were less happy with the overall pattern of media coverage. They objected in general to the way that journalists select and cover social science research and criticized the image that was given to social science disciplines by the media. Their complaints about media coverage of social science fall into five categories; two of these reflect issues in the media's *selection* of stories and three deal with the *content* of the coverage.

On the selection process, social scientists reported *inadequate scrutiny of the quality of the research* and criticized the journalists' choice of topics and experts. In validation of these perceptions, the authors note that the journalists themselves did not cite the quality of research as an important criterion in their selection of studies. Indeed, journalists may not even think of themselves as reporting social science, focusing instead only on the substantive topic, such as crime or interpersonal relationships (Weiss & Singer, 1988). These differences in approach, of course, do not necessarily mean that poor science will be selected but only that good science may come to the reporter's attention for reasons that are peripheral to those of the scientists (Dunwoody & Stocking, 1985).

The social scientists in Weiss and Singer's (1988) sample also complained of *biased selection of topics.* Journalists were seen as having an a priori preference for quantitative research findings, for findings that suggest reform of social institutions, and for findings that are "middle of the road" rather than liberal.

The social scientists most frequently claimed that, while the content was not necessarily inaccurate, it was *oversimplified.* The journalist's need to appeal to a broad audience, to highlight the human interest aspects of the story, and to convey information briefly and quickly interfered, they felt, with adequate attention to the complexities and subtleties of the research.

From the scientists' point of view, the need for a story that makes an impact led reporters to *exaggerate the certainty and conclusiveness* of the research. Reporters often failed to report the fact that findings were tentative and part of a process of ongoing inquiry.

In another example of the media's failure to see research in context, the social scientists complained that each story was treated in isolation from other studies. They saw coverage of research as *fragmented*, failing to tie in results that were not tied to earlier work on the same topic.

When Weiss and Singer conducted a content analyses of news stories, they found the same omissions that concerned the social scientists. In more than half the media reports of research, there was no reference to a published source that would provide further information about the research and, although a research organization was usually mentioned, the identity of the researchers was rarely cited.

The theme throughout these complaints is that media representatives operate outside the norms of science or, at least, are not constrained by them. Rather, their selections are based on such criteria as the newsworthiness and novelty of the study or the topic's relation to other news (Best, 1986). In particular, journalists appear uninterested in scientific methodology, the processes that led to specific findings. This is critical because methodological considerations are of primary importance to scientists. The norms of science constitute the means by which we conduct our work and make design choices, and they provide the principal criteria by which we evaluate our results and those of other scientists. Thus, when the media make decisions about which research to cover and how to cover it without necessary reference to the norms of science, researchers have cause for concern. This is particularly critical when the methodology of the work is complex and has a bearing on the interpretation of the data.

To those whose research involves sensitive issues, there are additional issues not covered by Weiss and Singer, who conducted their analysis without specific reference to the specific topics of the social science research they investigated. First, inaccurate and incomplete coverage may have consequences that extend beyond any effect of the initial media report. For example, if the research findings are reinterpreted for policy debate or for application, if they play a role in shaping public perception of a topic or a segment of the population, or if individuals consult the findings for personal information about their lives, then the media coverage must be evaluated for its role in these subsequent events. In situations such as these, reports on poor quality research and reports that are inaccurate, oversimplified, or that fail to acknowledge the tentative nature of the conclusions are additionally worrisome to the researcher.

Second, the media are the major route for communication with general audiences, so scientists who would like public exposure of their research results have little choice about whether or not to cooperate with the media. Further, the media's audience is varied: Citizens, public policymakers, and even other social scientists learn of social science research from the lay media (Best, 1986; Dunwoody & Stocking, 1985; Walum, 1975). Consequently, the scientist must be aware of the varied expectations and uses to be made of the research reports by these constituencies. Prohibiting the media from covering research on sensitive topics is rarely a desirable option.

Thus social scientists with applied research on sensitive topics face the additional difficulties that come with little choice and greater risk in such exposure, as well as sharing more general concerns with other social scientists whose work catches the interest of the media. Advice to social scientists about dealing with the media reflects the shared concerns, but, while useful, it usually focuses on what to do after the research is completed. Social scientists are advised, for example, to summarize the findings for the journalist, perhaps in a press release (Best, 1986; Stocking & Dunwoody, 1982); to learn of the journalist's assumptions, constraints, and particular interest in the story; and to educate the journalist about the importance, context, and limitations of the research (Stocking & Dunwoody, 1982).

Less attention, however, is given to the fact that there are also important considerations about the *research methodology itself,* issues that should be considered when the researcher plans for media coverage. Our research on predictors of treatment of individuals in the criminal justice system is a useful example of some of the issues that arise in planning the research design with eventual media coverage in mind.

Our Research on the Criminal Justice System

The original purpose of our research was to search for an explanation for the large numbers of African Americans and Hispanics found in all stages of Connecticut's criminal justice system (these groups constituted about 60% of those involved in the system at a time when they were about 11% of the population). We expanded our analyses to address the effects of income and gender and focused in particular on the disparities that occur at the bail setting stage. Our sample was drawn from those arrested for a felony and interviewed by the Bail Commission. We began with information on criminal charges and recommended bail amounts; to this we added criminal history information from state police files, data on the resolution of the case from the judicial department files, demographic information about the individual's census block group from the U.S. census, and length and type of sentence served from the Department of Corrections. Data from these sources allowed us to follow individuals as they progressed through the criminal justice system and to identify the factors that predict decisions at each stage.

The media coverage of our work was varied. We first presented the results to newspaper representatives at a press conference arranged by the community agency that sponsored our work. After this coverage, we gave interviews to other newspapers in the state, to a representative of the Associated Press, and to several radio stations. Others covered the study on the basis of these initial reports. We were asked to address specific issues of Hispanics and African Americans in the criminal justice system in a television talk show and a community panel presentation. The media coverage led to several requests, from legal professionals and from families of criminal offenders who sought assistance in specific cases. We had several fairly limited talks with government representatives after the media coverage brought our research to their and others' attention. Several years later, the local newspaper again covered the issue and used our study in their report.

Methodological Issues in Applied Research

Richard Berk (1977) emphasizes the fact that scientific standards for research are not specific enough to direct all the methodological decisions that an applied researcher faces; even within the standards of scientific rigor, there are numerous choices facing the researcher. In discussing these choices, Berk urges that researchers recognize that "applied research exists in the world of actual problems, not in the theoretical world of academia. Methodological decisions are at least de facto political decisions. Moreover, it is only when these practical considerations are carefully weighed that sound methodological choices can be made" (Berk, 1977, p. 331). Berk also argues that, while working within the boundaries of acceptable scientific standards, the research methodology should include the means to address criticism and protect findings from unwarranted attack.

Based on Berk's remarks, it is clear that throughout the process of research on sensitive topics, including in the initial design and planning stages, *we should make our methodological decisions with the intended audience and uses of the information firmly in mind*. In this way, we can ensure that we have made decisions that are within the standards of our disciplines and at the same time are relevant to the anticipated media coverage and the audiences reached through these media. If one wishes to communicate with lay audiences through the media, it is not sufficient to simplify and summarize findings that have been designed for professional audiences. One's audiences and the eventual uses of the information should be considered even in initial decision making about how to conduct the research.

I turn now to a number of methodological issues in our research on the criminal justice system that had a bearing on the eventual reports we were able to make to the media. These examples illustrate Berk's points about the discretion that exists within the norms of science and the need to make early decisions with specific audiences in mind. They also show the close connection between methodological decisions and the subsequent information we convey to the media. In the sections below, a number of topics are covered: measurement of critical variables such as race/ethnicity and income, identification of the various forms of racial and ethnic disparity, selection of control variables, and the labeling of disparity and discrimination.

Measuring Critical Variables

Race and Ethnicity

No topic within criminal justice research is more sensitive in nature than that which focuses on the differences in treatment of racial and ethnic groups. Yet, much of the research on racial and ethnic disparity suffers from a lack of theoretical development and proceeds on the basis of unexamined assumptions about these categorizations (See & Wilson, 1988). An important, recent improvement in criminal justice research is a coding of race/ethnicity that separates African Americans and Hispanics. In the past, these two groups often have been combined to form a "minority" or "nonwhite" category, or, in other instances, minorities other than African Americans have been excluded from the analysis.

The fact that we were able to distinguish between these two minority groups proved to be critical in our research: We found very different patterns of treatment of African Americans and Hispanics. Failure to distinguish between these two groups limits the researcher's ability to identify or understand the experiences of either (Zatz, 1985).

In their own experiences, black and Hispanic individuals make even finer distinctions of race and ethnicity than those recorded by most criminal justice systems. For example, there are important differences between Hispanics from Mexico and those from Puerto Rico, in addition to the fact that most Hispanics are not themselves "from" somewhere else at all. Some reporters who interviewed us about our work revealed a misconception about Hispanics in their belief that many have other homes in Puerto Rico to which they could flee, thereby justifying harsh bail treatment. Blacks who are not African American have resisted their inclusion in the category and argue that research and media descriptions of "blacks" do not reflect their experiences. These distinctions are particularly important in this sensitive area of criminal justice research because the stigma of high crime rates contributes to the image and disparagement of all minorities.

Income

Our attention to the variable income is an example of the need to design research in anticipation of the intended use and criticism of the work. We met immediate resistance from state officials who did not want to release their data on the grounds that the state does not collect income information.[2] They feared that the media would incorrectly assign a label of racial discrimination to inequities that were, in fact, due to income. This is an important distinction because discrimination on the basis of income is not prohibited by law and remedies through the courts are not available. In addition, disparity on the basis of income does not bring with it the same public concern that surrounds issues of racism, so these findings are often less controversial and less newsworthy.

A good deal of research in this field lacks a direct measure of individuals' income. Farrell and Swigert (1978) used occupational prestige as their measure of social class and criticized the fact that, in practice, criminal history may be used as a proxy for minority and poverty status. Spohn, Gruhl, and Welch (1981-1982) relied upon whether or not the defendant made bail as an income proxy; others have relied upon the use of a public or private defender (Pruitt & Wilson, 1983).

Fortunately, we were able to construct an estimate of income by obtaining the respondent's street address and matching it with census information to determine the median income of each individual's census block group. Clarke and Koch (1976) in their own work have defended this choice as objective in nature and therefore superior to self-reported income, especially in the study of alleged felons. Of course, this proxy is valid only to the extent that census tracts are homogeneous by social class, and the measure does not reflect the rate of unemployment or unreported income. But the use of this proxy decreased resistance to our use of the data and allowed us to proceed with research on what has been a politically sensitive topic.

Identifying the Forms of Racial and Ethnic Disparity

The subtleties of disparity on the basis of race/ethnicity provide another good example of the need to design research and data analysis with the specific audience and uses of the research in mind. As noted, the initial impetus for our research came from interested parties who sought information about the state criminal justice system. The research was only secondarily aimed at the professional readership of our own disciplines (and may not even be of much theoretical interest to them). Further, the initial questions reflected an understanding only of direct bias and a simple answer was expected.

Simply providing a description of the magnitude of differences in treatment of blacks, whites, and Hispanics is too limited and overlooks the fact that disparity may result from several different processes: Inequities may be the result of *direct* effects, where race/ethnicity has an impact after other variables have been controlled; disparity may be due to *indirect* effects, where the impact of race/ethnicity on an outcome is mediated through an intervening factor; or disparity may occur through *interaction* with another variable, where the impact of race/ethnicity, for example, differs for men and women (Taylor, 1985; Zatz, 1987). In our analyses, we found instances of all three forms of inequity in the treatment of blacks and Hispanics within the criminal justice system (Channels & Herzberger, 1988; Herzberger & Channels, 1988).

Given the expectations and interests of the general public, it is important that the initial question of direct disparity in the treatment of racial/ethnic groups not be ignored. But neither can we ignore the fact that, while direct effects are most easily understood and identified, and are most "newsworthy," there are other social mechanisms by which disparities also occur. A study of direct effects alone may distort the findings of racial/ethnic disparity (Zatz, 1987); it is important that research on direct effects always be accompanied by investigation of disparity in its indirect and interactive forms. In explaining research findings to the general public, we should emphasize that "subtle" biases based on race/ethnicity can be as serious in their impact on individual lives as overt ones and that remedies to these patterns of behavior are possible.

Selection of Control Variables

In the initial planning of the analysis, the researcher must face the fact that the choice of control variables to include in a model may be a key determinant of the conclusions drawn from the research. When conducting research on sensitive topics with implications for social change, it is important to recognize that these choices may have far-reaching consequences. Taylor (1985), in reference to research on disparity for affirmative action purposes, has noted that relatively little attention is paid to these critical choices; instead, researchers tend to rely on conventions in the field or to use whatever information is available. In making choices of control variables for analyses designed to address each kind of disparity, both the inclusion *and* the exclusion of specific variables must be given close attention.

A common criticism of research on disparity focuses on the *omission* of variables considered important. We regretted, for example, that we did not have data on the quality of the evidence or on traits of the victim. The statistical effect of omitted variables, a type of specification error, may be biased coefficients of the included variables or biased estimates of their significance, depending upon whether the omitted variables are correlated with other variables in the model (Pedhazur, 1982). In our research, the problems are particularly critical if the omitted variables are correlated with race/ethnicity. Then the unavailability of some variables may mean that we will fail to identify indirect disparity or interaction of race/ethnicity with other variables. Equally important, if the omitted variables are legal factors that are relied upon in the decision-making process under study, our findings have diminished relevance to the applied audience to which our findings are directed.

Considerably less attention is given by researchers to the decision about what variables should be *included*. Yet, in the determination of direct disparity, a coefficient reflects only the importance of a variable *after* the impact of all other variables in the model have been removed or "partialed out." So the control variables chosen have a bearing on the amount of effect that is "left" for the variable of interest. If these control variables in practice represent a "proxy" for race/ethnicity, or the route by which race/ethnicity leads to disparate treatment, simply to control for their effect can lead to extremely conservative estimates about the overall differences in treatment of whites and blacks and Hispanics (Pedhazur, 1982; Taylor, 1985).[3]

In our research on the direct effects of race/ethnicity, it was important to include as complete a listing of the *legal* variables as possible, because we wanted to know the effect of race/ethnicity above and beyond those factors legitimately considered in the criminal justice system. We faced the decision, however, of whether or not *income* should be routinely included in all analyses. The inclusion of such an extralegal correlate of race/ethnicity is not a neutral or apolitical decision; the decision may influence the findings of disparity between African Americans, whites, and Hispanics. Similar issues could, and should, be raised for other possible control variables.

In response to these issues, the applied researcher *should make separate decisions about control variables for each specific question to be addressed by the analysis.* A measure of direct discrimination, intended simply to describe the differences between African Americans, whites, and Hispanics, might use only legal variables as controls. Other personal traits could be introduced in later analysis, where they are of interest for their possible role in indirect and interactive disparity. Furthermore, the choices of control variables for research designed for media exposure to general audiences or for policy discussions might differ from those for academic research, where the variable selection may involve fewer political considerations, and more esoteric research questions may predominate.

Clearly the selection of control variables for the model has implications for the extent and type of disparity identified. To reiterate Berk's (1977) critical point, the norms of science alone are not sufficiently directive to guide the decisions that face the researcher. Taylor (1985) reminds us that these decisions are political in nature, arguing that insufficient recognition is given to "the fact that inclusion of a particular control variable in an analysis designed to estimate discrimination is not a technical matter: It is a policy statement about what portion of inequality in outcomes a given social institution ought *not* be held responsible to remedy" (p. 147). Although the courts are not responsible for the effect of race/ethnicity on income, their obligation to avoid racial/ethnic bias surely includes an obligation to address even those biases mediated through other factors.

Labeling Disparity and Discrimination

In early discussions of our research findings with community groups and with the media, as well as with other academics, we took care to emphasize that we found significant indications of *disparity* in the treatment of African Americans, whites, and Hispanics as they progressed through the criminal justice system. Our point in this was to highlight the fact that one cannot "prove" that differences between African Americans, whites, and Hispanics were due to *discrimination*; the finding could result from limitations of the data.

Our caution on this sensitive issue stirred some debate and criticism. Journalists were frustrated at our inability, or unwillingness, to assign the "obvious" (and more newsworthy) label to the patterns of treatment that we identified. Other discussion centered on the definition of "discrimination," usually pointing to the issue of whether motivations were a necessary component of discrimination, paralleling the legal debates about "disparate treatment" and "disparate impact." Some of the focus was quite specifically on whether these findings would "hold up in court."

In the end, we came to have second thoughts about our approach; to many in our general audience, our caution seemed to convey a message that we considered our findings to be insubstantial and easily dismissed. We began to see that research in this area is "bogged down" by these distinctions and that we should focus instead on the point made earlier in this chapter: that discrimination can manifest itself in many forms, some *overt* and some *subtle,* all with consequences for the people receiving such treatment (Zatz, 1987). We began to recast our discussions, to emphasize that we had the best and most complete data set available, including to decision makers and, while not ignoring methodological limitations, not undermining the value of social science research either.

Conclusion

Social scientists who conduct research on topics that are socially and politically sensitive, with findings that are relevant to general audiences, must acknowledge that the media will play a key role in the review and interpretation of their work. This is especially important when the consequences of the media coverage extend beyond the simple conveyance of information to have an effect on public opinion, public policy, or the personal lives of individuals. This recognition of the role of the media must shape the research process itself and the resolution of methodological issues; it cannot simply influence the release of results at the end of the process. Research designed to identify differences in the treatment of African Americans, whites, and Hispanics in the criminal justice system, a topic that attracts a large amount of media attention and that evokes a strong response from a variety of audiences, is a far more complicated matter than in past decades, where discrimination was not legally and socially proscribed. Discrimination is more subtle now and may result from complicated social processes; racism may work in conjunction with other factors in a way that makes it more difficult to identify. Anticipation of media coverage must be a central part of the research process and communications with the media must reflect the complexities of current scholarship as well as the view of racial/ethnic disparities held by many non-social scientists.

Notes

1. A newsletter, *UPLINK: The Forum for Computer-Assisted Reporting,* published by the Missouri Institute for Computer Assisted Reporting, is useful for understanding journalists' perspectives and experiences in the acquisition and use of data analysis.

2. Because researchers so often use existing data in these analyses, knowledge of the subtleties of disparate treatment advances only to the extent that higher quality data are gathered by criminal justice officials. Thus the need to monitor decision making is often hindered by dependence on these same decision makers for data gathering. In my view, this limitation is an important political point worthy of emphasis in media coverage; public opinion may have an influence on the type and extent of information collected and made available to social scientists.

3. See, also, Briere (1988) for a discussion of this same point in reference to controlling for family characteristics in studying the effects of child abuse.

References

Berk, R. A. (1977). Discretionary methodological decisions in applied research. *Sociological Methods & Research, 5,* 317-334.

Best, J. (1986). Reflections. Famous for fifteen minutes: Notes on the researcher as newsmaker. *Qualitative Sociology, 9,* 372-382.

Briere, J. (1988). Controlling for family variables in abuse effects research: A critique of the "partialling" approach. *Journal of Interpersonal Violence, 3,* 80-89.

Channels, N. L., & Herzberger, S. (1988, May). *The effects of offender characteristics on progress through the criminal justice system.* Research commissioned by the Hartford Institute of Criminal and Social Justice.

Clarke, S., & Koch, G. (1976). The influence of income and other factors on whether criminal defendants go to prison. *Law and Society, 11,* 57-92.

Crespi, I. (1980). Polls as journalism. *Public Opinion Quarterly, 44,* 462-476.

Dunwoody, S., & Stocking, S. H. (1985). Social scientists and journalists: Confronting the stereotypes. In E. A. Rubinstein & J. D. Brown (Eds.), *The media, social science, and social policy for children.* Norwood, NJ: Ablex.

Farrell, R., & Swigert, V. (1978). Prior offense record as a self-fulfilling prophecy. *Law and Society Review, 12,* 437-453.

Herzberger, S., & Channels, N. L. (1988, November). *The predictors and consequences of bail decision making.* Paper presented at the meetings of the Society of Criminology Conference, Chicago.

Krumholz, N., & Cogger, J. (1978). Social science research and public policy: Bridging the gap. *Sociological Symposium, 21,* 34-45.

Pedhazur, E. J. (1982). *Multiple regression in behavioral research: Explanation and prediction.* New York: Holt, Rinehart & Winston.

Pettigrew, T. F. (1985). Can social scientists be effective actors in the policy arena? In R. L. Shotland & M. M. Mark (Eds.), *Social science and social policy.* Beverly Hills, CA: Sage.

Pruitt, C., & Wilson, J. (1983). A longitudinal study of the effect of race on sentencing. *Law and Society Review, 17,* 613-635.

See, K. O., & Wilson, W. J. (1988). Race and ethnicity. In N. J. Smelser (Ed.), *Handbook of sociology.* Newbury Park, CA: Sage.

Spohn, C., Gruhl, J., & Welch, S. (1981-1982). The effect of race on sentencing: A re-examination of an unsettled question. *Law and Society Review, 16,* 71-88.

Stocking, S. H., & Dunwoody, S. L. (1982). Social science in the mass media: Images and evidence. In J. E. Sieber (Ed.), *The ethics of social research: Fieldwork, regulation, and publication.* New York: Springer-Verlag.

Taylor, M. C. (1985). Science and politics in affirmative action research. In R. L. Shotland & M. M. Mark (Eds.), *Social science and social policy.* Beverly Hills, CA: Sage.

Walum, L. R. (1975). Sociology and the mass media: Some major problems and modest proposals. *The American Sociologist, 10,* 28-32.

Weaver, D. H., & McCombs, M. E. (1980). Journalism and social science: A new relationship? *Public Opinion Quarterly, 44,* 477-494.

Weiss, C. H., & Singer, E. (1988). *Reporting of social science in the national media.* New York: Russell Sage.

Zatz, M. S. (1985). Pleas, priors and prison: Racial/ethnic differences in sentencing. *Social Science Research, 14,* 169-193.

Zatz, M. S. (1987). The changing forms of racial/ethnic biases in sentencing. *Journal of Research in Crime and Delinquency, 24,* 69-92.

Author Index

281

Subject Index

Abortion, as sensitive research topic, 63
AIDS:
  as sensitive research topic, 3, 9, 19
  behavioral change and, 161-162
  developing community sample of gay men for epidemiological study of, 82-97
  epicenters of, 161
AIDS epidemic, 16, 30, 82, 83, 160-161
  evaluation of an emotional and behavioral functioning of gay men, 84
AIDS prevention research, 105, 160-175
  community-based, 165-166
  contribution of social scientists in, 162
  grounding the research process in, 164-165, 166
  research enterprise and, 163
  use of focus groups in, 165-167, 168
American Psychological Association, 24
Annang women, 229, 236, 238, 239, 244
Anticult movement, 110, 116, 121
Art, sociology of, 216
Associated Press, 272

Associative writing, use of in feminist methodology, 179

Battered child syndrome, 33
Bayview Hunter's Point Foundation (San Francisco), 167, 173
Beijing University, Institute of Comparative Law and Sociology of Law at, 75
Bereavement, as sensitive research topic, 6, 8
Brainwashing, psychological, 109
British Association Scandal, 253
British National Front, 149
Bureau of Economic Analysis, 60

Child abuse:
  aggressive behavior in children and, 45
  and self-destructive behavior, 45
  as sensitive research topic, 3, 28, 34, 48
  cross-generational transmission of, 34
  cyclical hypothesis of, 39-46

About the Contributors

Patricia A. Adler is Assistant Professor of Sociology at the University of Colorado, Boulder. She has written and taught in the areas of deviance, drugs in society, social theory, and the sociology of children. A revised and updated version of her book *Wheeling and Dealing* (Columbia Uni- versity Press) will be released in 1993. Her recent publications include "The 'Post' Phase of Deviant Careers: Reintegrating Drug Traffickers" (*Deviant Behavior*), "Street Corner Society Revisited: New Questions About Old Issues" (*Journal of Contemporary Ethnography*), and "Personalizing Mass Education" (*Teaching Sociology*).

Peter Adler is Associate Professor and Chair of Sociology at the University of Denver. His research interests include social psychology, qualitative methods, and the sociology of sport and leisure. Recent publications include *Membership Roles in Field Research* (Sage), "Intense Loyalty in Organizations" (*Administrative Science Quarterly*), and "The Gloried Self" (*Social Psychology Quarterly*). With Patricia A. Adler, he edits the *Journal of Contemporary Ethnography* and *Sociological Studies of Child Development*. Also with Patricia A. Adler, his most recent book is *Backboards and Blackboards*, based on a 5-year participant observation study of college athletes (Columbia University Press, 1991).

Marybeth Ayella is Assistant Professor of Sociology, St. Joseph's University, Philadelphia, Pennsylvania. Since completing her Ph.D. at the University of California, Berkeley, in 1985, her research has focused on the topics of radical resocialization, psychotherapeutic abuse, regulation of psychotherapy and medicine, and the social construction of human sexuality. She is currently at work on a book about her research with members of a psychotherapy cult.

Gillian Bendelow worked in a wide range of clinical nursing posts, including two years as a Community Psychiatric Nurse for City and Hackney Health Authority in London, before entering higher education. Since 1988, she has been conducting research for her doctoral dissertation, "Gender Differences in Perceptions of Pain," with funding from a Ph.D. studentship provided by the Economic and Social Research Council (ESRC). She is continuing to develop this work at the Social Science Research Unit, Institute of Education, University of London, by conducting a follow-up study, again funded by the ESRC.

Benjamin P. Bowser holds a Ph.D. in sociology from Cornell University and is Associate Professor of Sociology at California State University at Hayward. He is Associate Editor of *Race Relations Abstracts* (Sage Ltd.). Other books include *Impacts of Racism on White Americans* (Sage, 1981) and *Black Male Adolescents* (University Press of America, 1991). He has published other chapters and journal articles in race relations, community studies, and AIDS prevention.

John D. Brewer is Reader in Sociology at the Queen's University of Belfast and was Visiting Fellow at Yale University in 1989. His research interests outside the sociology of policing cover extreme right politics, the sociology and politics of divided societies, and the sociology of everyday life. His publications include *Inside the RUC: Routine Policing in a Divided Society* (Clarendon Press, 1991), *The Royal Irish Constabulary: An Oral History* (Institute of Irish Studies, 1990), and *Police, Public Order and the State* (Macmillan, 1988). He is also editor of *Can South Africa Survive?* (Macmillan, 1989) and is currently writing a book on the South African police titled *Black and Blue* to be published by Clarendon Press.

Pamela J. Brink is Professor and Associate Dean of Research, Faculty of Nursing, University of Alberta, Canada. She is the Founder and

Executive Editor of the *Western Journal of Nursing Research* and an Associate Editor of *Medical Anthropology.* She is a board member of the Alberta Foundation for Nursing Research; a past member of the Executive Committee of the Society for Medical Anthropology; Distinguished Lecturer, Sigma Theta Tau; past president of the Council on Nursing and Anthropology; and past president of the Alberta Multicultural and Native Health Association. Her publications include numerous articles and three books: *Transcultural Nursing: A Book of Readings* (Prentice-Hall, 1976; reissued by Waveland Press, 1990); *Basic Steps in Planning Nursing Research* (Jones and Bartlett, 3rd ed., 1988), and *Advanced Design in Nursing Research* (Sage, 1989).

Noreen L. Channels is Professor in the Department of Sociology, Trinity College, Hartford, Connecticut, and Adjunct Professor at the University of Connecticut Law School. She has an M.A. in social work from the University of Connecticut and a Ph.D. in sociology from Michigan State University. Her professional work is in the uses of social science methods and information in nonacademic contexts, especially legal settings. She has published a volume titled *Social Science Methods in the Legal Process* (Rowman & Allenheld, 1985). For the last several years, she has been conducting research with Sharon D. Herzberger on the effects of race and gender on treatment in the Connecticut criminal justice system.

Sandra Cook is on the faculty of the School of Legal Studies, LaTrobe University, Bundoora, Australia. Her doctorate is also from LaTrobe University. In addition to her research interest in China, her work focuses on public policy formation, particularly as it relates to juvenile justice and education.

Daniel J. Curran is Professor and Chair of the Department of Sociology, St. Joseph's University, Philadelphia, Pennsylvania. He is currently involved in the development of a collaborative research program with the China Research Society of Juvenile Delinquency and the East China Institute of Law and Politics. He has written *Dead Laws for Dead Men: The Politics of Coal Mine Health and Safety Legislation* (University of Pittsburgh Press, 1992), several other books, and numerous articles, primarily in the area of the sociology of law.

Laura Dean, Associate Research Scientist at Columbia University, is the Director of the AIDS Research Unit in the School of Public Health,

Division of Sociomedical Sciences. She succeeds John L. Martin as the principal investigator of a longitudinal study funded by the National Institute of Mental Health regarding mental health and behavioral effects of the AIDS epidemic on New York City gay men. Prior to 1984, she directed fieldwork operations for numerous cross-national psychiatric epidemiological studies at the Center of Geriatrics and Gerontology, Department of Psychiatry, Columbia University College of Physicians and Surgeons. She has written or cowritten scholarly works that have appeared in the *American Journal of Public Health, The Gerontologist,* the *International Journal of Aging and Human Development,* and *Social Science and Medicine.*

Rosalind Edwards is currently Research Officer at the National Children's Bureau in London, having been a Researcher in the Department of Social Sciences at South Bank Polytechnic. Her main research interests focus on "the family" and preventive state intervention as well as feminist methodology. Her publications include *Mature Women Students* (Falmer Press, forthcoming) and, with Miriam David, Mary Hughes, and Jane Ribbens, *Mothers and Education: Inside Out?* (Macmillan, forthcoming).

Nigel G. Fielding is Senior Lecturer in the Department of Sociology, University of Surrey, Guildford, England. His research interests are in criminology and the sociology of deviance, police studies, and qualitative methods. He has been editor of the *Howard Journal of Criminal Justice* since 1985.

Sharon D. Herzberger is Professor of Psychology at Trinity College, Hartford, Connecticut. Her work on child abuse, perceptions of discipline, and issues of measurement has appeared in numerous scholarly journals; among them are *Applied Psychological Measurement, Child Development, Journal of Marriage and the Family, Journal of Family Violence,* and *Journal of Personality.* She recently conducted a longitudinal study of criminal justice decision making and is currently working on a series of studies of sibling conflict.

Raquel Kennedy Bergen is a doctoral candidate in Sociology at the University of Pennsylvania. She is also a counselor for battered and sexually abused women. Currently, she is working on a project that focuses on the experiences of marital rape survivors and how they cope with the violence.

Raymond M. Lee is Lecturer in Social Research Methods in the Department of Social Policy and Social Science, Royal Holloway and Bedford New College, University of London. Previously, he held posts at the University of Surrey, University College, Swansea, and St. Mary's College, Twickenham. His broad areas of interest include research methodology, the sociology of religion, and the sociology of labor markets. His previous research encompassed a number of "sensitive" topics including a study of Catholic-Protestant intermarriage in Northern Ireland and the operation of the underground economy. He is currently working on another book that addresses the problems and issues raised by sensitive topics.

John L. Martin held a Ph.D. in psychology from the City University of New York and an M.P.H. from Columbia University School of Public Health. At the time of his death from AIDS in January 1992, he had just completed a year as a fellow at the Center for Advanced Studies in Behavioral Sciences at Stanford. He initiated a pioneering study of the mental health effects of the AIDS epidemic on gay men in 1983 and, in 1990, he won a five-year research scientist development award from the National Institute of Mental Health. His research findings on bereavement, sexual behavior, and the epidemiology of HIV have appeared in a number of anthologies and scholarly journals, including the *American Journal of Public Health, Social Science and Medicine,* and the *American Journal of Community Psychology.* He was a consultant to local, state, and national agencies, including the National Institute of Drug Abuse and the Academy of Natural Sciences.

Claire M. Renzetti is Professor of Sociology at St. Joseph's University, Philadelphia, Pennsylvania. She is the author of *Violent Betrayal: Partner Abuse in Lesbian Relationships* (Sage, 1992) and coauthor of *Women, Men, and Society,* 2nd ed., Allyn & Bacon, 1992; *Social Problems,* 3rd ed., Allyn & Bacon, in press; and *Criminology,* Allyn & Bacon, in press. Her research on domestic violence, the women's movement, and women and economic development has appeared in various scholarly journals, including the *Journal of Interpersonal Violence, Family Relations, Sex Roles,* and *Contemporary Crises.*

Joan E. Sieber is Professor of Psychology, California State University, Hayward. A social psychologist by training, her area of specialization is the study of emerging value problems in social research and intervention. Her main interest is in the development of procedural and methodological solutions to ethical problems that otherwise would limit the value of social science. Her current work focuses on problems of developing culturally sensitive approaches for outreach, research, and intervention with populations at risks for HIV infection, problems of research on powerful people, and issues of data sharing. She is the author of *Planning Ethically Responsible Research* (Sage, 1992) and coeditor of the Sage volume *The Ethics of Research on Children and Adolescents* (1991).

J. J. Thomas is Senior Lecturer in Economics, London School of Economics and Political Science. Prior to 1984, his research focused primarily on applied econometrics and macroeconomic model building. Since 1984, he has made a number of visits to South America and has taught econometrics at universities and research centers in Brazil, Colombia, Peru, and Venezuela. As a result of his experiences in South America, he has been researching "informal" economic activities and has published articles on the informal sector in developing countries and the underground or hidden economy in developed countries. These topics also provide the focus of his book, *Informal Economic Activity* (Edward Arnold, 1992).